^{THE}
MOLE PEOPLE

SHORTY AND FRAN

THE
MOLE PEOPLE

LIFE IN THE

TUNNELS BENEATH

NEW YORK CITY

JENNIFER TOTH

CHICAGO
REVIEW
PRESS

Library of Congress Cataloging-in-Publication Data
Toth, Jennifer.
    The mole people : life in the tunnels beneath New York City /
Jennifer Toth.
            p.   cm.
    Includes index
    ISBN 1-55652-190-1 : $19.95; pbk ISBN 1-55652-241-X : $13.95
    1. Underground homeless persons-New York (N.Y.) 1. Title.
    HV4506.N6T68   1993
    305.5'696-dc20
                                                93-23912
                                                CIP

Photographs © 1993 by Margaret Morton unless otherwise credited.
Illustrations on pages ii and 254 © Chris Pape.

First edition
Published by Chicago Review Press, Incorporated
814 North Franklin Street, Chicago, Illinois 60610

Printed in the United States of America
ISBN 1-55652-241-X

15 14 13 12 11 10 9 8

To my father who teaches by example and love
and
To Kristen, Dericka, Richard, Julie, and all the children in the
tunnels in hope that they will carry the lesson with them

"If you have built castles in the air, that is where they should
be. Now put the foundations under them." —*David Thoreau*

Contents

Author's Note   ix
Introduction   1
1 Finding a Home   7
2 Seville's Story   11
3 Mac's War   29
4 The Underground Population   35
5 Underground Spaces   43
6 The Bowery   49
7 Living with the Law   59
8 Hell's Kitchen   73
9 Children   77
10 Roots   87
11 Bernard's Tunnel   97
12 Tunnel Art   119
13 Graffiti   129
14 Runaways   135
15 Tunnel Outreach   151
16 Dark Angel   165
17 The Underground in History, Literature, and Culture   169
18 Wanderers   181
19 Harlem Gang   183
20 J.C.'s Community   191
21 "City of Friends"   203
22 Women   213
23 Jamall's Story   229
24 Blade's Piece   237
Epilogue   249
Acknowledgments   255
Bibliography   257
Index   261

Author's Note

I THOUGHT A GREAT DEAL ABOUT THE TITLE OF THIS BOOK. AL-though there are several communities of tunnel dwellers who call themselves the mole people, there are many individuals living in the tunnels who take issue with the term. In homeless circles aboveground, the tunnel people are commonly referred to as "mole people." Sometimes the term is used in such circles disparagingly, to establish higher status within the homeless community.

Graffiti artist Chris Pape and photographer Margaret Morton each raised concerns about "The Mole People" because it is regarded as a pejorative term among homeless advocates, and more important to us all, it is insulting to some tunnel dwellers. Bernard Isaacs and his community under Riverside Park were those we most wanted to protect from this title. For years, Bernard has objected to the term because he feels it is a label that portrays him as an animal, not as a person. Yet when I talked to Bernard about the title of this book, he agreed "The Mole People" was the right choice.

I chose the title for several reasons. The people of New York City who live underground are most commonly known as mole people. And it is no accident that the term conjures freakish images. I hope this book will reverse the horrible and striking image of "mole people" simply by showing what I saw and found. I hope

ix

the stories from the tunnels will bring a better understanding of the underground people. By writing their stories, I hope to dismiss the myth of animal-like underground dwellers, so that you, the reader, can come to know that mole people don't exist beneath the surface of New York City, but people do.

Introduction

MY TEN-YEAR-OLD FRIEND KRISTEN WAS THE FIRST TO TELL me about the "mole people." She was one of my students when I volunteered in the Harlem tutorial program during my year of graduate school at Columbia University. We met every week. She taught me about street life in New York, while I helped her with multiplication tables.

One Saturday morning we sat together on a thick red couch in the plush hall of the International House at a great bay window overlooking Riverside Park. Outside the weather was cold but bright, and the sun reaching into the room made us warm and happy. Kristen, bored by her school work and hungry for attention, searched for distractions in the high ceilings, the polished piano, and the wall paintings.

"I know this girl at school, Julie. She don't live like this. She live underground in a tunnel," Kristen announced. Her eyes grew wide and excited as they did when she began one of her tales. I laughed.

"Really, it's true!" she insisted, straightening her slouched back. "She live in one of them tunnels."

I asked if she were a friend of Julie's.

"No, she nobody's friend. She dirty all the time, and she be stinky too," Kristen shivered. Her eyes lit with a familiar smile that was never far from her. Then she added with a giggle, "She

1

be one of them *mole people.*" She wiggled her fingers near her mouth to indicate whiskers, squinching up her nose and eyes to look like an imagined mole. She looked more like my cat than a rodent, however, and I laughed again and she laughed with me.

While I was dubious about her story, I asked her for more details about Julie, including the name of the school, and then Kristen arranged for me to meet Julie and her father at the swing set in Morningside Park on a Saturday morning. They found me and told their story, one of many to come on the following pages, but they refused to take me to their underground home.

I WAS UNEASY TALKING TO HOMELESS PEOPLE. ALTHOUGH I HAD served in soup kitchens in high school and college, coming from St. Louis, I found New York City's homeless wild and frightening. They seemed to multiply three-fold on each corner during my 1989–90 year at Columbia and their squabbling over the same turf seemed threatening as I passed by. Then, too, young girls were attacking pedestrians in the area with needles and everyone was terrified that the tips were AIDS-infected.

However, two experiences made me less reluctant to talk to the homeless. My friend Robert Meitus, also at Columbia that year, had an extremely open manner with those we met on the street, even embracing them at times. He and his band sometimes gathered near midnight on the long white steps of Columbia University's administration building next to the school's statue and played for the homeless who gathered in the sweeping white moonlight. He wrote some songs for and about homeless individuals in the area. He broke my fear of a population that seemed untamed and dangerous. The other experience was more pointed. One night I was feeling upset as I left my room, and I saw a homeless woman with a shopping cart of trash bags filled with empty cans and old clothes. She asked me for money. I said I had none. She thanked me and smiled. Then, seeing my tears, she began giving me advice with a gentle look and soft eyes until at the end, she reached into one of her garbage bags and handed me a limp and fading white carnation. I, in turn, spoke to her as more than a something on the street asking for money. She had lost her apartment a few days earlier, her children were with friends, and she was combing the streets "for cans and luck," she said.

After our talk, I became less afraid of approaching the homeless on the street and talking to them. The homeless on the streets near the university, while they had heard seemingly fantastic stories about mole people, had never met any.

The following summer I interned at *The Los Angeles Times* bureau in New York and continued the search. Many of the homeless in Grand Central Station, not far from my office, claimed they had seen mole people or even visited their communities. Several promised to take me up the tunnel tracks to them, but, to my relief, none came through. One of them, however, directed me to St. Agnes' Soup Kitchen nearby, where I spoke with the director.

"I've heard some stories," he said at first. "I haven't been down there." Then he began to hedge. "I'm not saying there are such people, but I'm not saying there aren't," he smiled when pressed. Finally, as we walked out, he quietly suggested that I visit Sergeant Bryan Henry, the Metropolitan Transit Police officer in charge of homeless outreach in Grand Central Station.

Finding Sergeant Henry's small office was not easy, and when I did, another officer stood by when I explained that I wanted to write a story about the underground homeless. "You mean the mole people," the two men laughed. "No one is living underground," Henry said flatly, "they're just stories."

When the other officer left and I continued recounting the various tales I had picked up, Henry listened more seriously. When I said that some homeless men had offered to take me into the tunnels, he asked for their names. While I was telling him about conditions at different locations in the tunnels, as they had been told to me, a woman officer walked in. She looked stunned.

"You told her about all that?" she accused Henry. "What is going on?"

Henry looked from her to me, covered his face with his hands, and took his feet off his desk. He rose, ushered her out, and shut the door.

"OK," he began. "I'm going to tell you about this. It's big. There's a city beneath the streets . . . "

Henry was frustrated, like many others, at the inadequate city and state efforts to deal with the underground homeless population that increased year after year. He finally took some photographs of the conditions, which he showed to me, and brought those pictures to Albany in an effort to see the governor. He was advised to keep quiet and told help would come, but it did not.

Initially *The Los Angeles Times* was lukewarm toward the story, probably because I was fresh out of school. Perhaps they are pulling your leg, one reporter laughed; maybe they are luring you into the tunnels where you could be raped or killed, another warned. But several other reporters, particularly Karen Tumulty, encouraged me to pursue the story, especially after I brought J.C. to the office.

J.C. was the self-described spokesman for a two hundred-member underground community under Grand Central to whom Sergeant Henry had introduced me. Karen and editor Roger Smith gave me confidence to pursue the story. My drive was also fueled by denials that the underground homeless existed—even by those who clearly knew better. After months of research, I received, anonymously, a list of officials—mental health and substance abuse specialists who met with each other several times to discuss the underground homeless situation. The story unfolded easily. I became more fascinated by the homeless I met, their warmth and friendliness, as well as the way they interacted with one another through their quick communication network. I enjoyed being recognized on the street by those I had interviewed and even those who knew me by word of mouth. One night while waiting for the D train to take me home to Brooklyn, a homeless man came up to me and suggested that I pass up the waiting train for the next one. "There's going to be trouble" on that train, he warned me. I took his advice. Hours later while stuck on the stalled train, I learned that there had been a shooting on the previous train that I had passed up.

Immediately after my article appeared on the front page of the *Times,* I was deluged with calls from advocates of the homeless, some of whom were furious that I had quoted them. "It doesn't help the homeless to be portrayed as 'mole people' living underground," complained an official at New York's largest organization for homeless people. "It makes them look freakish." He intended to phone an editor and claim he had been misquoted by me. I asked if he intended to lie. "Sure I'd lie," he told me without equivocation. "I'd lie to help the homeless."

I wondered if I really had done harm. "Don't worry about them," Bernard Isaacs advised. A veteran tunnel dweller from the West Side, Isaacs is very critical of these groups for the homeless. "They're as bad as the city government," he said. "They have their agenda and we have ours. They need money to keep their jobs at their organizations. They make up the truth to support their platform so they get donations. We don't have a platform. We need the truth."

So I went back into the tunnels for more firsthand accounts and experiences of underground life for this book. With the help of Bernard, Sergeant Henry, and Blade, I had encounters that will last me a lifetime. If I had it to do again, I wouldn't. The sadness and the tragedies were overwhelming, and, in the end, the danger to myself was too great to want to relive. Too many friends I made in the tunnels have died or regressed almost beyond recognition. Too few have made it back aboveground. The excitement of dangerous tunnel adventures lasts only until you get to know the people of the tunnel and understand their plight.

In describing the dangerous world of the underground homeless, I've sought to bring up to the reader not only their personal histories but also the sparks of friendship and caring that help light their dark world. The stories tell not only of their present lives in the tunnels and the communities they form, but also of their communication networks, and of the encounters with government agencies, charitable programs, and nonprofit advocacy groups. All, I hope, make up the larger truth about the homeless underground that those who have never approached these people will find difficult to credit, let alone comprehend in its entirety.

Finally, few of the homeless in this book are identified by their real names. This was their choice.

"We leave our pasts and our failures with our names above-ground," explained the self-styled "mayor" of an underground Penn Station community. While they gave only their street names or invited me to invent one for them, virtually all of them wanted to talk about their lives, hoping that it would bring some understanding and perhaps help others. These people and their lives represent the worst of New York City and, I argue, the best. These are their stories.

1

Finding a Home

HE'D HEARD ABOUT THE TUNNEL. SOME MONTHS EARLIER A corpse was found in it, not far beyond the tracks, its face half-eaten by rats, one eye scratched out and punctured with small teeth. The fleshless cheek swarmed with maggots and flies. They said a fat white worm, or perhaps only a maggot, crawled in the empty eye socket, while the other eye stared in unblinking horror. A veteran police officer threw up at the sight of the dead man who was just one of the homeless frequently seen but little known. He never fit into any place or plan. Even in death his body refused to be useful even to medical science. He had been dead only a few days, but his body was too decomposed to determine the cause of death. Or so they said. He might have been killed in a robbery or a drug-crazed beating or from natural causes—as natural as they come to a man of about fifty who had been living on the streets and sought a place to rest. It didn't matter much. There was no one to cry over him or claim his body. All that was left was a burial by prison inmates at Riker's Island in the Island cemetery, a government-issued number, and the folklorish memory of his hideous corpse circulated among the homeless.

That story about the tunnel was accepted as truth to him and the other homeless who lived in the area. Now as he enters a dark tunnel away from the tracks, he fears he is entering that corpse's tunnel. He considers working his way back out, past the mounds

of broken cinder blocks and clumps of debris and refuge, back to
the dark tunnel entrance he had stumbled into in his search for
solitude. A moment ago he stood at the mouth of the tunnel
silhouetted in the last of the day's red light, not yet committed to
the underground. Now he finds himself enveloped in its darkness,
his bravery receding with the light as he walks deeper into the
tunnel. The dark is not much worse than the night in the city, he
tells himself, and the danger can't be greater here than it is for men
like him on the streets.

Three nights earlier he was stabbed while being robbed by a
man he had considered his best friend, just after they had shared a
Meals-on-Wheels sandwich and a park bench in East Side Manhattan's Alphabet City. Two nights ago a man tried to rape him at a
city shelter where he hoped for sleep to heal his bandaged arm. Last
night, as he lay curled in a doorway to stay warm, a group of young
thugs kicked him in the head until blood filled his eyes. They tore
the pint of cheap whiskey from his hands and poured it over him,
then tried to ignite him with an iridescent yellow lighter until a
woman began screaming. He could have gone to the cops, but
what for? He couldn't identify them and he wouldn't risk fingering
the wrong kids. That had happened to his brother once and it just
wasn't right.

The names they called him hurt more than their kicks and
blows from a pipe across his back. "Nigger" and "worthless leech"
and "sorry shit." "They should round up all you homeless fuck-
heads and shoot you dead, exterminate you like roaches, and then
they should hang your mother for having you," one kid yelled
while kicking him. He remembers the sharp pain of each kick and
the smash of the pipe until he had given up fighting, and each blow
in turn passed to thuds against his body that he heard but did not
feel. Only the terror of being set ablaze made him cry out.

He still cringes, not because of the pain, but because he had
urinated in his pants and because he needed the woman's scream
to help him, and because she had seen his weakness.

As bad as the streets are for a homeless man with a clean face,
they are far more hostile for one with still-weeping scabs and eyes

swollen into slits from the beating. People cleared a path for him, and their eyes, when not indifferent, showed anger that he would expose them to his misery. Worse still was that his slowed movements and visible wounds made him easy prey for other vicious youths looking for violent ways to express their frustration and hatred.

So how can this tunnel, even if it were that tunnel, be more dangerous for him than the streets this night?

He walks deeper, quietly, like a ghost, he thinks, and his heart gradually stops fluttering like a netted butterfly. It belongs to him again, his own. He stops and then he hears what he will remember as "echoing darkness." It's the only way to describe what he hears, a velvety blackness that rebounds from side to side, and then wraps around him gently as he sinks to the floor at the wall, a spot that now feels safe and his own. With his back comforted by the wall, he draws his knees up to his ribs and lingers with his thoughts as he drifts toward sleep. The quiet is broken only by the patient fall of dripping water in the distance, a soft and pleasant sound that he knows would be lost to the noise of New York's busy streets. He is soothed despite the dampness that seeps through his frayed jacket and torn trousers. All the way down, he muses, are layers upon layers upon layers of tunnels, with no bottom. This layer is safer than the street above, the one below even safer, and the one below it is even safer, and so on, beyond thought, all the way down. A soothing numbness takes him. Nothing really matters. It could suddenly start snowing up above, or raining, or there could be warm sun. Nothing matters because all of that would change, it would pass. He feels his breath condensing, but he is content with simply being, and being without being seen, secretly in a new world, sensing he could see out to watch those who could not see him. He was living a life that others were afraid even to imagine.

In such a life, he thinks, there is a truth. You can be so cold that you can't get colder, so wet you can't become wetter. You can feel so deeply that you are saturated, numb but still intensely alert—beyond fear—as if living a memory. Beyond living, he thinks. Surviving.

The morning brings a splinter of light through a hole high in the wall opposite. He stirs and moves into the mote-filled beam. He persuades himself that it warms him. He feels he never slept so well since he became one of the homeless. So what if this is that tunnel, he thinks. He has found a home.

Home on a catwalk. *Photo by Margaret Morton*

2

Seville's Story

S EVILLE WILLIAMS IS AS UNIQUE AS ALL TUNNEL AND TOPSIDE
people, but his personal history mirrors those of many others
in the tunnels. The path he took from the streets to the
underground, and his struggles to climb back up are common to
many tunnel dwellers.

At thirty-one years old, Seville's story is far from over. Although the life expectancy of a man on the streets isn't much
beyond forty-five, he believes with his unending optimism that his
life is just beginning. He refuses to let his past define him or limit
his hopes for the future. He talks about getting a full-time job as
a welder, a trade he learned during two years in prison for dealing
drugs, with the same enthusiasm and conviction of a high school
senior who talks about becoming a doctor after failing chemistry.
At times an inward shadow dims his bright eyes, as if he recognizes
that his past still influences his life like an old habit. Then, with
the marvelous resilience that allows him to care for others, his smile
is suddenly brilliant again. Every day is new to Seville, and anything can happen as he struggles to survive and climb out of the
underground.

"I gotta believe there's a purpose for me still being here when
I've come so close to death so many times you wouldn't believe,"
he says with his broad smile and light shake of his head. "You just
wouldn't believe it. Most of my friends—Shorty, Teather, Flacko,

11

Big D—they're all dead now. Some of them, it was their own doing. Some of them, it weren't, but they be dead anyway," he says and then sucks air through his teeth. "Don't know why I'm here, really don't. I done everything they done and worse. Times I tried to kill myself, I mean, not suicide or like that, but put myself in situations I was sure to be killed. It didn't work," he smiles happily, lifting his hands in mock disbelief. "I'm still here. Don't know why, but there's gotta be a reason."

Like many tunnel people, Seville comes from a dysfunctional family, torn by drugs and violence. He has emotional and physical scars from the years, but they have not callused his humor, which is open and without bitterness. He remains generous to others on the fringe, especially those in the tunnels. When he passes an underground homeless person in need, he usually stops to help.

"We got to take care of ourselves down there cuz ain't nobody else gonna do it," he shrugs again. "Know what I'm saying? You just got to accept it or reject it," he says of the homeless condition. "Take it the way you can. Know what I'm saying?"

I met Seville on the concourse in Grand Central. He was one of a group of homeless whom Sergeant Bryan Henry of the Metropolitan Transit Police approached with me in tow, but he stood apart from the group, a bit aloof, in an old Harris tweed coat with the middle button missing. He leaned with two crutches against a small constructional work truck, suspicious and defiant, with half-closed eyelids. He sucked his breath in slowly and evenly in a reverse hiss, but with barely a sound. His short beard is well kept, and if he could stand without crutches, he would look tall and healthy.

If being articulate is not Seville's strong suit, humor is. Finding the humor in underground situations is not only a gift but a necessity in order to remain sane in the tunnels, a survival technique, Seville says.

"You have to keep laughing. If you don't you fall apart. Sometimes you gotta smile when you don't want to, you laugh at terrible things that nobody should laugh at, but it's like your mind has to find something funny or you'll go crazy." Then, tired of speaking seriously, he smiles broadly again. "I know that too. I know it all; I been through it all." He stretches his arms wide and high with self-satisfaction and pride at being alive.

Seville keeps the tunnels lively with his humor. Once while he was panhandling in Grand Central Station a commuter gave him a bag containing a loaf of bread and a pound of baloney. He thanked the man and then, after looking into the bag, shouted out after him, "Pardon me, sir, would you happen to have some Grey Poupon?"

Commuters cracked up with laughter, not least the donor. "He fell out," Seville remembers. "The man had a ball all the way out of the station. I loved doing it. That's what it's all about."

With the same sense of humor, Seville goes on to tell about doing drugs and living under Track 100 in Grand Central Station. He was once so exhausted from the drugs and his feet so swollen and sore from injecting into the veins in his feet, that he could barely get himself across the street for a free meal. One time he collapsed while running toward a Meals-on-Wheels van.

"I just lay there and yelled, 'I'm hungry, but I'm too tired to move.' And the lady she come up to me laughing and she say, 'We'll bring it to you. But just don't try to run; you look so funny when you run.'" He grins briefly at the image in his mind of himself as a disjointed, uncoordinated scarecrow. "Boy, I was really messed up bad then."

"I don't mind making people laugh, makes them more generous sometimes," he goes on. But some of his black friends dislike some of his enterprising, humorous acts and see them as demeaning to his race.

"We don't need no handouts from no white people looking to stay out of trouble," says Malcolm, who hangs around Port Authority Station. "They the ones who put us here. We don't need to be cleaning their shit pots."

Seville explains his enterprising scheme differently.

"We have this thing called Volunteers of the Bathroom where we clean up the toilets in Grand Central or Penn Station or Port Authority, and then we tell the people in a little speech." He begins, sweeping his hand gracefully after tipping an imaginary hat, "'Good afternoon, ladies and gentlemen. I'm a Volunteer of the Bathroom, keeping the bathroom safe, clean, and organized. As you know, most of the volunteers are homeless, like myself and this gentleman with me. Your donations help us eat and stay out of trouble. We do not get paid for our services, but we do it in the hopes that you good people can use the bathroom most effectively and appreciate it. Any donations, large or small—cuz I couldn't live with myself if I didn't ask—are appreciated.'

"Some people get a kick out of it [the routine] and give us something with a smile, but my own kind rarely ever gives me anything. Once in a blue moon maybe. They won't even look into my face. . . . I'd rather they tell me they don't have it, or don't ask them than not look at me, you know?" He resumes earnestly, "Phoey! People like that think I'm like them and they got no respect for themselves so they don't look at me—maybe that's it. I don't understand it. Seems to me that if you make people laugh, they treat you normal. They're not afraid to look at you. That's what it's all about, ain't it, a way to get some respect, to be treated like a regular person?"

Seville calls the eighties the "decade of the tunnels, because that's when we all found them. There were people in the late seventies who used the tunnels occasionally to get high or whatever, but it wasn't until the eighties that people started settling in, living down here.

"It's the decade of crack and homelessness. It's the decade of the tunnels," he repeated. "People've been down and out since the beginning of time, but we's the first to actually live in tunnels. There's been nowhere else to go," he laughs. "There was too many of us. We got no families that can help us or want to, whatever, and no place to go, so we come to the tunnels. Even people who don't like the tunnels come down here to be with their own. And I don't mean color. I mean people who grew up like me."

How Seville grew up came out piecemeal, over time and many conversations, amid laughter and jokes with which he conspired to ward off pity and "break up the blues."

"Well, just say it wasn't no 'Father Knows Best' situation or 'Leave It to Beaver,'" he says with a little laugh. "Man, I used to love those shows. It was like sci-fi to me; they were on a different planet from me."

Seville tried to run away from home several times before, but at the age of nine, he succeeded. By then he had been deserted by his mother, attempted to shoot his father, and seen more violence between parents than most children see on television. He also fathered his first child when he was barely a teenager.

When he was seven years old, his mother left him in West Hampton, Virginia. His parents separated and reconciled often, and were separated at this time when his mother decided to take a bus to New York. His father was apparently also in New York, Seville recalls, and maybe she went searching for him, but probably not. Whatever her reason, she left Seville in the house alone.

"I just stayed in the house," he remembers. "I knew how to cook; my grandmother had taught me. Then the guy next door—he was a priest—came over and asked where my parents were. We called my father and he came down immediately to get me and brought me to New York. He was mad, boy," Seville laughs. "He wanted to kill her for leaving me, and he probably would have if she'd been there."

His father, an Air Force enlisted man, was large and his mother was small, but when they argued, "she'd chase him around like a little bird pecking on him, her head bopping like a pigeon. It was funny, boy. She'd nag him to death. He'd try to run away, and he was big and she was tiny but he'd be the one running. But once in Brooklyn, he turned on her and I had to hold the door closed to keep him from getting at her while she got away.

"My mother threw acid on my father's head one day, and he almost strangled her. They almost killed each other so many times, it was pathetic. That's why I had to leave; too much fighting for me and I got caught up in it. I almost shot my father with a sawed-off shotgun my grandfather gave to me. It's called a loophole, an Italian gun. He was lucky, my father. I was too small to hold the gun, and he ducked. That's when I left. I couldn't take it no more."

Seville slept on rooftops, in doorways, halls, and basements throughout New York—in Queens, Brooklyn, and the Bronx. "I lived everywhere you could live. It wasn't too bad. You got used to it. . . . It's bad when you get too used to it though, cuz then you don't try to get out of it. That was my problem. After a while I couldn't get used to sleeping in a room. I felt closed in with no escape."

He stole to support himself. "Sometimes I stayed with an uncle of mine, Uncle Louis, but he kept trying to take me back to my mother's house, and each time I'd leave again. I got so tired of family court."

Seville claims he went to school regularly even when he lived on the streets because, he says, there was nothing else to do. His parents tried to catch him there. Once his father did corner him on the second floor of a school, but he jumped out a bathroom window and onto a car hood to escape. Somehow his father ran down the steps faster than Seville could get away. "I remember I couldn't believe a fat dude like him could run so fast. When he caught me, he said, 'I'm not gonna hit you, just come on home.'

"But I got out again. I got tired of being around them. They were just too busy fighting to pay attention to me. My father be there, my mother would move out. My mother be there, my father move out. It was like a revolving door."

Without brothers or sisters, he learned early to be alone. He didn't miss company; in fact, he almost sought to escape people "because people disappoint you. I had some friends here and there, but most times my best friend was myself," Seville says. "You don't need too many people around you, cuz when you got too many people, you don't know who's for you and who's against you. When you're alone, you don't have to worry about that cuz people will flip on you like at the International House of Pancakes. They'll be your friend and the next minute they'll try to kill you for money. If they're thirsty enough, and if they think they can get away with it, they'll try to kill you. That's a fact."

He lived well in his early teens by stealing cars, which is how he met Iris, whose father had a white Cadillac.

A friend was auditioning with a ventriloquist act, and Seville, while waiting for him outside the club, was sitting on the hood of the Cadillac when Iris and her father came out. Her father spoke gruffly to Seville in a foreign language—Dutch, it turned out.

"He had these thunderclouds in his face," Seville says, "Very unhappy. Didn't like me. He thought I was a hoodlum or something. I guess I am, but I know how to put it aside. I said to Iris: 'Yo, what's up with this? Is he cursing at me?' She laughed and said, 'He just wants you to get off his car.'"

To anger her father, Iris invited Seville to go into the club with her. She was a stunning redhead with green eyes, according to Seville. "She was real tall and thin; her dad was short, fat, bald, and ugly."

"We hit it off pretty well, and she asked me to show her New York while they were visiting. We stuck around each other for two weeks. Then I got locked up for selling reefer in Queens. I didn't call her—didn't want her to know—and when I got out, she was gone. I didn't know she was pregnant with Naga.

"When she got back to the Netherlands, she had to do something fast, so she married this guy Earl [an American serviceman] to bring her back over here. He kept beating on her—real nasty attitude—and she got him arrested. I had told her where I sold reefer and she moved there, to 163rd Street between 89th and Jamaica Avenue in Queens. She was looking for me, and I was there but I didn't see her or recognize her and I guess she didn't see me.

"Would you believe, I was giving my own daughter a dollar every day for three months, and I didn't know she was my daughter! She was so cute. I used to deal across the street from where they lived, and I used to call Naga over when she was going to school cuz she was so cute. I love kids and I wanted to mess with her.

"Naga'd say: 'What them people give you money for? What you giving them?' I'd say, 'None of your business. Here, take a dollar and go to school.'

"Every day I used to give her a dollar. I didn't find out she was my daughter until one day I thought, man, she's so cute her mama's got to be nice. So I followed her upstairs one day so I could get a look at her. When she came out of the apartment, I just stood there. 'Iris?' I said."

He nods his head now in a pleasant memory. I wonder how fanciful it is but keep silent.

"Boy, we had a good time after that. I was fourteen years old when Naga was born. Iris was twenty-four. Count it up, Naga is seventeen now, and I'm thirty-one."

Seville sent Iris and Naga back to Holland in 1981 when the police shut down his reefer operation. The tickets cost him $842, he remembers, and he gave them $5,000 more. "I asked her father to take care of them until I got things back together again," he says. "Sure I want them back. But I just haven't gotten it together again yet."

Seville is inconsistent with some pieces of his biography and omits key facts while traveling down one avenue of his life, disclosing them later when they serve to embellish another tale.

He fathered three more children by two other women: two other girls and a boy named after him. The boy, whom he called "Little Seville," was born to Candy in March 1981, the same year Iris went home to Holland.

He was not present for the birth of his son, now seven years old. "I was in jail," he says, looking down as if ashamed. "I had to tell on myself to get Candy off the hook because I didn't want my son born in jail. I sent him to live with her relatives in Saint Croix. He's my only son and I want him to grow up. You know what I'm saying? I don't want him dying on one of these streets. Most kids do."

The boy's mother, Candy, was eight months pregnant when Seville and a friend burglarized a jewelry store ostensibly to help support Candy and their coming child. "We got $25,000 in cash and $40,000 in jewelry, and I got caught because of a jealous girl who saw all of Candy's rings and stuff and she called the police," he explains. It was then, apparently, that Seville admitted to the crime to keep Candy from going to jail. Iris and Naga are not mentioned again.

"People have to do what they have to do," he shrugs. "You

can't blame them for that; you can't look down at them. They do what they have to do to take care of themselves and their own, no matter what.

"When the judge locked me up, he asked, 'Mr. Williams, do you regret doing this?' I said, 'No, cuz to take care of mine, I'm going to do it again. Now if you don't want me to do it, get me a job, and not that minimum wage stuff—you can't support no family on that.'"

"I had to tell him straight up what was real. He said he respected that." Then Seville smiles. "But he still put me away for three years. It would have been less but I had been in [jail] for so many other things so many times, he had to do it. I respect him for that. Since 1975, I've been arrested so many times I can't count. I used to get into trouble cuz there was nothing better to do. I used to be good at stealing cars, even when we didn't hardly know how to drive. Once me and my friend Bill—he was crazy, Bill—we drove up an exit ramp the wrong way, and a police car looked over and just didn't believe it. We went fast against traffic on the highway for two exits, with the whole precinct after us. We were having fun, whooping it up. You don't take it seriously when you're a kid. You get thirty days, ninety days, they throw the case out, it don't matter."

SEVILLE HAS LIVED FOR TWELVE YEARS IN THE TUNNELS, VIRTUALLY all of his adult life except when he was in jail. He was sleeping on subway platforms at nineteen, and a year later moved to the hollow areas under the passenger platforms of commuter rail lines under Grand Central Station terminal. The homeless had knelt along the tracks and pick-axed holes in the walls, usually high under the overhang so they could not be seen by anyone standing on opposite platforms; he lived in these burrows first alone and then with many "communities," as Seville calls them.

Each move took him deeper into the tunnel and underground life. From beneath the platforms, he went along the train tracks as they leave the station into the tunnels that spread like veins on the back of a hand. From there, he moved into the tunnel network of the subway system, and into the tunnels under Penn Station, and then the more distant and peaceful reaches of the Amtrak tunnels along the Hudson River in upper Manhattan. Seville moved deeper, too, downward into the darkest reaches of the underground.

"Once you've lived in one tunnel, you've lived in them all," Seville says half-joking. "They're all connected. The people are mostly the same, too. Homeless is homeless. The tracks are just another place to live, that's all. Same people. Attitudes change. Some people will do anything for you, some of them are bad. Most of them don't care, not about you or about themselves. They are totally unhappy with themselves. They won't say that, but you can see. They can't see it, but you can see.

"The tunnels are old. They look like catacombs. It's a whole 'nother world down there, separate from this one. Believe that. The worries you have up here, you don't have down there. You don't have rent worries, for one. You don't have any bills to pay. You have a whole different attitude. Everyone's on a different wavelength down there, and then every time you join a new group of people and move in, you find the direction they're going—it's like a circle. It's family in a way, but limited, very limited. Like your family to a certain extent. You take on a role, and then you become like them even when you don't know it's happening."

In some ways, tunnel life closest to the surface is the worst. "Under the train platforms," Seville says, "you have to worry about rats. You can light small fires to keep them from jumping on you." Police once found a body by the smell; he had died of an overdose and been picked at by rats. Seville shivers with the memory. The compartment, stretching the length of the platform and about ten feet deep, was home to about twenty men at the time, all heavily into drugs. They urinated and defecated where they lived. The odor was gagging.

After a year, Seville moved deeper underground to "the Condos," a kind of natural cavern where over two hundred people lived. He had become friendly with a few men who lived there, and they

convinced him to stop taking drugs. When he did, he said that
they invited him to join their community, which is accessible from
the tracks in Grand Central.

Few "did drugs" in the Condos. "Some were homosexuals,
some straight, but mostly it was called the 'Condos' because the
living environment was so good. It was easy to get water from a
sprinkler pipe. You could set up shacks on the ground and find
electric wires to screw in light bulbs. You could run clotheslines
to dry your clothes. It was quiet and peaceful."

The cliff was set back from the tracks so that beyond it, train
noises could barely be heard, and police seldom had ventured that
deep into the tunnels.

"I'd been looking for mole people for years, been patrolling
those tracks, and never saw them," Sergeant Henry once confided
to me. "I only found them when I overheard people talk about the
Condos in the terminal."

Sergeant Henry and the Transit Police cleared out the Condos.
Seville moved even deeper underground.

"The further down you go, the weirder people get, and I mean
real weird," Seville says. "There are people down there, man, I
swear they have webbed feet. . . . Can't hardly see them at times,
they're so sneaky. They make strange noises and sounds, like trains,
but they aren't trains; they're communicating with each other.
They said I could stay but that I could only be allowed to go back
up with their permission. I ran from that place man, and I ain't
never going back. They're the *mole people*."

SEVILLE NOW FAVORS AN AMTRAK TUNNEL RUNNING UNDER HELL'S
Kitchen along the West Side. The area is considered extremely
dangerous by graffiti artists who paint flashy mosaics on the walls
in tunnels as well as on the surface. For Seville, the most dangerous
aspect is getting into the tunnel from the street. He usually slips
through a gate in a chain link fence atop a natural rock crevasse.
One day the gate was chained shut by police.

Trespassers had made a new entryway by bending up the lower section of the fence at one spot. "We used to crawl in feet first and then slide under, and the rocks on the side of the wall were like steps to get down part way. But you got to hold on. If you fall," he says of the thirty-foot drop to the tracks, "you might not get killed but you'd be hurt something terrible. You climb down the side part way and then jump the last part. I fell once and broke my wrist. It was hanging like this, only backward," he laughs, swinging a listless hand as if unjoined. Mechanics who work in the auto repair shop outside the fence saw him fall and climbed the fence to help. "One said, 'Man, after that fall, I thought you'd be dead.'"

Even when he gets into the tunnels, as experienced as he is, Seville is not safe.

"The biggest danger is crossing tracks. They got tracks that interlock, and if your foot gets stuck, trapped, that train won't be able to stop. It's happened, and the people down there won't risk their necks to help you out. I hate to say it, but I doubt they'd help you out.

"The people down there, I wouldn't say they're bad, but most of them are strung out. There is some kind of unity, but it fluctuates. It's a mood thing. Whatever mood they have, they'll act on and their mood changes twenty times a day, mostly because of drugs—coke, speed, and now heroin, if they got enough for it."

After a while he continues, "Those people down there, they're not used to people helping them—or them helping people. Like this guy who just got hit by a train up here last week." The man was so drugged that he apparently did not hear the warning whistle of a train behind him. The train was moving too fast to even slow down. "There were people around who could have helped him, gone get him off the tracks but they don't really care. They're not going to risk their necks for you. That's a fact. His girlfriend was there. She's like most of the girls up here. They're whores. She only with him cuz she think he can protect her." He shakes his head and stays quiet for a minute.

"I knew this girl down there," he resumes with a small smile. "Pretty little one. She'd be so strung out she would almost starve herself to death. I used to make her clean herself up. I used to drag her up top and she'd be crying, 'Fuck you!' But I'd get one of the gas station people to let her into their toilet and I wouldn't let her come out 'til she was clean. Man, she was so pretty, she didn't need to be turning tricks. She was in her early twenties maybe," he remembers. "Maria."

"She found a man," he says, vaguely again, "that didn't want nothing from her but to help her, and she came and surprised me. Came down to my couch in the tunnels and woke me up. 'Wake up, Daddy, I got something for you,' she said. Brought me lunch and everything. Looked clean and straight, real nice. Said she wasn't coming back no more, and I haven't seen her again," he says wistfully. "I hope she made it."

SEVILLE HESITATES BEFORE AGREEING TO TAKE ME DOWN INTO HIS tunnel. Because of his recently crippled foot, he can't use the regular entrance over the eighteen-foot fence and down the steep, rocky tunnel face to the tracks, and he won't let me go on my own.

"I don't want that on my conscience," he says, shaking his head. "If we see Franko or Shorty, I'll let you go with them, but not on your own. There are people who are bugged out and people who are real crackheads and they'll try to rob you, at least. That's a fact, and you being in the tunnels alone, I don't think there's too far they wouldn't go. No way I want that on my conscience. But I'll show you where it is."

He hobbles through Grand Central, and we take the shuttle to Times Square, emerging into a bitterly cold January. Seville's hands are cracked and bleeding. "It's that Hudson wind," he laughs as we walk along 48th Street toward 10th Avenue. Between 10th and 11th avenues is an almost unnoticed bridge over a gully through which run railroad tracks some thirty feet below street level, the spot where Seville fell. Access from either side of the bridge is barred by chain link fences, but these can be climbed or slid under, and the weeds—poison sumac, goldenrod—grow freely to the top of the sheer rock face of the crevasse before it drops to the gravel road bed of the tracks.

"Nothin' in the world like that old Hudson wind blowing off the river. I should know; I've lived with it for four years now."

At times the wind is so strong it almost knocks Seville over. We find none of his friends so we duck into a restaurant, Lee's Chinese Food. The sign is short of one *e* and soon to lose the slipping *h*. It has two tables, a counter, and a loud kitchen.

"Chicken and fried rice, Mr. Lee, and don't hold the grease!" Seville calls out on his way to the counter.

Lee laughs. "How're you doing, man," he asks. The black patois somehow doesn't sound odd coming from this middle-aged Asian man; perhaps it is becoming the universal language, the Esperanto of urban slums.

A huge, white mechanic from a nearby auto repair shop joins Seville at the counter. When Seville asks for a cigarette, the man insists he take several. Seville seems to have friends wherever he goes.

"Wha' happen to your foot, man?" asks Lee in a thick Chinese accent. "You fin' trouble?"

"No, Mr. Lee," replies Seville in his courtly manner, "it found me. I never look for it, but it finds me," he says with a mischievous shake of his head.

"Yeah, yeah, I know," says Lee, looking skeptically at Seville, "you din' do nothin'."

"Nothing but living my own life, Mr. Lee," agrees Seville, and does not protest when a courtesy bowl of wonton soup is placed before him.

Seville contemplates his foot which, under a huge blue sock, appears encased in a large plaster cast. In fact, his foot has swollen to twice its normal size.

Two nights before, he explains, a man demanded money from him and his friend Cindy. "I said, 'Look, man, I give you what I got, but I don't got nothing.' And it was the truth. Look at me. Do I look like I carry money? I just keep myself clean, that's all," he shakes his head at the senselessness of the incident that followed.

"But this guy is all strung out. 'I'll take the girl then,' he says. Now Cindy, she knows her way on the streets. She lives in the tunnels, too, but she does the streets to make some money for drugs and stuff. But this guy got me mad.

"I used to know a little karate when I was young, so I thought, what the hell, I'll try it," Seville smiles like a mischievous child. As he raised his foot to kick, the would-be thief flicked open a knife and split Seville's foot from ankle to toes. Seville thinks he passed out briefly, and when he came to, Cindy was screaming. The assailant had run away.

"That Cindy, man, she can scream. Had I known that, I wouldn't have done nothing, just let her scream. That's what made him run anyway." He laughs, but not for long as he recalls the medical treatment.

Cabs refused to stop for them. When one did, it refused to take Seville. "Man said he didn't want blood in his cab." Cindy finally persuaded the driver to take them to the hospital where most homeless go for care.

"Saint Clemens, man, they are the worst!" Seville flares. "I seen people die in their waiting room." In his case, he waited six hours for treatment, by which time the foot was too swollen for stitches so the wound was stapled closed. The doctor asked him to return when the swelling disappeared. Seville means to go back, he says, but he just doesn't have the time to spend commuting and hanging out in the waiting room. "I got to spend all day getting food and ready for the night, and then I got to spend all night staying warm."

Seville's tunnel is one of the city's more dangerous places because most of the community are heavy drug addicts. Seville once dealt drugs and still knows how to procure them, so he says people respect him, or at least don't mess with him, against the day when they may want his services. Seville himself does drugs sometimes, but he's very cautious about getting addicted, he says, having seen how they destroy lives. He refuses all alcohol because he remembers his father and mother were alcoholics.

"Last time I was dealing [drugs], a girl tried to give me her baby's food stamps and diapers for a hit," he remembers, shaking his head. "She was holding the baby, and the baby and her little boy standing next to her, both was crying, and they looked half starved. So I gave her the stuff and then turned around and called HRA [New York's Human Resources Administration] because that just ain't right. They needed help. After that I stopped dealing. Nothing's worth that. I had enough of it."

SEVILLE ALSO EXPRESSES DISTASTE AT TIMES TOWARD SERGEANT Henry and his Transit Police, which is surprising because as police go, Seville often says, Henry's not as bad as others. So as we sit, I ask him directly why he doesn't like Henry.

"Because I seen him do things he shouldn't be doing," Seville says flatly.

"He's like the rest," Seville continues, growing angry with some memory. "If he has a bad day, he'll beat up on people who are too weak to stand up. I seen him do things to people that were not necessary, not necessary at all. That's why I look at him the way I do sometimes. Cuz I seen things he done, seen them when he didn't know I was there.

"Yeah, I know he done good stuff, too, for some people, got them jobs or into rehab or apartments and other stuff, but he isn't a saint by any means. That article in *The New York Times* about Henry and Grand Central, you see that? Didn't say anything about the tunnels, but Henry loved it cuz it had a big picture of him and made him out a hero. He sure as hell ain't no hero."

Could you do a better job than Sergeant Henry? I ask.

"Hell, I wouldn't want that responsibility," he leans back comfortably, stretching his hands in the air and laughing. "I do what I can [for others] everyday, which is more than most people. Even when I was smoking and doing it up, I brought people stuff to eat. One thing about being homeless in New York, you can't starve. There is just too much food around.

"One time I had this deal with Flacko with a restaurant in Grand Central that has a hot salad bar. When they closed, they packed up all the leftover stuff for us, and it was good—squid, ravioli, meats, sushi, first-class stuff you wouldn't believe—and we would pass it out in Grand Central to others who were also homeless tunnel people."

He pauses, recalling my question. "If I was in charge," he says, with a mischievous grin starting, "if I was in charge, I'd put up a big sign on the platforms saying, 'C'mon down! Everyone welcome! Come live free—rent-free, tax-free, independent, free like Mandela!'"

When he stops smiling, he turns earnest and leans over our table in the Chinese restaurant, spilling his now cold wonton soup, "If you write this book," he says, "you tell them the tunnels rob you of your life. No one should come down here. There's lots of reasons they do. They think they can just get out after the police stop looking for them, or when they get off drugs, or when they feel better and can face things again. You can't go back up. Man, I wish I knew that twelve years ago.

"I just want you to tell them that. The tunnels take your life. That freedom stuff is bullshit. Everyone down here knows it. They won't say it, but they know it."

But you have left the tunnels several times, I remind him.

"I never really left them," he says. "I took vacations from the tunnels," he smiles lightly, "but I never really left them. I guess they're my home. Their people are my people. They are what I know best. They are who I know best.

"Think about it," his eyes dim. "You gonna just stop living where you live with your friends and your job and your family, learn a whole new way of life with nothing waiting for you there? How you expect me to do it after twelve years of doing what I do?"

We look at each other for a moment. Then he broke the silence with a smile.

"Tomorrow will be different," he rights his Styrofoam soup bowl. "Maybe I'll win the lottery and turn the tunnels into an underground resort area: 'Challenge your survival techniques!' Maybe tomorrow will be different. Don't you worry about me."

3

Mac's War

I N THIS RECESS OF THE TUNNEL, MAC DOES NOT NEED A TRAP
with stale food or a feces-soaked rag to catch "track rabbits,"
as rats are known to the underground homeless. They come
because the garbage is as dense as its stench. The light is very dim,
but Mac is well accustomed to it all.

Many newcomers vomit here, he warns. No use wondering
what the smell is, he says. It'll just make you sick thinking of the
possibilities. Ignore it, he advises.

I bury my nose and mouth deeper into the collar of my turtle-
neck. The cloth seems to filter the stench a bit. At least my eyes
stop watering and my senses recover slowly from the shock.

A shuffling sound penetrates the quiet darkness, and Mac
crouches low to the ground, like a wrestler preparing for a new
round. This, he says, is how you hunt track rabbits.

A brown rat the size of a small adult raccoon sniffs its way out
of the refuse and lumbers past Mac, undeterred by the stark beam
of my flashlight pointed aimlessly at my feet. He is in no way
frightened by humans and is prepared to ignore us.

"See," Mac says proudly, "the biggest, healthiest, and boldest
sons of bitches you've ever seen live down here."

The rat turns at the sound of his voice and, teeth bared, darts
toward Mac. In a sudden, graceful movement, Mac's hand sweeps
down as if throwing dice and seizes the base of the animal's tail.

29

The rat shrieks and claws the air as he lifts it high above the ground.

Mac lets out a short, powerful laugh. "He doesn't look so almighty up there, does he?" he asks triumphantly. He flips his wrist with a snap and the rat's body flies off into the dark and makes a dull thud as it strikes the wall.

"Shit," he spits. "Where is that son of a bitch?" He allows that it's harder than you expect to break those track rabbits' necks.

"Sometimes I think they're stronger than we are. They're as mean, that's for sure," he says, walking toward the wall. Down here, the point is survival. "We're both fresh meat. If I hadn't grabbed him, he would have bit me."

He spots the rat, which is still and bleeding from an ear. Dead.

"Dare's da wabbit!" he mimics Elmer Fudd with a goofy grin.

When Mac picks it up, the rat hangs limp—as soft and unthreatening as a puppy. Its eyes are closed and its teeth, which were so sharp and menacing a few seconds ago, are clenched shut.

Mac drops the corpse into the blood- and dirt-stained white canvas bag he carries everywhere, and throws the bag over his right shoulder. He is a white man in his early fifties, small and wiry, filthy and bearded, with sandals that flop loosely against the bottom of his feet, which are blackened by tunnel soot.

He adds pieces of wood and metal to his sack as we walk back toward his camp. The wood will feed the fire, he explains, and the metal will serve as a leg for a table he is making, or maybe a club, or maybe part of a new trap. Everything has a purpose, he says, and if he can't use it, he will give it away or just leave it for another tunnel dweller to discover.

"You may not be able to see what its purpose is," Mac says, "but everything has a reason for being."

We reach his camp, far beyond the operating subway tracks, and he walks behind a raised bunker, a ten-foot-high concrete wall that once served as a rest and tool shack for track maintenance workers. After a sharp, chopping sound, he returns with the headless body of the rat, its blood flowing freely over his hands. With a proud smile punctuated with crooked and rotten teeth, he strings the carcass by its hind paws in a corner of the tunnel beyond his space.

"Can't leave them there too long or the other rats will eat them," he explains. Quickly he builds a small fire and then skins the rat, shaving off the skin a strip at a time. Carefully and almost affectionately, like a small boy with a large fish he has caught, he skewers the rat from its neck through its anus and sets it over the fire.

"I took his head off for you," he smiles. "You probably wouldn't want to see it, but when you're hungry, it's very good. Juicy. Reminds me of pig's feet. Tasty. But the fun is sucking out the gook. You can even eat some of the finer bones."

As the rat cooks, he tells me about his favorite book, Thoreau's *On Walden Pond*." He carries a worn, paperback copy of it in the back pocket of his jeans and is able to quote long passages from it.

I ask, dizzy from the scent of burning flesh and cracking hair that haunts the campsite, if he is a Transcendentalist.

"I am, myself," he says, then pauses to look from the rat to me. "But that's a surprisingly dumb question from you," he says aggressively. "I am simply being myself, living for myself, so I can have things down here established when others come down and need me. It's my calling, you might say.

"The one thing I can't stand is labels," he adds, as if growing even more irritated by my question. "I am simply a person. I don't conform to any caste or group of people who are too lazy to think for themselves. Everyone up there has a self, but how many of them know it? How many define themselves by what society says?"

The belly of the rat is smoldering. One of the feet catches fire and quickly turns into a blackened claw of carbon. Mac rotates the spit to cook the back, and returns his attention back to me with a gentle smile.

"Please excuse my impatience," he says carefully, adding an almost courtly element to his urban mountain man persona. "Sometimes I forget that it took me a good year to forget what society up there taught me."

I'm not sure I know what he means, but I remain silent. I'm frightened now.

He watches the meat as he turns the spit to avoid overcooking the animal. Flames periodically lick up to envelop and claim the fresh body, igniting a few remaining hairs. Mac lifts the rat off the fire, pulls out the hairs, and places it back.

"The world's going to end soon," he announces. "There'll be another holocaust. Men up there are too evil and people will come down here and ask me for help. We'll be the presidents and heads of state. We'll be the ones to teach them how to survive. That's why I'm here."

Do you feel you are sacrificing yourself for this vision? I ask. Aren't you missing out on life?

"Hell, no," he answers quickly and fiercely, as much because he seems prepared for the question as because of his certainty. "I am living my life to the fullest. 'Only those who suffer can understand what life is about.' Some guy wrote that—Patrick White, I think. He won a Nobel Prize. 'We are betrayers by nature. We disappoint high hopes. The healthy tear the sick apart. Only those who suffer can understand what life is about.'

"That man knew the truth and wasn't afraid of it," Mac continues after a moment, toying again with the spit. "Happiness is for the weak. It's an escape from life." He mistakenly spears his thumb with the hot tip of the spit. His own deep red blood bubbles forth.

"Look, Miss," he says, suddenly louder and sharper. His eyes seem to flash with anger in the firelight. "I don't need your pity and I'm not asking for your help. Don't mess with my mind or my plans!"

He looks away sharply, into the blackness beyond the fire. After a second, I follow his stare but see nothing. I hear only the sizzling rat.

"It's alright," he says, not to me but to the darkness. "She's OK."

I stare even harder, trying to catch the momentary glow of eyes. They are gone, as if the lids were closed to extinguish them.

Why didn't he come forward? I ask.

Mac shrugs away any explanation. "It's Smidge. He's been guarding me."

All the time?

"Yeah. That's his job. He watches over me."

Can't he come and sit with us?

"He doesn't trust you," Mac says.

I can't understand why, I say. You've already searched me for guns and knives.

"He's afraid I might tell you some of our secrets. We have plans, you know. He wanted to watch you to see how you move. We tell everything by the way people move. We don't just let anyone come in. You could be a spy."

For whom?

"For another group that wants to start a war with us," he says evenly. "Here, let me show you something."

He rises, but seems to have second thoughts. He takes the rat from the fire, touching the browned meat with his fingers but quickly jerking them back. He soothes his fingers in his mouth.

"Mmmm," he licks his lips and places the cooked animal on a section of newspaper. For a moment, it looks like fish and chips bought from a London stand, but then my mind sees the headless rat twitch. I flinch.

Now Mac looks at me. "C'mon," he orders.

We walk farther along the tunnel, away from the direction we had come, and through a small arch into another recess. Mac begins pulling loose bricks from the wall. Inside, on a floor covered loosely by garbage bags, is a small arsenal of guns and ammunition. Some are pistols; others look like the semiautomatics used by street gangs.

Mac pulls me back after I get only a quick look and replaces the bricks.

How many guns are in there? I ask.

"That's not the point. The point is we're building our security. Not just Smidge and myself but a whole group of us. This is far more extensive than you'd believe."

Aren't you afraid of people up there knowing you have this stuff?

"No," he says firmly. "We'll move them when you're gone in case you try to find them again, which you wouldn't. Besides, they won't believe you. They're not the danger to us. It's the few other communities down here who are trying to destroy us, take what we've got. It's all a struggle for the future. They want to be the leaders of the future, but we are the ones destined for leader-ship."

It sounds like something out of a science fiction movie, maybe *Road Warrior,* I say, suddenly worried as the words escape me that he might become furious.

He hasn't seen the film, he says, and then adds with a smile that terrifies me, "You got a lot to learn, Miss, but at least you know where to come when the holocaust begins."

The air begins to stifle me and I feel I have to leave for fresh air. I silently promise myself I'll never return to this place, and never be tempted to visit Mac again.

Mac senses my discomfort and quickly begins to guide me up and out. I still can't see Smidge, I say.

"He doesn't like questions," Mac says. "But he must like you. You're the first outsider he hasn't thrown bottles and rocks at."

We climb two levels up, one by a wall ladder, the other along pipes, before he leaves me still one level from the surface. He never goes to the first level, he says apologetically. On the first level, he advises, it's only about one hundred feet until the exit to the street. I turn back to ask him which direction I should take, but I can no longer see him through the darkness, only the outline of two fig-ures.

"Right or left?" I yell into the darkness, my fright verging on panic. "Right or left?"

"Right," a voice much deeper than Mac's says. I think it was Smidge, but I never saw him.

4

The Underground Population

OMELESS PEOPLE HAVE BEEN CALLED MANY NAMES AND DE-
scribed in many ways—unseen men, forgotten men, dere-
licts, hobos, vagrants, bums, beggars. They have lived in
Hoovervilles, shantytowns, boxcars, and sewers. They are a problem in every modern industrialized country today. In Japan, homeless people are called "johatsu," meaning wandering spirit or one
who has lost his identity. "They" are not only men, but also
women and their children. And they live not only in the streets
where you see them but also under the sidewalks where you don't.

New York's underground homeless are only the latest in a
long history of people living below the surface of the earth. In
ancient times, men were forced to live underground. Slaves of
Egypt and Rome lived, worked, and died in their mines. Other
peoples have chosen for one reason or another to make their homes
underground voluntarily, such as the Cimmerian priests who attended the subterranean oracles of the classical world.

"They [the priests] live in underground dwellings which they
call argillae and it is through tunnels that they visit each other back
and forth," Nigel Pennick writes in *The Subterranean Kingdom: A
Survey of Man-Made Structures Beneath the Earth,* quoting Ephorus,
who wrote around 500 B.C. Like many monastic orders before and

since, the Cimmerians lived in cells cut from rock and emerged only to minister to pilgrims visiting their shrines. They had a rule that they should never see daylight, and so they left their burrows for the surface only at night, returning before the break of dawn. "Pits with vertical entrances were once a popular form of dwelling," Pennick writes. "The indigenous inhabitants of the Crimea lived in them."

During the Tatar invasions in the Middle Ages, Crimean peoples hid in these old holes. Early Armenians lived in well-like homes, too, as did the people of prehistoric Britain. A series of cylindrical pits near Highfield, one mile south of Salisbury, England were found on a high chalk ridge. More than 100 such pits have been studied. They vary in depth from seven to fifteen feet, with widths from six to twelve feet. Some experts date them to the Neolithic period; others put them in the Bronze Age. They were probably used mainly in the winter, according to archeologists. Similar structures for winter use are still found today in remote parts of the Himalayas.

In more modern times, subterranean houses were built in Scotland and Ireland, the Souterrains of France, and the Erdstalle of Germany. In some cases the underground dwellings were inhabited by poverty-stricken workers of the nineteenth and even early twentieth centuries. They were often viewed as subhuman. "Modern Troglodytes" was the title of an article by Robert Garner in *The Reliquary* in 1865 about his discovery that "whole communities live in subterranean villages, and in our own times, and in mid-England. The New Red Sandstone is particularly tempting for the formation of such dwellings, and was thereto excavated very largely in former times, for instance in Sneinton, and on the Lene in Notts, Nottinghamshire. Also the lime debris near Buxton has been burrowed for the same object," he writes.

The largest remaining village at the time, Garner found, was at Dunsley Rock, known locally as Gibraltar, where seventeen separate underground dwellings housed forty-two people. Other nearby cells cut out of the rock were used as byres or styes for animals.

He reports asking one "troglodyte woman" how many people

lived in one cavelike dwelling. "Nine of we," she replied, with rent three shillings a week. In a pretentious aside, Garner wrote, "We were satisfied with what we had seen of the troglodytes without feeling any strong desire to become a member or any class of them ourselves."

Probably the last underground village in England were the "lime houses" at Buxton in Derbyshire. Lime workers, who were paid pittances and treated much like slaves, burrowed their homes into the spoil heaps from the lime-burning industry. French geologist Faugas de Sant-Fond left this account of a 1784 visit to Buxton: "I looked in vain for the habitations of so many laborers and their numerous families without being able to see so much as one cottage, when at length I discerned that the whole tribe, like so many moles, had formed their residences underground. . . . Not one of them lived in a house."

"Wretched and disgusting are these caves in the extreme," according to an unnamed correspondent Pennick quotes in *The Subterranean Kingdom*. "And but for having their entrances closed by a door, [they] might be more easily taken for the dens of wolves or bears than the abodes of humanized beings."

Secondhand reports suggest these subhuman conditions existed as late as 1928. "Fortunately," Pennick concludes, "they have now been relegated to the annals of the Industrial Revolution."

Unfortunately, however, they still exist and even flourish—in a different form—in the tunnels and caverns under today's biggest cities. Few are as inhabited as in New York, but many have the potential for the same kind of derelict population to find and settle in them.

Paris, for example, is honeycombed with a network of tunnels beyond those of its famed Metro subway system. Some date from the Gaulist period in prehistoric times. Most are the abandoned workings of mines from which much of the city's building stone was quarried. During the eighteenth century a series of collapses on the surface led to the rediscovery of the abandoned tunnels, which were then used as charnel houses—repositories for the bones of Parisians who had been taken from the graves of overcrowded cemeteries to make more land available for development in the city. The skeletal remains of over three million individuals are said to be deposited in these tunnels known as the "Catacombs."

Rome, London, and Moscow are just a few of the cities where the digging of long subway lines uncovered long-abandoned tunnels. In Rome, workers found cellars, caves, galleries, catacombs, and underground chapels. In Moscow, a warren of tunnels was unearthed that was said to be the semilegendary Secret City of Ivan the Terrible. Moscow's subways are already said to be home for tens of thousands of postcommunist homeless. In Japan, the homeless frequent Tokyo's subways.

TODAY, NEW YORK CITY'S UNDERGROUND HOMELESS LIVE IN THE secluded tunnels that run beneath the busy streets in an interconnected lattice of subway and railroad train tunnels, often unused now, that in some areas reach seven levels below the streets. Often shunned by the street homeless, the underground homeless are outcasts in a world of outcasts. They go underground for many objective reasons. The housing shortage and inadequate welfare budgets are only two. Some go down for safety, to escape thieves, rapists, and common cruelty. They go down to escape the law, to find and use drugs and alcohol unhassled by their families, friends, and society. Some families go into the tunnels to avoid giving up their children to foster homes. Some, ashamed of their poverty and apparent "failure" in society and impoverished appearance, go to escape seeing their own reflections in passing shop windows. Some fall into the tunnels to deteriorate slowly, out of the way of people aboveground and in a place they can call their own home.

Underground, they live often in groups, as if huddled like prehistoric men against the elements—as well as against the rats, human predators, and the dark. One community has a formal hierarchy, with a "mayor" and "spokesman" who are elected, and "runners" who are appointed; it seems to desire some semblance of societal structure from aboveground. There are communities of families, runaways, homosexuals, and diverse independent individuals. Some are loose-knit associations of individuals. Some are gentle and welcoming; others are violent and hostile. The largest single category is substance (drug or alcohol) abusers. The next largest category is the mentally ill.

"THEY CALL US THE 'MOLE PEOPLE.' IT GIVES US AN AIR OF MYSTERY wouldn't you say?" laughed Squeeze, a thirty-two-year-old man who earned his nickname squeezing through pick-axed holes and between the forest of pipes that have been the burrows and trees of his world on and off for eight years. "Sure, they think we're animals. We use our instincts down here. Outcasts? Well, we is. We don't belong up there no more," he shrugged. "If they scared of us, more power to us. We know what we are, most of us anyway. We human too, more human than most I would say. More human than most. But you, let them call us the mole people, cuz that 'bout sums it up, how they view us and how they treat us. We are the mole people."

The population of the underground homeless is not known precisely, and estimates are controversial. Transit and welfare authorities prefer to give sanguine estimates, in part to reduce fear among commuters about the potential threat of these tunnel people, in part to mute criticism of their efforts and their budgets to attack the problem. No census of the underground population has been taken, but a 1986 study for the mayor's office estimated that five thousand people lived in the subway system alone. This was a rough estimate at best, according to Marsha Martin who authored the study, because homeless people are often evasive. Her figure did not count the homeless in the railroad tunnels, both those still in use and those long abandoned. A 1991 survey by the New York Health Department counted 6,031 homeless in the Grand Central and Penn stations alone.* One transit official dealing with the problem privately contended that the total underground population was about twenty-five thousand at that time, but my research leads me to conclude that the number is closer to five thousand.

---

*Both of these studies were internal and unpublished. Individuals provided them to me.

MANY AUTHORITIES SEE TODAY'S UNDERGROUND HOMELESS AS ESSEN-
tially irretrievable. The executive director of New York's Mental
Health Association has compared the difficulty of rehabilitating the
underground homeless to "taking a wild animal and attempting to
domesticate it." The issue appears to center on whether a significant portion of homeless people, wherever they live, can hold jobs.
Sociologists Alice Baum and Donald Burnes concluded that 85
percent of the homeless are "too crippled by mental illness or
substance addiction to benefit" from the various programs and
services. In a letter to *The Washington Post*, Suellen L. Stokes, the
director of the Eleanor Kennedy shelter in Fairfax, Virginia, says
she once believed most of the homeless were "employed or employ-
able," but after almost two years at the shelter, she reversed that
view. "Denying or minimizing the extent of mental illness and
substance abuse suffered by the homeless does them a great disser-
vice," Stokes says, "and prevents the channeling of limited resources toward programs that may make a difference for some (i.e.,
other) people."

Transit authorities would like to ignore the issue, both quan-
titatively and qualitatively, and they would prefer that the media
did the same, lest their accounts frighten off riders and give the
city a bad name. Homeless advocacy groups are also reluctant to
deal with the underground homeless openly—or at least to publi-
cize their plight—for fear the public will lump all homeless people
with the most violent and dangerous of the underground homeless
and thereby lose their sympathy and support. The issue will not
go away with ignorance. Nor will it be solved or even successfully
managed by treating the underground homeless as people just down
on their luck. Certainly silence will not prevent that underground
population from increasing.

Deep in the tunnels under New York, there are people struggling to survive. Here rats run in dark waves toward, not away,
from people and the crunch of roaches underfoot is as familiar as
the stench of sewage seeping through the rock walls. Here the thin
streams of daylight filtering through the occasional overhead grate
barely penetrate to the floor in the stagnant blackness. "They eat,

sleep, and defecate here," one policeman says with a mixture of pity and disgust. "Your eyes are seared at times by the smell of urine until sometimes you can't breathe. It almost knocks your brains out."

Some of the homeless live on the catwalks just a few feet above the rushing roar of subway trains and in holes chopped out of walls that support platforms on which commuters wait, but most of the homeless find their homes far enough away from operating tracks where they hear only a slight tremor when trains pass. Still others live in relative splendor—in the frescoed waiting rooms of a few long-abandoned subway stations, at least one of which is said to contain a piano, a fountain, and mirrored walls.

They die of AIDS and overdoses, but also of common colds that turn into pneumonia, of physical violence, and of tuberculosis, hypothermia, and diabetes. Their life expectancy is three to five years, one health-care official estimated. Or perhaps only two years. "If a knife, bullet, train, or live [high voltage] wire doesn't get them," he sighed, "some illness that should only be lethal in medieval times will."

Whether New York's underground homeless are harbingers of the future is an open question. They are a crisis of our time which, with help, the future can overt. The homeless appear to be overcrowding; they seem attracted to, or at least more numerous in, huge urban areas where they can better live within the cracks, as it were. A great deal of food in cities is thrown out, particularly from restaurants, and a good deal of it reaches the homeless in one way or another. The large gaps between the wealthy and the destitute in cities also makes begging more successful and in some cases more profitable than a minimum-wage job. However, urban housing will always be in short supply, and accessible tunnels will always hold an attraction to some homeless.

Although virtually all large cities of the world have seen some of their inhabitants go into the subway tunnels and below, New York may be exceptional in its high proportion of substance abusers and mentally ill in the underground population. If society again decides to institutionalize the homeless mentally ill, and if the present easy access to cheap drugs could be curbed, the underground population of New York might be shrunk significantly and the spread of this phenomenon to other cities would be less likely. But these are big "ifs."

The notion that the underground homeless people are "irretrievable" is refuted by their hope and caring for one another, which reaches far beyond the harsh environment in which they live. I know many people who attest to it. Theirs is a strange and foreign world, but it is very near and largely of our making.

5

Underground Spaces

"THERE IS A CITY BENEATH THE STREETS," WRITES ROBERT E. Sullivan, Jr., in his introduction to Harry Granick's *Underneath New York,* and the description has been used many times since. Sullivan meant it to encompass the vast networks of cables, gas mains, water and sewer lines, and the subway and train tunnels that serve as the nervous system, intestines, and bowels of New York City. However, when Sergeant Henry of the Metropolitan Transit Police uses it, he means the people who have made homes and communities within the subway and train tunnels, and the natural and man-made passages accessible to and from those tunnels, which are the dwellings of New York's underground homeless. He means the burrows, large and small, that are not just under the streets but also plunge seven stories underground, and the interconnection between the homeless communities that exist there. The underworld of Manhattan is far more complex and extensive than dreamed about by most of those who walk the sidewalks of New York.

Manhattan is an anthill-like structure, its granite bedrock honeycombed and crisscrossed by almost endless cavities and burrows. Some of the monuments are like mountains, as deeply rooted underground as their peaks are high. Concrete, bomb-proof tubes are sunk eighty stories below the Chrysler Building, for example.

In order to understand the structures, the city should be peeled back layer by layer.

Below the first three inches of asphalt and ten inches of concrete—both drenched with toxic chemicals seeping down from the roadways—are channels carrying all kinds of wires for telephones, for electricity for homes and offices, for street and traffic lights, fire and burglar alarms, and the rest. Below the wires are the gas lines and then, some six to ten feet down, are the water mains that run for hundreds of miles in all directions. At the next deeper level are steam lines, more than one hundred miles of them, and then the sewer lines and sewer tunnels, which are not level but slope downward to get gravity's help in disposing of city waste and rain waters.

The underground networks are not only vast but chaotic. "Computer graphics are too calculated to capture the randomness of the world beneath the avenues," Sullivan writes. In the mid-nineteeth century, New York had fifteen different gas companies, each with its own network of mains. Their consolidated successor, Con Ed, retired the oldest lines to preclude accidents and, since 1970, more than fifty thousand feet of old mains—some ten miles—have been replaced. Channels are often left vacant, and into them slip the homeless.

New York's subway lines wind through 731 sprawling miles of New York's five boroughs, in tunnels that burrow down to eighteen stories below ground at 191st Street and Broadway in Manhattan. These miles are divided among 23 lines and 466 stations. New York's subways constitute the largest urban railroad system in the world, with 6,100 cars that carry a quarter of a million pounds of flesh and blood each day—"the greatest moving mass of human tissue in the universe, apart from the planet earth," as Jim Dwyer wrote in *Subway Lives*. The eight-car trains move at up to forty miles an hour, and if you stand next to the tracks deep in the tunnels where they hit maximum speed, they take about ten ground-shaking, ear-shattering seconds to pass.

No complete, single blueprint of New York's underground exists. Construction crews installing yet more lines and tunnels must sift through the archives of old maps to guard against breaking water mains and electrical wires, and then dig test pits to verify the picture they glean from the many different and often contradictory maps. Even they are often flabbergasted at what they find when excavating.

A ninety-two-foot-long merchant sailing ship from the eighteenth century was found under Front Street, part of the landfill when Manhattan's lower tip was being extended. Its bow is in a museum in Newport News, Virginia, but its stern remains buried under a filigree of utility cables under Front Street. One excavation found the wall that gave Wall Street its name—a long stockade of upright wooden timber designed to keep out intruders, presumably Indians, three hundred years ago. Underground latrines from Revolutionary days are not uncommon. From more recent times, mysterious vaults are sometimes hidden just below the crust of the sidewalks.

There are also disused subway stations and abandoned tunnels of various kinds. In 1912, workers digging the BMT (or the Brooklyn Manhattan Transit, known by graffiti artists as "the ding-dong line" because the doors used to make a ding-dong sound when they opened) tunnels found the city's first subway line twenty-one feet under Broadway between Warren and Murray Streets. It consisted of a single pneumatic tube 312 feet long and 9 feet wide, in which the cars were pulled or pushed along by huge fans at the ends of the tunnel. Noted inventor Alfred Ely Beach, the founder and one-time editor of *Scientific American* magazine, built the subway in 1870 and it ran for only a few weeks before New York's infamous Mayor Boss Tweed shut it down. Other early underground transportation systems included a terminal for trolleys, which is still visible under Essex Street off a modern subway line, and a tunnel by which President Franklin D. Roosevelt traveled from the Waldorf-Astoria Hotel to Grand Central for a train ride to Hyde Park. Beach's is the only one of several experimental subway lines uncovered, so far as known. One of its features, a waiting room furnished with a crystal chandelier and grand piano, was found intact when the line was rediscovered.

Into it and other large, abandoned underground waiting

rooms have moved the homeless, sometimes only at night but also living there throughout the day. They are similarly encamped in some abandoned subway stations, like that at City Hall, which is now not long enough to host the modern trains. They also live in what is probably the newest abandoned underground structure—a six-lane stretch of highway built in the late sixties beneath Christie Street, which was almost immediately sealed, abandoned, and forgotten.

Some of them are fortunate to find shelter in burrows and tunnels near the restrooms built for the subway rider but long since closed. At one time 932 such facilities were open, but since 1981, only one hundred remain available to the public. Ingenious homeless people use many of the ostensibly closed restrooms and the toilet facilities built below the theater district on Broadway and long inaccessible from the streets.

With hundreds or thousands living underground, many die there, either in accidents or from disease, or perish because they lose their way. To sniff out dead and rotting bodies, the Transit Authority has Beau, the only dog in the state trained for the purpose.

Today's transit employees who work underground repairing track and cleaning debris are just as afraid of the world below the streets as those workers a century ago who, as they dug the tunnels, feared cave-ins, whirlpools of sand, and sudden water flows from springs below and rain above. Now the fear is more personal—rats, roaches, leaking sewers and water mains, loose asbestos, hypodermic needles that might be contaminated with AIDS, human waste, and ordinary garbage. They also fear the people they encounter in the netherworld.

Sullivan considers the presence of people living underground to be a significant change from 1940 when Granick wrote the first edition of *Underneath New York*.

"Homeless people who now live underground by the thousands were more an oddity than an issue back then, as the city was close to full employment," Sullivan said of the immediate pre–World War II period. Now, although some maintenance crews get to know squatters in certain tunnel areas and even bring extra sandwiches for them, most workers believe the underground homeless are dangerous—criminals on the run, insane people, drug addicts, alcoholics, AIDS cases, tuberculosis patients—all of whom represent threats of one kind or another.

Most frightening to the workers is the area between 28th Street and Canal Street on the Lexington Line, and the abandoned stations like those at City Hall, 18th Street, 91st Street, and Worth Street—in all of which communities of homeless have settled. Only a bit less dangerous, they believe, is the Second Avenue Station, which is popular because it is an unusually warm tunnel and is situated near a couple of food kitchens and welfare shelters.

The train tunnels under Grand Central Station contain perhaps the largest collection of squatters. There, in a mere three-quarters of a square mile, thirty-four miles of track stretch out along seven distinct levels before funneling into twenty-six main rail arteries going north, east, and west. Police have cleared out as many as two hundred people living in a single community like "the Condos"—short for condominiums and so named because they consider it very posh—and "Burma's Road" and "Riker's Island." Those evicted from Grand Central went mainly to the tunnels under Penn Station on the West Side, and into tunnels under the Port Authority bus terminal. Some went deeper under Grand Central, down below the levels of subways and trains.

The first of the inhabited tunnels to get publicity was one near the Lafayette Street Station. Several dozen people lived there in 1989. One underground home consisted of a "little living room" with a mattress, table, and couch. A group shared a television set and a VCR, using electricity diverted from the nearby station. Another group enjoyed a stereo set. One area was wallpapered. Kitchen utensils and food supplies were also found.

Finding ways into these small and large burrows associated with the subway lines has always been rather easy. Thousands of stairways lead into subway stations and hundreds of others serve as emergency exits from tunnels. Locks were placed on most entrances to prevent unauthorized entry, with only four hundred keys made for Transit Authority personnel. There is a Brooklyn hardware store within walking distance of Authority headquarters that sells the key for a dollar. During rush hours, when some station turnstiles are crammed solid with commuters, homeless people who have settled in abandoned side entrances sometimes open their "homes" to the rushing passengers who, in gratitude, are invited to drop a subway token or some coins into a proffered cup.

"I consider it my public service," says Hammer with a broad smile, tipping his Mets cap to commuters as they pour like lemmings through his door. They ignore his neat bedroll piled in the corner and the small box that serves as a table. The waxy black residue on the box supports the remains of a candle. Hammer's long, thin frame seems only a little thicker than the vertical iron rods in the gate he obligingly holds open with one hand. In the other hand is his Styrofoam cup.

6

The Bowery

COLD RAIN FALLS ON THE APRIL NIGHT AS A POLICE CAR WEAVES through the heavy traffic of lower Manhattan. By 8:30 P.M. the Bowery is already deserted. The crowning lights of New York's Chrysler and Empire State buildings brighten the skyline to the north, but in the Bowery, where gray sheets of metal close like heavy eyelids over the sweatshops for the night, only headlights and flashes of red and blue police lights reflect off the wet streets.

"Please, you go," a cabdriver calls in a thick Russian accent through his unrolled window to the police cruiser. "You go. American wonderful. You wonderful. You make the streets of American wonderful," he enthuses, waving his bare forearm through the rain, his shirtsleeve rolled up beyond his elbow as he yields the right-of-way at the intersection to the merging police car.

Sergeant Steve Riley nods and smiles, but Officer Neil Farrell behind the steering wheel looks suspiciously at the cabbie, seeking a trace of sarcasm. He finds none, and we move on.

"This is a crazy area," says Farrell. "You can expect anything. It looks OK because it's been done up, well lit now and all, but you got bad elements here." He glances toward poorly dressed men and women with beaten or angry expressions peppering the sidewalks.

Off West Broadway, the police car turns onto Hudson Street, still paved with cobblestones and grooved with the silver tracks of

49

a bygone era over a century ago, when the filigreed steel network of elevated subway trains dominated the scene. By the end of the nineteenth century, the Bowery had acquired the seedy reputation that still hangs over its name, with roaming prostitutes, flop-houses, pawnshops, and "slave markets" where manual workers were hired off street corners. For decades the Bowery was the single acceptable place for New York's outcasts, and the disaffiliated found outside of the Bowery were ushered back within its bound-aries by the law enforcers. It was the most infamous of the nation's skid rows through World War II.

"No other road in North America has been disreputable for so many decades," historian Richard Beard wrote of Bowery Street in *On Being Homeless: Historical Perspectives,* the two-way street after which New York's skid row was named. The street runs for sixteen blocks in lower Manhattan, but the actual skid row section encom-passes a larger area of side streets and avenues.

In 1949 almost fourteen thousand homeless were counted in the Bowery. Through gentrification and cleanup efforts, the popu-lation was more than halved by the early sixties. In 1987 another census claimed fewer than a thousand homeless lived in the Bowery.

Not all of them left as the census would suggest. Some went underground.

By day, many can still be seen on the streets. Some beg for change, some scavenge in refuse bins on corners, some pick through garbage behind restaurants. Some are bolder, approaching cars stopped at red lights with muddy wet rags, to "wash" windshields before demanding money. At night, the streets are clear. Some have gone to homeless shelters. Many have gone into the subways system and its network of dark, protective, and yet dangerous tunnels.

"I was pushed from a hotel into the street," Joe, a Bowery tunnel dweller says, trembling either from anger or alcohol a few days earlier, "and I was pushed from the streets into these tunnels." Joe, who says he's seventy-two years old, has a grizzly gray beard and angry eyes. His face is lined with a constant scowl.

"You ask me why I'm here?" he said earnestly. "You go ask

them," he pointed a crooked finger ingrained with dirt toward a police car. "Ask them where I should go. They'll say to hell. They'll put you in a death house they call a shelter if they don't kill you themselves. They don't know anything about who lives down in the tunnels, how many of us there are. You ask and they'll say no one. Well, I ain't no one down there," he spit, "only up here. You go, you ask them."

Inside, the local police precinct house looks bleak and functional, lit by cold fluorescent tubes, but the atmosphere is congenial and lively. Officers bat about friendly insults and exchange serious compliments. They also volunteer, once they learn my purpose, the casualty list of officers who go into the tunnels: one beaten to death with his own nightstick by a tunnel dweller; another left with an eight-year-old mental capacity after a similar beating; and two officers killed with their own guns as they escorted tunnel people out of the Bowery tunnel. "The motherfuckers shot them dead," an officer says, shaking his head. "You always got to be careful of those people."

They show me mug shots of the most notorious graffiti writers—Smith, Reese, and Ghost—who mar subway cars and tunnel walls, and on particularly bold days, even walls next to the precinct or the bathroom of the precinct house with fingerprint ink left from a booking—Smith's notorious trademark. Smart kids, they say, kids that could go somewhere if they would clean up and shake this addiction of smearing paint to gain dubious fame.

Lieutenant John Romero stands tall with a mustache and unflagging warm brown eyes. He offers me a firm handshake and his beaten leather chair. His desk, sunk in the corner of the squad room and laden with papers and pictures of his young family, is separated by a thin, head-high divider from three other desks in the cramped room. Six officers stand around, waiting to take Romero and me on a night tour of the tunnels.

Romero is responsible for policing Bowery subway tunnels for the New York City Transit Authority. He explains the "tunnel situation" with a mixture of smooth public relations phrasing and sharp street-smart remarks.

"We first found people living in the tunnels in the seventies," he begins, "and by 1989, when we believe the problem reached its highest peak, we estimate that there were five thousand homeless persons living in the subway system. That year, seventy-nine homeless persons died in the subways—some hit by trains, some electrocuted, some died of natural causes."

By that time, much in the same way as graffiti-covered cars and seats had done, "the behavior of the homeless in the system contributed to public perception, commuter perception, that the subways were out of control," he continues. As the problem grew, police officers began resisting efforts to oust the homeless. "Some cops felt it wasn't police work. Other cops felt it was morally wrong to eject destitute people."

Through special information sessions and videos, "we made our officers see that by enforcing the law [against trespassing], they were interrupting the behavior of these people that was causing them harm. And also by enforcing the rules, we were forcing these people to make a decision about their future. A lot of them chose to get out and accept the services for the homeless aboveground."

Another program was needed to provide outreach services to the homeless in the tunnels, those who lived not in moving cars and on subway platforms but went into the tunnels, along the electrified tracks, to find some sort of sleeping place in the darkness underground.

"We've had a homeless outreach program since 1982," Romero says, "but prior to 1990, it was only five officers and a sergeant. They worked with the New York City Human Resources Administration, which supplied two social workers, a driver, and a bus." The officers and social workers would go into the tunnels only if a track worker had been seriously assaulted, or if a motorman driving a subway train spotted a person who was a threat to himself and the train. Then the team would search for the homeless, bring them up from the tunnels, and bus them off to shelters.

"That was a Band-Aid approach to a problem that was growing and growing. There was no regular patrolling into the tunnels, going in constantly to try to help these people," Romero says.

"We asked for more officers, but the city was in a financial crunch. Still, we managed to assign thirty officers to the job."

That year, 1990, more than four thousand homeless were ejected from the tunnels, according to Romero. "It's been cleaned up," he says. "You'll find pockets of one or two persons here and there, but a few years ago, in just a two-block stretch of tunnels under the Bowery, there were as many as two hundred people. It would take us six hours to clear them out because we'd constantly have to shut down the power [of the third rail]. Now we go in there with the power on."

Throughout Manhattan, Romero claims, over seven thousand homeless were transferred from tunnels to aboveground shelters in 1990, and another four thousand in the first four months of 1991. "But it's not enforcement," he emphasizes, "it's outreach."

"Many homeless advocates saw this as a crackdown on the homeless," he says. "It wasn't. It was a crackdown on violators. We have a responsibility to our ridership to provide a safe environment in the subways. We see a lot of track fires set by people cooking down there in the tunnels. We know that debris they leave around causes fires when sparks from the trains hits it. So we target violations, not homeless."

Officer Al Logan describes a typical encounter: "When you ask them if they want to go to a shelter, they say no, that's not for me. You ask them three or four times, they say, maybe I'll give it a shot. If they still say no, we eject them. Most of them won't go to shelters; a lot are afraid of being beaten or robbed or raped there. But we never put our hands on them."

How tunnel dwellers can be ejected without being manhandled is puzzling, but I let it go, just as I do Logan's comment—which contradicts Romero's—that most tunnel homeless do not go to shelters after being rousted.

"You'll hear stories about the shelters," Romero says, "and I'm not saying city shelters are the Ritz, but they're a lot better than what you see in the tunnels. The real reason these people don't want to go to shelters is that shelters have rules, and these people don't want to abide by any rules.

"You see crack vials, hypodermic needles down there. You can't shoot up in a shelter. You can't drink in a shelter. The simple fact is these people choose this kind of environment because they don't want to abide by any rules.

"Most people living in the tunnels under the Bowery are hard-core. Mostly male but some females, 95 percent are males between twenty and forty-five years old. At least 80 percent are mentally ill or chemically dependent," Romero continues. "I've heard of families down there, but in seven years with this unit, the closest I've come to seeing one was a woman about sixty and her son about forty. Really, there are no families in the subways.

"We're going to walk underground from Broadway-Lafayette to Second Avenue, about four blocks, and you'll see firsthand. One guy described it as the closest thing to hell he's ever seen. Really, it's hard to describe. You have to see it to believe it."

The officers making the patrol don fluorescent vests, cloth gloves, hard hats, flashlights, and masks to combat the stench and tuberculosis. "You don't want to touch anything or anyone down there," Logan warns me when I'm outfitted like them.

A few officers check their guns. "They are not all hostile," Romero says. "We've never really had a problem. They know us down there."

We enter the Broadway-Lafayette subway station, pass through the turnstiles, and walk down several flights of stairs to the lowest platform. We jump off the platform to the tracks, carefully crossing the third rail. There is no space, absolutely none, for a person to stand between the wall and a passing train without being struck.

"Don't step on the third rail," Sergeant Steve Klambatsen warns me. "I hate to see that happen. Sparks fly everywhere, but the worst part is that the electricity blows off the extremities. Hands, head, whatever, explode. It's disgusting."

"That's enough," says Romero. There used to be over two hundred individuals living in the few blocks of this Bowery tunnel, Romero says. "You can see how we've cleaned it out, but we still have to police it twice a day." Many of the hard-core tunnel dwellers moved farther into the tunnels, especially into the Port Authority and Penn Station tunnels, where they are not yet disturbed by police.

The sound of rain pounding on the street can be heard, and wind whistles through the grates, but neither penetrates into the tunnel, which is noticeably warmer. Romero says that on average, tunnels are twenty-five degrees warmer than the street. I feel somehow more secure despite the danger.

The tracks are cleaner than I expected: a few crack vials with colored tops, as promised, as well as a few bottles of spilled pills, some needles, and an occasional piece of clothing. The air becomes fouler as we go farther. Against the wall, a flashlight beam picks up fresh feces that lie on a glass dish, and wet urine stains a spot on the cement wall nearby.

A mouse, its eyes squeezed shut and its paws curled tightly under its head, lies dead near the tracks.

"That's good," says Klambatsen, who normally leads the night patrol. "That means there are no rats. They spray powerful chemicals down here to kill the rats. We don't come down for three days after that because it's so strong. We clear the people out before they spray, of course. . . . Yes, I suppose some do come right back and live in the spray, but, as far as I know, there've been no fatalities from that."

The officers search the tunnel as if for animals, stirring blankets and looking into cardboard boxes. Eight homeless men are roused, shielding their eyes from the flashlights. They are asked repeatedly if they want to go to shelters. They are angry at being awakened and refuse. Two prefer the rainy streets, while the rest agree to be shuttled by a white van to a shelter.

The Bowery tunnels once held some of the largest underground homeless groups, or communities. Now we find a couple of men share the night here and there, some singles, and a woman on her own, but rarely are there more than three people in one space. In the mid-eighties, several communities of forty or fifty people set up camps underground along the Lexington Line, but they remained essentially separate, even aloof, from each other.

"I think that was because there were no women there with them," says Dale, a formidable and friendly homeless woman who lives aboveground in the Bowery. "They always expect someone to rob from them, even their friends. They didn't have women to soften them. They didn't live like a family or nothing. They lived like alcoholic men, sometimes angry, sometimes dangerous, but mostly depressed and asleep," she says. "They didn't trust each other, only people like social workers on the outside sometimes." Few of the Bowery's tunnel people say they have friends. In referring to someone they drink with or can be found hanging out with, they usually call them "an associate."

Gary Bass is one of the more established tunnel dwellers of the Bowery. Bass is well known to the officers on the patrol. He is friendly to some; for others, he has bitter distaste. He is evicted almost every night, he says, but always refuses to go to a shelter.

He enters the tunnels through emergency exits to the street, which by law cannot be sealed. One exit hatch that lifts a section of the Broadway sidewalk is part of the roof of his home, a duplex spanning two levels of the subway. The stairs to the lower floor are well swept, and the living quarters neat. His clothes drape neatly on hangars from a pipe. He shows me his working iron plugged into the tunnel's electrical system, standing atop a full-size ironing board. To read, he detaches the exit sign over a naked bulb to get its strong light. To sleep, he unscrews the bulb for complete darkness. On the top level of his duplex, where he sleeps, a passing subway sounds like the distant rumble of a country train. The entrance off the tunnel is marked by crossed brooms and guarded by a trip wire that can bring down a five-gallon water bucket, which is sometimes full and sometimes empty but always warns of an intrusion. The police have dismantled his home many times, but each time he reconstitutes it the next day, he says.

On our trip this night, eight of the homeless sleeping in the tunnel choose to take their chances in the cold rain rather than a city shelter. Six agree to go to a shelter but only after some cajoling and promises that they will be taken to Bellevue rather than the Fort Washington shelter.

TOM AND HIS FRIEND DENISE (WHO IS ALSO MALE) CONSULT WITH one another about the Bellevue promise.

"That's cool," Tom says, "but when you leave us off at Bellevue, they drive us off to Fort Washington cuz Bellevue's full. We ain't gonna stay in that Murder House." Farrell, a kind- and honorable-looking cop, convinces them that they can stay at Bellevue and promises that he will wait with them until they are admitted, so they finally agree to go.

Among the homeless in New York, the Fort Washington shelter shares with the Armory shelter the worst reputation of the city. Stories about the violence at Fort Washington, the "Murder House," seem too numerous to be fiction.

"I'll tell you about Fort Washington," a homeless man later tells me. "First, all those stories about homosexuals there, well, they are all true. The shelter people, they always watch everyone in the showers, but still I know a few guys who got raped there. I only stayed two nights. After the first night I got lice and had to throw all my stuff out. The second night I was in bed and felt something spraying across my face," he says, making a spurting motion. "I was mad, killin' mad. I was sure some guy was jerking off on me. I jumped up and was gonna kill him, only I saw it was blood that was all over me. Some guy had come over, then stabbed the guy in the next bunk to steal his shoes, and his blood was spraying on me."

THE FARTHER INTO THE TUNNELS, THE LESS EASY IT IS TO ROUSE those sleeping. Some are poked and shaken awake and are angry at being disturbed. Few run from police as they do in the Port Authority, Pennsylvania, and Grand Central tunnels. Most in the Bowery tunnel don't seem surprised by the police officers. Their reflexes are slow and wary, fighting the effects of fatigue or drugs. An officer nudges a sleeping inhabitant who snarls and grunts, clawing at the officer's hand.

"Sometimes it's hard to see them as anything but animals," the police officer confides after the incident, as we near the end of the tour. "They're trying to survive, and that can be the most dangerous instinct an animal has. But one time I found this man in the tunnel crying over the body of his lover. He wouldn't leave. The autopsy said the man had died of AIDS two days earlier, and the lover wouldn't leave the body, even to go eat."

He paused.

"That changes the way you think a bit. At least until the next one threatens you or your buddy." He smiles briefly before putting his mask back on to resume combat with the stench.

7

Living with the Law

"**S**TOP! FREEZE!" YELLS SERGEANT BRYAN HENRY, HIS DEEP
voice edged with fear.

Henry's flashlight darts blindly at movement more
heard and sensed than seen.

"Come forward! Slowly!" he orders. His hand has already
unhooked the leather safety strap over his nine-millimeter revolver
and is poised tensely above its handle.

There is hardly a sound in the tunnel, just the regular dripping of water from the streets and the whispered scurrying of rats.
The silence is as overwhelming as the tunnel's blackness.

"Shit," he says finally, his voice firmer now as he comes down
from the adrenaline rush of preparing for violent action and enters
familiar frustration. His flashlight is steadier as it ranges across
sections of wall that shield the tunnel's farther passages from its
prying beam.

"Fuck," he shouts in exasperation, thrusting the gun more
securely back into its holster. "They're so fucking fast!"

Henry runs nimbly across four subway tracks, ignoring the
third rail in pursuit of the underground homeless. When he was
first assigned to tunnel work, he bought shoes with the thickest
rubber soles he could find, he says, hoping they would insulate him
from the high voltage if he stumbled onto the rail. Now the danger
of electrocution is all but ignored as he seeks the elusive human moles.

Sergeant Henry scoping an area beneath Grand Central Station. *Photo by Margaret Morton*

The movement that roused him may have been a ploy, what tunnel people call "running interference," in which one or more individuals distract an intruder while a larger group escapes. But Henry doesn't know about that.

A dozen steps beyond the walls, he finds a thin, rusty ladder climbing a sheer cement wall. Tracing it upward, his beam circles a dark region of the wall that begins to shimmer and stir. Winged, cockroach-size insects excited by the light buzz angrily and scurry about, climbing over one another. Grimacing, Henry shores the flashlight into his belt, pulls on a pair of heavy black leather gloves, and starts cautiously up the ladder, his bulky shoes at severe angles to the shallow rungs.

On top is a recessed compartment the size of a small square room, perhaps nine feet by ten feet. Henry's roving flashlight, out again, stops in a far corner, exposing several white plates resting on a small refrigerator. A clothesline with two pairs of jeans and three T-shirts stretches diagonally from one corner to an overhead pipe. On a makeshift table consisting of a crate supported by books stands a toaster oven, open and still warm to the touch. On another such table, this one with flowers, lies a book of poetry open to W. H. Auden's "On This Island." Layers of old clothes and paper-filled garbage bags carpet the floor, serve as insulation from the dank, underground cold.

Henry kicks at the clothes and plastic bags in frustration, and then shatters the silence by striking his nightstick repeatedly against the pipes. He overturns one table and knocks the books and plates from another, savaging the dwelling with his club and feet. He is following orders to roust these homeless, who are a danger to themselves as well as the transit system, but he seems to be acting out a larger anger, and perhaps even enjoying his strength.

"They were just here," he says, pointing to a bowl in which a few drops of milk remain.

A doll with a smudged face has been left behind. Her large eyes seem to stare at me. Books and plates litter the floor. I turn over a paperback, *Winnie the Pooh*.

Henry seems to feel the anxious eyes of hating witnesses. "They're probably still here, watching us," he says, looking about challengingly, and he attacks the pipes with renewed vigor.

This is a typical trip into the tunnels for Sergeant Henry and for other officers of the Metropolitan Transit Police, not according to them but to J.C., an underground dweller who has watched their regular forays.

"Actually, Henry ain't as bad as most of the others," says J.C., who describes himself as "spokesman" for a community of two hundred homeless who have settled under Grand Central Station.

"Some of them will kick people around when they find them sleeping, and break up their stuff," he explains. "No reason at all. They take out a lot of their aggression down there, I'll tell you that much, 'specially when they're having a bad day."

J.C., a small, lithe, and sneakered black man in his middle to late twenties, clearly remembers with lingering bitterness the first time he met Henry. Henry, a large muscular man over six feet tall in his early forties, also recalls the meeting, but he sees it as one of his more amusing tunnel experiences.

Henry had been after J.C. for months, knowing he was living illegally in the tunnels but unable to catch and evict him. He would follow J.C. into a tunnel only to lose him in the dark underground mazes and back out before he got in too deeply. He'd wait at the entrance for J.C. to reemerge, but J.C. knew too many ways in and out of the tunnels for the cop.

One spring day, however, the sergeant saw his quarry step out of a tunnel and into an alleyway. Henry, shouting and drawing his revolver, began chasing J.C. up the alley at full run. J.C., after an initial sprint, realized that he was in a dead-end trap and, hearing the ominous hammer click on the policeman's gun, he stopped abruptly. He stopped faster than Henry could pull up, and, before each knew what happened, the big cop had his cocked revolver cold against the skin of J.C.'s face.

"I had him against the wall," Henry laughs. "It was so funny. We were both shaking. Neither of us knew what to do. He was so scared he wet his pants."

"Yeah, we were both shaking," J.C. grimly agrees later. "The difference was he had the gun. He's always been quick to grab his gun."

Henry didn't arrest J.C., he only made "contact" with the tunnel person.

From the dangerous encounter, the two men developed a wary relationship. They remained merely nodding acquaintances for a long time before Henry persuaded J.C. to enroll in a vocational school and live in an apartment aboveground. J.C. says he appreciates the sergeant's help but does not trust him enough to guide him to the underground community in which he then lived.

"He could lock me up for the rest of my life and I wouldn't tell him where it is," J.C. insists. "That's just the way it is, and he knows that, too."

J.C. now lives aboveground much of the time, working as a janitor. In his spare time, he is a volunteer in the Parks Department's youth program. He still visits his community, however, and speaks for them to outsiders. When he lived in the tunnels, he could be contacted only by leaving notes under a certain brick at a certain tunnel entrance. In order to talk to him about the tunnels, he insists on the same system again.

"I don't like to confuse the upstairs with the downstairs," he explains. "And I don't want any of my people up here to know about my people down there. It's safer for them that way, and better for me, too," he says. "Because people don't believe me, anyway, about my community."*

THE BEHAVIOR OF POLICE UNDERGROUND IS AS CONTROVERSIAL AS on the streets. Brutality stories are so common that rarely a conversation occurs among tunnel people without some new incident being brought up, sometimes marginally but often seriously. Violence is part of the way of life in the darkness under the streets, perhaps even more than aboveground.

Its victim one day was Peppin, an illegal Latino immigrant who lived under Platform 100 in Grand Central Station. He was a familiar figure to the police, and usually ignored. On this day, they began beating him, apparently because he couldn't stand up and move on as they ordered.

"I saw it all happen," says Seville. "Me and others—four of us—was standing down there, a ways back. No one saw us but we saw them.

"He was a nice guy, Peppin, didn't bother nobody, kept to

*J.C.'s community is described in chapter 20.

himself pretty much," Seville recalls. "He didn't do no drugs or nothing, but he was crazy because he wouldn't take much food. Didn't speak much English. Sometimes he'd take something to eat when he was desperate, but he was depressed all the time. I think he was embarrassed to eat food from garbage bins. He could barely walk because he was so weak from not eating.

"And that day he couldn't even stand up. One of the officers kept yelling, 'Get up! Get up!' But he couldn't.

"So they picked him up and threw him around. His head hit the third rail and sparks flew everywhere. His body just bounced up like you never seen, like a big dummy bouncing up, like he was on strings or rubber bands. There was blood all over the place. We thought they killed him. They thought they killed him, too, cuz they got scared; they talked about what to do with the body and what to say happened, what their story was gonna be.

"They were gonna say they chased off a gang of punks who were beating him up and when they got there, that the punks threw him on the rail and ran. That's what they were going to say," Seville shakes his head incredulously.

"We wanted to do something, watching all that, but we were afraid to go forward. I don't know. We should have. But we just stood there.

"Then the medics came, and they took him to a hospital and he lived. Peppin's still alive, but he's not the same. He can't even take care of himself no more. He just wanders around. I guess those officers were having a real bad day, but they shouldn't have been doing that shit."

Not all police are brutal, of course. Even those who brutalized Peppin are not always nasty, the homeless say. Also, many of the police are repelled by such behavior by fellow officers.

"It's no wonder these tunnel people don't come to us for help," says one cop. "If I heard those stories, I'd be hiding, too. But they're not true, or, if they are, they're exaggerated.

"I mean, people get scared down there. Policemen, too. And they act in unacceptable ways at times. No one's perfect. But if anyone has the advantage, they do, those people in the tunnels, not us. The people who live down there, they can see in the dark, and they can hide, and they throw things—steel bars and bottles and chunks of concrete. And they come right up behind us without us knowing. All we got is a gun. It doesn't do us much good if we can't see them."

Sergeant Henry bleeds, too, in his own way, although it doesn't always show.

In 1988 he became the first officer ever assigned to deal exclusively with the tunnel people, and he was told to keep them a secret. His task was described vaguely as "homeless outreach," without admitting these homeless lived underground. For sometime he told those who asked, including reporters, that no one lived in the tunnels, that the stories of "mole people" were a kind of underground folklore concocted by homeless people for their own amusement. Yet now he admits that he and his officers had cleared about four hundred peoples from the tunnels under Grand Central Station.

Henry often jokes with the homeless he encounters, in an effort to neutralize their fear and hostility. His large, loose frame conveys an image of comfortable friendliness. Like his body, several homeless people describe his shiny brown eyes as "soft."

When he and I come upon a group of homeless in the northeast corner of the station, Henry staggers backward in clowning disbelief, one hand to forehead, when he recognizes a man in a handsome trench coat over worn Reeboks.

"Man, oh, man, what happened to you?" he asks, grasping the man's frail hand in a firm, warm handshake.

"He got himself a job," explains another of the homeless group happily, still giggling at Henry's surprise. The cop is pleased—sincerely so, it seems to me—that one of the homeless is getting up and out of the tunnel life.

Despite his easy way and rapport with most homeless on his beat, some tunnel people do not trust him. Borrowing from psychological jargon, some accuse him of being on an "ego trip." One claims he likes his gun and black leather gloves "too much" and that he likes the credit and the publicity, including his picture in newspapers. Another broadly hints that Henry has taken part in beatings of homeless people, but he won't say it outright.

On the other hand, Henry has helped many homeless like J.C. to escape the tunnels, to get into job training programs, and to find housing aboveground. He asked for the duty. When he found out the great size of the problem, he asked for more officers but was refused. He took pictures of the underground people and their communities to the mayor's office and to the governor's office, he says, but he got little additional help. It may be that he shows me his pictures and leads me to some tunnel people because of his frustration with the authorities.

Henry sometimes makes extra sandwiches at home, which he gives to the homeless he meets in the tunnels. His job is to wean people away from the tunnels, to accept help aboveground. If they refuse to leave voluntarily, he has to evict them, but he prefers not to.

He takes his work home with him, too. He has experienced more than one episode of profound depression because of his job and has had to take time off to recover. He blames it on the darkness, however, rather than on the sad condition of the people he works with.

"You don't get enough light working down here," he says. "You get depressed. One time I was getting desperate. I used to sit so close to a light bulb that it singed my papers. A doctor told me what I had was depression and that light helps, any kind of light, and I should try to get more of it."

Another time, after some diligent work, he found a homeless community deep underground where one tunnel opened into a huge cavern. The scene was peaceful, with shacks and campfires, well protected and virtually hidden behind a thirty-foot-high cliff of rock between it and the tracks. The community called the site "the Condos," because the living environment was so good. The cliff even drowned out the noise of passing trains, and an electric wire had been diverted to actually allow some of the cardboard and wooden shacks in the Condos to have light. Water was available from a convenient sprinkler system that leaked.

"It was the only environment where I thought that 'Hey, once, maybe, these people are better off down here because what they get upstairs is a hell of a lot worse,'" he recalls pensively. "That's when I knew it was time to take a vacation, so I went to Jamaica and started light therapy," he smiles.

The Condos, where more than three hundred people once lived, have now been cleared of the homeless and most of their camps.

Some social workers also believe that at least some of the police brutality stories are exaggerated, or even fabricated, by the underground homeless. Harold Deamues is one of them. A worker for the outreach program of the Association for Drug Abuse Prevention and Treatment (ADAPT), Deamues contends that the stories primarily reflect the hostility and tension between the tunnel people and the police.

"The problem is that the police go down there assuming all these people are crazy or bugged [drugged] out. There's no trust between them at all," he says.

"These people don't have any belief in themselves, and if you don't believe in them or trust them, they know, they sense it, so how are you going to help them? I always feel like if I can look them in the eye, they're not going to hurt me," explains Deamues, who holds ADAPT's best record for persuading tunnel people to go aboveground. "If they have a gun in their face, that's not helping."

This philosophy is built into ADAPT's outreach effort, which is funded by the Transit Authority. The program's director, Michael Bethea, said none of his team takes a weapon or wears protective gear when they work in the tunnels.

"We got to get through to them, and convince them that they're not untouchables, not animals. That they're people just like us, and we're people like them. I don't know how you can do that by pulling a gun all the time," Bethea says.

SOCIAL WORKERS MUST COPE WITH LEGAL REGULATIONS IN ORDER TO help the tunnel homeless. Families found underground are often split up. The children are usually put in foster homes on the grounds that the parents cannot adequately care for them, which causes families to avoid seeking any welfare help.

For the past several years, welfare agencies across the country have warned that families—usually mothers with children—account for the fastest growing group among the homeless. This is a particularly severe problem in New York City where housing is very scarce and expensive. During July and August of 1992, a total of 13,994 families asked city officials for shelter, almost double the 7,526 families in the same months a year earlier.

"It's an explosion," according to Ken Murphy, deputy commissioner of the city's Human Resources Administration. "Two or three years ago we had to place maybe seventy-five families each night. Last night we placed 210 families and still had 143 left over in the offices at 8 A.M.," he told *The New York Times*.

The pattern is reflected underground. Shelters for families are usually full, so parents seeking help are sent to an adult shelter, and the children usually go to foster care or are even put up for adoption.

Sonya and Rodney had their two daughters taken from them when they were found in the tunnels.

"They's in foster care," says Sonya, a slim woman who ties her hair up neatly in a navy blue cotton cloth and away from her high cheekbones, accentuated by sunken cheeks, thin nose, and full lips. Even fatigue and hunger cannot take much away from her attractive face. "They [welfare officials] were supposed to put them together, in the same family. They promised they would," she complains, "but then they said they couldn't, so they's in different houses.

"We used to go see them a lot, but it hurt too much. The older one, she see I was crying and she says, 'Mama, don't come see me no more, because I just make you sad and crying.'"

She breaks off, weeping, and hides her face in Rodney's bony chest.

"We don't see them no more," he says, pain lining his face. "Not 'til we can get them back to ourselves completely."

"It's not easy," Sonya resumes. "They just don't give them back to you. The social worker says sometimes they never give them back to you. Maybe we have to start again," she says, sniffling. Rodney nods.

"It's a very hard call," explains a sympathetic social worker. "On the one hand you don't want to leave them without hope by telling them the facts—that most families pulled from the tunnels and split up never get back together. But at the same time, you want them to know it won't be easy; it's not just going to happen, getting back together. They have to work at it.

"The parents don't want to let go by putting the kids up for adoption," she continues, "so while the parents float around trying to pull themselves together, the child grows up in foster homes, pushed from one house to another. The parents don't want to let go, to cut the cord. So it's the worst of all worlds for the kids, who would be best off with loving parents who can provide for them. Or second best, adopted into a family that could provide for them.

"But this way they are worse off. And as they get older, by the time the parents realize they won't get them back, the kids are too old to get adopted. If they're black, it's even harder to get adopted," she sighs.

Overworked social workers—in New York City, the average caseload is almost ten times the size recommended by the National Association of Social Workers—are taxed with decisions that determine the fate of such underground families. Sometimes they see the choice as cut-and-dry where tunnel dwellers are concerned.

"No child can live a normal, healthy life in a tunnel," says one flatly. "If that's the best the parent can do, well, that's just not good enough."

Underground couples without children are also encouraged to separate sometimes.

Trey, a tall, slim man with a powerful frame, works in a soup kitchen with his girlfriend LaJoy, whom he calls his wife. The two live in a box shack at the mouth of a tunnel with several other people, mostly men.

He is a large, gentle man who speaks softly and smiles often, but he is usually too busy watching LaJoy to join in any laughter with the kitchen staff. LaJoy, who is twenty-five but looks forty, is an obvious addict. Her eyes are darkly ringed above heavy bags, and her dark skin looks chalky. Her movements are quick and jittery. Even to the untrained eye, she seems dangerously thin and fragile. Trey tries never to let her out of his sight.

Even while talking and peeling potatoes, he watches her. She speaks loudly without warning, and his hand slips over the potato into the sharp peeler. Blood gushes from a deep gouge in his middle finger, but he ties a napkin around his fist and rinses his red blood from the potato, almost without noticing it, eyes still locked on LaJoy.

"I try not to let her do it [both shoot up and smoke crack]" he said as he resumes talking, hardly letting his eyes fall from LaJoy. "But I can't watch her all the time. Sometimes she does drugs right when I'm there, and I don't even know it, don't know how she did it." He tries to explain.

"They say people can be like cancer. When it's in your arm or leg, you amputate it to get well. It hurts like hell, but you got to do it to live. But you see, it don't work for me with LaJoy. My wife is my life. What's the point of living if she ain't around. I don't want to live without her. She can't stop doing drugs, even for me. So I got to be with her while I can."

Trey has his problems, too. Alcohol. Most times, he gets drunk every night, which he feels is an improvement from the past when he was oblivious all day long. He tries not to drink, at least not too much, he says, so he can take care of LaJoy.

Some of his friends believe LaJoy encourages Trey to drink, maybe because she has more freedom to take drugs when he is drunk. She insists they live in the box where drugs and drink are very common. The pattern reinforces their addiction. Some couples overcome their addiction together, but usually one brings the other down with her or him.

"When it comes to choosing between a person whom they love, or their own health and life, they pick the person," according to Yolanda Serrano, the executive director of ADAPT. "So how do you help people like that? When it comes to aiding the addict, our system says they got to do it alone. There are no provisions for family and loved ones to do it together.

"What it comes down to is we don't see them as persons with feelings. We may lack the experience. The police see them as threats. The system pulls them apart, their family, their friends. It's all sink or swim, and a lot aren't strong enough to swim. A lot of them don't understand that we're trying to help. For that matter, a lot on our side, our people, don't seem to know they're supposed to help.

"When it comes down to it," she says sadly, "you can't really blame either side. Neither side really understands the other. We need to have that understanding. But we don't have the time or the compassion to see where they're coming from. And they don't have the trust."

8

Hell's Kitchen

SMITH, A GRAFFITI WRITER WHO OFTEN PAINTS UNDERGROUND, takes me into Seville's tunnel, which begins on West 48th Street, between 10th and 11th avenues, near an almost unnoticed bridge over two railroad tracks thirty feet below street level. It is the spot where Seville fell and broke his wrist.

We climb a chain link fence from the top of a dumpster, slide halfway down a rock-faced wall, and then drop about eight feet onto the gravel roadbed of the tracks where they run briefly in the open before disappearing underground. There are several such places on the West Side where the tracks are in a gully, not a tunnel, and can be seen by those who know what to look for. The path for the tracks was blasted out of the Manhattan rock perhaps a century ago and the tracks were abandoned for some years because of declining rail traffic through New York City. Trains now run through them again, largely carrying freight.

Clothes, mostly women's miniskirts, litter the tracks, along with glass bottles and aluminum drink cans. We pass a pair of corduroy pants, one leg crumbled and the other almost straight, that has been soaked with blood and is stiffening and turning brown in the sun.

Then comes the first underground passageway. Once inside, as the light is disappearing behind the last turn, a woman's voice calls out shrilly: "Who's there? Who's in the tunnel?"

Smith ignores the voice, stepping like a cat over the rubble despite the blinding darkness. Searching for a body to go with the questions, I seem to turn an ankle with each footfall.

"Answer me!" the woman's voice demands. Almost at the same moment, a bottle flies past Smith, crashing against the far wall. We pick up our pace until well away. We've been lucky, Smith says. Often as many as fifteen bottles have been hurled at him from different directions in that same short passage of tunnel.

These people just don't like visitors, he observes unnecessarily. "Trains are a lot safer," he says dryly.

The tracks seemed particularly dark in contrast to several places where bright shafts of sunlight splash down through gratings to create stark, disorienting shadows. After the last warming bright beam from above, we come upon a huge boulder on which is scrawled a warning sign in the orange spray paint of track workers: "CHUDS."

Track maintenance crews call tunnel homeless "CHUD people," for "Cannibalistic Human Underground Dwellers."

"It's not all a joke," one railroad engineer insists. "We know they are there. We can see their eyes. And when you aren't looking, they'll steal your tools, your food. I had a pair of pliers right next to me once, and a few seconds after I put them down, they were gone right from my side. I swear it happens all the time down here. The boss doesn't even question when you put in a request for more tools because he knows they got stolen down here.

"And sometimes they'll even 'pipe' you," he complains, indicating a club smashing into his head, "usually to steal from you but sometimes just cuz they're wacked out or scared.

"I usually bring an extra sandwich or two when I work on the tracks here, and I leave them around so they can take them and not get nervous and bother me. When I leave, all the sandwiches are gone, but I never see them being taken.

"So I wouldn't laugh at the CHUD thing," he cautioned. "They eat dogs, I know, and I'd bet my life they'd eat people."

Out in full daylight again, farther up the West Side along the Hudson River, Smith and I walk along tracks cut in the side of cliffs of layered rocks that are stepped back as they rise. On these terraced ledges are the homeless version of the sweet life—recliners, beach chairs, mattresses, and discarded housewares of all types on which the tunnel people sit. Some say hello as we pass, others turn their backs and walk toward the rock face where they disappear from our view.

"We have twelve cubbies in this rock here," one woman explains helpfully as she looks down from her ledge. "You can come with me up into this one if you want," she offers, "but don't you go exploring on your own. People don't take kindly to that. These are our homes you know." Her cubby is a small cave in the rock, large enough for a mattress, a couple of framed pictures of her family, and a candle atop a plastic milk crate, but not high enough for her to stand erect.

We walk on along the tracks, going underground again. People sit on similar terraced ledges, but now in the dark.

"We could have light," Seville had told me, "but sometimes we're too lazy to screw in the light bulb. There is an emergency exit door from the tunnel there, and you can turn out the bulb in the sign if you want, or turn it on if you wanted light, and when people were too lazy to screw in the bulb, we sit there in the dark," he laughed.

"Track workers would come past every day, say 'how you doing?' but they didn't come over. I think they were scared. I know I'd be scared, looking into the dark and knowing people were there watching you. I remember one time a worker stopped and just stared at me from the tracks. He just kept staring until I said, 'Damn it, you all right man?' And he jumped a mile!

"'I just wanted to make sure you was somebody,' he said, 'cuz all I could see was this pair of eyeballs. I was about to break and run because I didn't know what it was.' I got up and turned on the light so he could see me. He didn't know what was growing down here. He thought I was some kind of animal or something," Seville guffawed, slapping his knee.

Farther north along this road is Bernard's tunnel—a world apart from this one—but I will enter it another way at another time.

9

Children

"And I'll grow up beautiful." —Julie, age eight

ON A FREEZING DECEMBER NIGHT, A WOMAN'S SHARP screams fill every recess in the abandoned train tunnel that more than a dozen people call home. The air is still, amplifying the shrieks as they echo through the dark cavern.

One by one and sometimes in twos, the nervous inhabitants come to its mouth, where the screams tumble out into the night air and are quickly lost.

"This ain't right, this jus' ain't right," says Shorty, a recent member of the tunnel community, a newcomer to its kind of suffering. His words create vapors that linger briefly before they disappear without effect. The half-dozen men with him study the rubble at their feet in silence.

Shorty is a soft-faced man with watery eyes so brown that their whites have yellowed. Now they are intense and demanding. "We should be gettin' help. This ain't right!" he insists.

His clenched fists chop the air in short strokes when a sharp beam of white light from a passing river barge catches him, suddenly illuminating the scene. He shrinks from the exposure and his fists seem to abandon their determination, opening into stubby fingers, cracked by the cold and ingrained with dirt. He shoves them into the pockets of his browned and oversized jeans whose frayed bottoms, cuffed several times, fold heavily over torn sneakers. Despite the cold, his clothes reek of the familiar smells of homelessness—spoiled and soured food from scavenged dumpsters, stale sweat, and the excrement and urine of the streets.

The beam sweeps past, and New Jersey's flickering lights reappear across the river. The men are poorly protected from the Hudson's cold winds. Butch, the beefiest among them and regarded as the leader of the community, shifts his weight to keep warm. His eyes are rimmed with tears from the cold as he hunches his shoulders against a new gust. He draws a switchblade from his jacket and fingers its edge gingerly. As everyone watches, he draws it several times across the face of a smooth rock, as if to sharpen it further, then closes and pockets it. His face resumes its vacant, distant look.

"Maybe we should pray," says Juan tentatively. A slim Latino man whose eyes never leave the ground, he is the most clean and neatly dressed of the gathered tunnel dwellers. By day he works a minimum-wage job at McDonald's. No one there suspects he lives underground.

Razor, a black man with face and neck scars, snickers at the mention of prayer. His midshoulder-length hair, matted reggae-style and knotted with dirt, looks especially wild in the darkness.

The rest of the men nod and grunt approval of Juan's idea, and, in a low monotone, he begins to speak of the coming child:

"Dear Lord, please deliver us this baby safely. His parents are good people. He's done nothin' bad, Lord. He's jus' a baby. He don't mean no disrespect being born underground. We'll take care of him when he's with us. Just deliver him and his mama safely, Lord, and we'll take care of the rest. Amen."

"Amen," several of the men repeat in whispers that overlap each other like the small waves slapping the river edge.

Above New York, white stars pierce the sky. Everything appears too sharp and dramatic in the sparkling cold, including the quiet when the screams abruptly stop. A small animal, probably a rat, shuffles through the dried leaves at the corner of the tunnel's mouth, but the world seems less hostile in the quiet.

Then the baby cries a strong, demanding bleat. The men look at the ground or at nothing, seemingly unmoved. They were familiar with death in the tunnels. Birth was something new.

"Should we go in?" asks Fred. His heavy-lidded eyes make him look dimly criminal and threatening, an effect he deliberately enhances on the street. Now, even while standing innocently outside a manger scene, he looks as guilty as a thief.

"Naw," Butch says. "Wait for Ronda."

A woman's figure walks almost bouncing out of the tunnel's mouth.

"It's a boy!" Ronda announces, her eyes tired but lively. "Sally's fine."

The group moves from the December night toward the underground home of Sally and Tim, their blank expressions thawing into avuncular pride.

"Man, our first tunnel baby! Man!" exults Butch, shaking his head and smiling brightly. He leans over and smacks Shorty on the top of his head. "Shorty, man, you was a mess, brother," he says, smiling more broadly.

"You weren't no calm chicken neither," says Fred, elbowing Butch as tension releases into exaggerated bonhomie.

The men gather wood as they walk deeper into the tunnel, adding it to the campfire they had left when Sally's screams became too near and personal. The flames leap and warmth returns with swigs from a bottle of Thunderbird that is passed around, and the men spend the last of the night expressing wonder and even awe at the idea that a baby has joined their community.

Sally and Tim live in the tunnel for a week after the birth, but when I return a couple of weeks later, Ronda says that Sally, a white woman in her late twenties, and Tim, a black man in his early forties, have gone back to Brooklyn. Sally is living with her sister, Ronda says, while Tim looks for work.

The baby was fine, but the tunnel community is glad they have gone.

"We'll miss them and all that," says Shorty, "but this ain't no place for a baby. A tunnel ain't no place for a baby."

Butch is most pleased that the couple left.

"It's too much responsibility having a baby," he says. "We always had to think about getting things for it, and making sure it was warm. I told Tim he had no business keeping his wife and baby underground. He was risking all of us. People up top were gonna start hearing the baby cry, and you know, if the cops came down and found it, they'd find a reason to arrest us all and shut down the tunnel."

Tim was reluctant to leave. "He liked it here," Butch says. "He didn't like to ask no one for help." Tim apparently wanted to raise the child in the tunnels, but the community threatened to alert the authorities.

"We would've told someone sooner or later," says Juan. "No baby could live down here with us."

Most of the homeless who attended the baby's birth have no intention of visiting Tim and Sally. Other underground communities are close-knit, but this one is more akin to being homeless on the streets, accepting the passing, fragile nature of relationships, willing to allow people to float in and out of their lives. Some also deliberately insulate themselves against disappointment in others by staying aloof.

Shorty, not yet callused in this way, hopes to keep in touch with the tunnel baby. "Sure, I'll see Little Shorty," he beams at the thought of his namesake. "They'll bring him down to visit his uncles." He entertains an idea fleetingly. "Maybe I'll pass him on the street one day."

"Naw," says Butch. "Little Butch is better off staying away. He wouldn't want to see your ugly face, anyway," he grins.

Everyone seems to name the baby after himself except for Ronda, who refers to the child as Joey—"because he looks like a little kangaroo," she explains. Eventually they accept that he is Little Tim.

A BIRTH UNDERGROUND IS A RARITY. PREGNANT WOMEN ARE USU-
ally urged by the tunnel homeless to get proper care. If they refuse
to go, authorities are usually informed where to find them, particularly if the women are addicts unable to care for themselves.

Nell, who is thirty-one years old, has been wandering in the
tunnels for days, stoned and asking for money for food. Her body
is emaciated, but she is hugely pregnant. She doesn't know it.

"I don't know why I'm hungry all the time," she says, looking
vacantly to the side. "It ain't drugs. I don't do no drugs no more.
I've gone straight," she says unconvincingly.

I ask if she is pregnant, and she looks at me, confused.

"You mean a baby?" she asks, muddled. "Naw, it ain't that.
My belly's always been big. Maybe though," she adds as the
thought sinks in. "Ain't bled for a while."

She turns out to be seven months pregnant. Her baby is born
in a hospital, trembling, addicted to crack cocaine.

Some expectant mothers in the tunnels are ignorant of how to
care for themselves. One refuses juice and even food at a soup
kitchen several times before a worker suggests she needs it for the
child.

"Really?" she asks, clearly delighted at the prospect of eating
again. "I thought I shouldn't eat."

The kitchen stays quiet for several minutes. "She didn't know
she could eat," a homeless man at another table explains to a friend
in a whisper. Soon everyone nods their understanding. No one
laughs.

LITTLE TIM WAS TAKEN FROM THE TUNNELS BUT MANY CHILDREN ARE
brought into them. Their parents are not abusive or even negligent.
They often want only to preserve their families, preferring the
tunnels to losing their children. These parents refuse shelters because there, they say, the children are taken from them by the
Health and Human Services Department. For this reason, many
homeless parents are as wary of social workers as they would be of
secret police. They remind me at times of dissidents in Moscow I
knew when I was a child living there in the seventies, who would

say nothing of substance when they might be overheard. Underground children usually have only one parent, the mother, who says she uses the tunnels only as temporary shelter until she can send the children to relatives or decide whether to put them in foster care or up for adoption.

Underground communities in which children live semipermanently, like J.C.'s community under Grand Central, are extremely secretive about their young ones.

J.C. told me initially that his community had no children, but when he allows me to visit it, I encounter several. "I didn't lie," he insists. "There are not children here. You can't be a child down here." After a moment, he adds, "We have adults as young as five."

J.C. and the mayor of his community refuse to say how many children live with them. On a visit, I counted at least four, but speaking to them is almost impossible. An adult is always present and intervenes by sending the children to play or standing directly between them and me.

OF ALL THE PEOPLE I MET IN THE TUNNEL, THE CHILDREN GAVE ME the most hope. Many of them seemed healthy and happy, undeterred and unaware of the implications of their environment.

Actually, it was their *absence* that made me upset, the evidence of their existence before I ever met them. I am still haunted by doll's eyes that I saw on my first trip into the tunnels with Sergeant Henry. I don't recall their color, but I will never forget their stare in a hastily abandoned recess above the train tracks that had served as home for a homeless family. She lay on the floor, her dirt-smudged face half-hidden behind well-stroked hair, lonely and deserted.

MY TEN-YEAR-OLD FRIEND KRISTEN GAYLE TOLD ME ABOUT JULIE, who lives with her parents and four-year-old brother in a shack in a tunnel. Julie is eight years old with a brilliant smile and tired eyes. She looks much like other girls her age, but perhaps she is a little slimmer. She boasts, with a mischievous little smile, that she has more secrets than any girl at Public School 125. No one at school knows she lives in a tunnel, she whispers. They think she lives in Harlem's Douglas Projects, but only her mail goes to that address where her mother's friend keeps it for them.

The hardest part, she says, is not letting anyone close enough to want to play with her after school. But that's not so difficult, she admits, because they already laugh at her clothes and sometimes at the way she smells. She says that it's not that bad; she has her parents and her little brother to play with.

"Papa says this is best," she explains earnestly. "We're proving ourselves and how strong we are. When we get enough money, we're going to move away from New York, and we'll have our own little white house. I'm going to have my own room. Everything in it will be pink and pretty. Everything I wish for I'm going to have because I've been such a good girl. And I'll grow up beautiful," she says, her large brown eyes sparkling with that dream.

When she feels too alone and sad, she has an itch to tell her secret, but then she thinks how much she loves her parents and doesn't want to be taken from them. She comes so close to telling, she says, drawing a deep breath, that she is ashamed. She thinks she'll burst, just burst, but she keeps it in, she says and smiles.

Julie isn't an American citizen. She and her family were born in Haiti and illegally entered the country in Miami. Paul, Julie's father, brought the family to New York looking for his sister-in-law's brother. When they arrived at his address, they learned he had just moved with his family to Minnesota. Neighbors allowed them to stay a few weeks, but then they moved to shelters and from there to the tunnels because of the constant fear they would be deported.

Paul does menial labor jobs while saving money to go to Minnesota. They do not seek welfare or other social services and go to soup kitchens only infrequently, to avoid drawing attention. For months Julie did not attend school, but her mother, who was once a teacher, insisted that she go. The family decided her education was worth the risk of exposure.

Julie's world, to hear her tell it, is full of only good things.

When she sees homeless people alone on the streets, she thinks how lucky she and her family are to have each other. When she hears children make cruel jokes about kids who live in shelters, she's glad she has kept her secret. Someday, she says, her brother will be the president of the United States and will change things.

What things?

"The way people treat each other, and he'll make sure everyone has a home, no matter where they come from. And," she giggles, "he'll make candy free."

When next I seek out Julie and her family, I'm told they have moved to Minnesota.

CHILDREN ADAPT BETTER TO LIFE UNDERGROUND THAN ADULTS, AC-cording to Harold Deamues of ADAPT (Association for Drug Abuse Prevention and Treatment), who found numerous children living with parents in tunnel communities. "They were running around like, you know, 'this is my house, this is my doormat,' like any other kid in his house. They were jumping off the walls. They get used to the roaches and rats as if they are pets. So I guess they are normal children until they get old enough to say, 'What am I doing here? There's more to life than this.'"

Before that self-awareness sets in, young children can become so secure in the darkness and so comfortable in their communities that the world aboveground, particularly crowds of people, is frightening.

Teresa, a young mother, meets me in Grand Central with her two young children. Even at rush hour they are easy to spot. The first words from four-year-old Dara is, "Mama, I'm scared." Her little hand clutches Teresa's finger more tightly, and the mother draws her closer to her leg. Her three-month-old son, Dwane, is snug at her breast.

They look as destitute as they are. Teresa, who is twenty-five, wears a blue cardigan ripped at the sleeve and missing a button. Dara is outgrowing her thin cloth jumper and is obviously un-washed. The baby is wrapped only in a white blanket, enough for the warm spring evening in the station, but perhaps not in a dank tunnel.

Despite their ragged appearance, no one seems to notice them. Yet Teresa feels everyone is looking at her and the children as if, she says, they are "mole people."

"We try to be neat," she says later, "but they can smell us. They know," she whispers with a nod toward the crowd. "They know we be tunnel people."

Teresa has tied back her hair neatly in a navy blue kerchief. Her face is young and clean but tired, her eyes unsure. She moves like a colt, an angular body with loose skin over sharp bones. Some movements are unsteady, ungainly, as if she is trying out each move. Her daughter, full of spirit and curiosity, sometimes appears stronger and more self-assured.

Teresa stops under the domed center of the terminal, looking upward as orange sunlight reaches through the windows, revealing a spring sunset.

"Been a long time since I've seen that," she smiles, but quickly looks down protectively on her child.

We sit at McDonald's as Dara eats, first her own food and then Teresa's. Only after Dara insists she can't take another bite does Teresa pick hungrily at the leftovers. Dwane won't drink the milk. He's not used to it, she explains, letting him gum and drool a French fry. Teresa normally chews his food. Baby food is as scarce as money in the tunnels, she says.

Teresa refuses to go to any outreach program for fear they will take her children, or worse, call her boyfriend who is the father of the children.

"I know what they say, and I know how it happens," she says fiercely. "They would say they take the kids for only a day or two but really, you never get them back. I seen it before. I don't trust no one with my babies."

Teresa came to the tunnels after a month on the streets. She ran from her abusive boyfriend. "He hit Dara, flung her across the room. He hit me a lot. I love him so much that when he hit me, I think at least he cares. But when I saw the marks on my baby," she shudders, "I had to leave."

He came after her to her friends' home, and not only beat her up but threatened to kill the friends as well. They asked her to leave, and she went on the streets. A tunnel dweller found her and the children in a cardboard box in freezing weather last winter and led her underground. She has been there ever since, living off the generosity of other tunnel people.

She wants to get out of the tunnels before Dara is old enough to remember them. "I don't want her to remember this," she looks down at her clothes. "I want her to know I always loved her and took good care of my children."

But Dara knows things are different. "My mama used to be like a teddy bear," she says, "all round and always laughing. Now she be all skinny," she feigns disgust.

Teresa says she is saving money for bus fare to her sister-in-law's home in the Midwest. I'm skeptical, but a week later I see her off at the bus station, en route to her mother, she says. A drug dealer worked a deal with the bus driver to get her free passage, and tunnel people gave her pocket money, she tells me.

10

Roots

"To be rooted is perhaps the most important and least recognized need of the human soul. . . . A human being has roots by virtue of his real, active, and natural participation in the life of the community, which preserves in living shape certain particular treasures of the past and certain particular expectations for the future."

—*Simone Weil,* The Need of Roots

MOST TUNNEL DWELLERS PREFER TO BE CALLED "HOUSELESS" rather than "homeless." More important than a warm apartment and cleaner life aboveground, many say, is belonging to a community, even if it is underground. I found most tunnel dwellers say they are members of communities of one kind or another, some with a barely recognized structure but others quite well-defined, including two types of "families." In one, members refer to each other in terms of kinship—as nephews and nieces, papas and mamas, brothers and sisters, and cousins. They use these familiar terms as nominal evidence of affection and closeness. In the other, members claim to "adopt" each other to form a "true family" among whom ties are stronger than among their biological (and usually estranged) relatives. Most members of underground communities have lost or abandoned their ties aboveground and welcome a new life below. Their community provides them with a sense of physical and psychological security and in their eyes also sets them apart, and above, the mass of homeless wandering the streets aboveground.

"I'm a better father to my family down here than I ever was up there," one man maintains. "I was never good enough up there. This gives me another chance."

Many of the underground communities simply evolve as people settle in. "You go down there, play with the wires, and get some light," says Dee Edwards, who lived underground but is now employed by the Coalition for the Homeless. "Before you know it, you got twelve or fifteen people gathering round you. They become like neighborhoods: you know the girls at the end, the family in the middle. Everyone watches out for each other. One person goes on line [for food] and brings it down for the rest. When someone gets sick, we put our money together for medicine. People team up. You can just about make it that way."

Even those tunnel dwellers who seem to live alone often belong to a loose community that resembles the tepid, nodding familiarity of urban neighbors who don't know each other's names. These loners prefer solitude and consider any affiliation an imposition. More often they are wary of others as a result of past experiences and choose not to make contact with those they live near though they may see each other everyday. It usually takes a crisis to form trust, but even they eventually need some relationship.

Bob, who lives under Riverside Park, would pass Bernard Isaacs in the tunnel several times a day before they spoke.

"I didn't want to get taken again," Bob explains. "You can't trust someone unless you look into their eyes, and in the tunnels, it's dangerous to look closely. I've gotten in trouble too many times. Being alone is better than being dead." Yet after a time— Bernard says it was a year—Bob warmed up and now describes Bernard as his "best friend."

Bernard is a generous and self-confident black man who once, half-joking, proclaimed himself "Lord of the Tunnels." He shares the meals he cooks at his campfire with anyone who asks, and more than a few of those who live around him credit him with saving their lives on cold nights by urging them to come to warmer spots and even bringing them food. Without advocating it, he is proud of life underground. He says the independence and self-sufficiency of the underground dwellers sets them above the street homeless.

"I would say we're the elite of New York's homeless," he declares. "We chose to settle down here, and we have made homes down here. We've made a life for ourselves."

As little as a regular chore done for the community, like going for water, provides a sense of belonging. Dwayne, who lives under Fifth Avenue, takes pleasure in having been missed by members of his community. He recalls that Mary, its oldest member, chased him with a rolled up newspaper for disappearing for more than a week without notifying anyone that he'd be gone. Some communities say they admit new members only after watching them for a time and discussing their suitability, a process that also contributes to a sense of self-worth.

For these reasons, the traditional definitions of the homeless may not be adequate to describe the underground dwellers. The *International Encyclopedia of Social Sciences* describes homelessness as "a condition of detachment from society, characterized by absence or attenuation of the affiliative bonds that link settled persons to a network of interconnected social structures." Whether it is because of limited space or a primitive need to huddle against the dark, most of the underground homeless have created communities that may be detached from most of the social structures aboveground but nevertheless strive to maintain substitute or alternative structures below the surface.

Many communities even maintain contacts with each other. J.C., the "spokesman" for a community under Grand Central, speaks about a "loose federation" of more than twenty communities in the network of tunnels within about a mile of the station, and he claims that perhaps fifty other communities farther afield also keep in touch. Designated "runners" shuttle medicine, old clothing, and information about welfare services—new drop-in centers or changes in soup kitchen schedules—among communities, he says. Often staff workers at new drop-in centers are shocked by the numbers of homeless who ask for their services.

"It's not at all uncommon for a new drop-in center to expect maybe fifty people the first day and when they open, have two hundred waiting. The network of communication among the homeless is amazing," says Beverly Israely, the director of Volunteer Services for the Grand Central Partnership Social Services Corporation.

"They've formed an alternative community down there," according to Rob Buckley, the director of All Saints' Soup Kitchen on the Upper West Side. "What would make them want to come back up when they feel they have no place in the world up here?"

Soup kitchens, churches and synagogues, and other small non-profit groups are the primary institutions aboveground with which the tunnel homeless have contact, and Buckley's program—small, but warm and not patronizing—is among the most highly regarded. Many homeless men and women volunteer here as cooks (like Bob) and servers. All Saints' serves eighty to a hundred lunches each day, and while the church must turn away some of the hungry when the demand is particularly high—usually toward the end of the month when welfare checks have been exhausted—it serves as many as two hundred dinners each Sunday with no one turned away.

Buckley, a twenty-something young man from a white, middle-class suburb in New Jersey, personifies the conflicting pulls that come from different religious denominations seeking to help the homeless. "The more liberal churches are doing good deeds by giving food, but there's a firm line between the donors and the recipients—we have and you don't. Then there's the evangelical side, which says don't worry so much about their material needs; work on their souls. A middle ground between the two is forming, or at least we're trying to find it," he says optimistically. He is himself evangelical, but focuses less on the spiritual than the earthly needs of his visitors.

"My personal belief," he explains, "is that someone's life is not going to get entirely fixed unless he or she finds Christ, but I'm not going to make them accept it. I can't go on my preconceived ideas of what a fixed life is. I've learned that here. I can't tell a homeless, fifty-year-old black man what his life needs. I have to ask what he's looking for, what he wants out of life. Some of these guys don't want a nine-to-five job and a home and wife and two children, and being a good, prosperous, productive member of society. That may be my idea of a productive life, but it's definitely a cultural thing out of my upbringing. I can't say you have to fit into my kind of mold, but I believe you have to be responsible and productive, and there's the catch. You don't need to fit my plan, but you need to find something that fits you in life."

Over the several years of working at the soup kitchen, Buckley observes different stages of homelessness. "You're either on the way up or on the way down. Some homeless are very clean all the time, very presentable and very articulate. Others are just at the pit, the bottom, those who can't even come out of the tunnels because they're afraid to be seen." He tries to tailor his advice to the person, watching him or her for a time before trying to provide a reason to return to a more conventional lifestyle.

Buckley is ambivalent about the underground communities because of the sense of belonging they offer.

"It's healthy in that sense that the communities give them some sort of identity, which some of these people never had, but it's not a healthy alternative," he says, "because there's no future in that kind of life. The longer they stay down there, the harder it is for them to readjust to life aboveground. Once you know that the communities offer them comfort and the self-esteem they can't find in shelters, it's difficult to say people shouldn't live down there. But once you go down there and see the way they live, like animals, you can surely say no human beings should live like that."

The other side of the argument comes from Bill, who claims he is not only content to be homeless but fascinated by the communal structure of his community and others that are underground.

He argues that the underground is the best option, far better than the exposure and isolation of the streets or the danger and separation for his adopted family in shelters.

Bill, a black man in his late fifties who is called "Papa," is deliberately sketchy about his background, except for his education. He earned a masters degree in economics, he says, after a business degree from Fordham University and some legal studies at John Jay College of Criminal Justice and Georgetown University. He was a senior mediator/arbitrator in the Bronx-Manhattan Summons Court until he retired, and he'll proudly volunteer that he's worked for the government all of his life. His wife died a decade ago.

Bill dipped into his pension to help two of his immediate family members in need. "That's all I'm going to say about that. They're grown adults and I have no right to tell you about the reason," he says, shutting the door on his personal history. He refuses to inform his family that he's homeless now, while he tries to save for an apartment with the government checks he says he receives as a disabled veteran from the Korean War.

"We're a community just like neighborhoods upstairs," Bill says with a professorial smile through a short, well-groomed beard peppered with gray. "To tell you the truth, it's adventurous, it truly is, to learn about the subculture and the subcommunities of America. I would say my community here in the Rotunda is the same as those in the tunnels. I know some of them, but I can't bring myself to go underground for long."

THE ROTUNDA COMMUNITY OF ABOUT FIFTY PEOPLE TAKES ITS NAME from the large, pillared structure overlooking the Hudson River. Fashion photographers often use the Rotunda to pose their models against the scenic backdrop. Each morning, Parks Department employees who clean up before the public comes to the park wake the homeless. An unspoken contract between the Parks workers and the community allows the homeless to populate the Rotunda area at night on two conditions: the morning cleanup and no public use of drugs or alcohol.

Bill had not recognized the extent of the Rotunda community before joining it. "I knew nothing about its family-like structure and its communal ways," he says, "no idea how close these people are to each other. It's a cross section like you find upstairs—bickerings and jealousies, love lives, hatreds, homosexuals."

In order to occupy a spot in the Rotunda, "you have to be invited," he says. "You'd be trespassing if you came uninvited, just like in a house. There has to be a vacant spot you can set up in. We share everything from food to clothing. If food is being given out somewhere, one person from the community will run back here to tell all. If a person is sick, people here will take him to a hospital and note when he's coming out and take care of him when he does. Some people cook, but in this setup, eating is done among the personal family.

"Almost everyone here has something to do in the daytime—cooks or maintenance men in churches—but some who come from the South have no skills and almost no education. But we also have some highly educated persons. He's got a masters in chemistry," Bill says, pointing to a man slumped in a stone corner. He stares out at the winter mist receding from the gray river. "He's got a Ph.D. in biology," Bill nods at another man, this one reading a book. "We have native Americans, a Yugoslav, an Irishman, blacks, Caribbeans, Latinos, male and female. We're just as diverse as people upstairs," he says, meaning people who are not homeless.

Society places the Rotunda homeless outside its traditional concept of community. "They call us a subcommunity the same way they say we have a subculture even though we believe we have our own culture in our own community," Bill says. This culture has its own pecking order. Among other things, the Rotunda homeless feel superior to the homeless who live in tunnels directly underneath them. Bill admits he stays aloof from the underground people.

"Their communities may operate like ours, but they are different. They have their own water, electricity, cooking arrangements. They seldom come up. Generally they're not as clean. They're further removed than we are," he says, as if his community is halfway between the underground homeless and traditional society.

Tunnel homeless resent the attitude of the Rotunda community. "I can't understand why they think they're better than we are," says Bernard Isaacs, who lives underground about two miles due north of the Rotunda community. "If anything, we're more highly developed. Our underground communities are tighter."

However, these communities are more like each other than either is like a traditional community. Sharing a cigarette is one example. "You light a cigarette, you pass it around here," says Bill. "It's part of the pattern." Also, culturally, the homeless communities have a great respect for privacy and are far less concerned with past and future. "We very rarely go into depth about each other's backgrounds because it's very personal, sometimes very painful. We build on everyday stuff. Sharing the past isn't the thing that brings us close. It's sharing the knowledge of how best to survive each day."

When day-to-day concerns are so paramount, there is virtually no sense of future in these groups. "These communities offer no long-term alternative to society, really," says Buckley, "because they become more and more isolated particularly as they go deeper and deeper underground, and it gets harder and harder for them to fit back into society at any level.

"They slowly die because they're cut off from the whole. I think that's what happens to them eventually. They get so isolated from society that it gets harder and harder for them to fit back in at any level. You've got to fit into society. You don't have to fit the mold, but you've got to be able to fit so that you can participate. Society is society with all its faults, it's still our culture and somehow you've got to be able to tap into it. You may want to change it or make an alternative, but somehow you got to be able to play along the main route."

Buckley says he sometimes gets frustrated and dejected watching a familiar pattern among homeless of recovery and falling out. "Sometimes it's hard to understand," he says.

"It's like leaving home," explains Sam, raising a cup of bitter coffee to his overgrown mustache. His leathery skin proves his claim to living on the streets and underground for fifteen years.

"You leave your space, all your friends. Your family really." He has left several times because he wanted to get clean and warm, but each time has returned.

"I want a better life, but I don't want to give up the friends here. There's no one up there for me anymore."

Tripper is an addict who personifies those underground homeless no longer striving for a better life. "Why should I go dry? What for?" he asks. "There's nothing up there for me. This is what I want. If it means I die early, then I die early. Who cares? What's the point of cleaning up to fit the myth that everything's better up top? You're only miserable a little longer up there."

MANY OF THE STRONGER ONES NOT ONLY WANT TO CLIMB BACK OUT but they also want to succeed.

Virginia is a slight, homeless woman with big, earnest eyes and hair that is pulled back smoothly. She was a secretary before losing her job, and then her husband, because of her drug use. She was expecting a child when she met Frank, once a featherweight boxer, who was just out of jail. They met at All Saints' Soup Kitchen, became lovers, and decided to go through drug rehabilitation together. They have slowly been rebuilding lives within society, falling back a few times, they admit, but making progress through persistence and mutual support. They now have an apartment and are seeking jobs. They come to All Saints' rarely now, only when welfare money has run out before the end of the month.

"It's hard to come back around people I was out drugging with on the streets," Frank says. Virginia, shy and mousy in a smart, fitted blue dress, nods agreement.

"They're good people," she adds sadly. "They're real happy we got our lives straight and all. A lot of them say 'I wish I could do that,' and I tell them they can but they don't believe me."

"It's hard for Frank and Virginia," Buckley says later. "They've had to cut themselves off from a whole group of people who were their support. Their struggle has hit a new niche, a transition. They aren't really here and they aren't yet there. They constantly try to take in old friends and help them to get straight, but they are constantly disappointed when the friends go back on the streets again after a month."

Virginia wants to speak to me more at All Saints', but I am preoccupied with the underground people in the room, rather than those who obviously do not live in tunnels. She looked as though she had no connection to the tunnel world. She follows me, even tugging at my sleeve to get attention. As I leave, I give her my business card.

She phones me several times before we get together again. "I just wanted you to tell them," she says of the homeless people I meet, "that they can do it. I didn't believe I could get straight. Nobody ever told me I could, so it's important that you tell them they can get themselves cleaned up and respectable," she says in a soft but insistent voice.

I'm taken aback by her, persisting with such a simple message, and I remember Tripper's chilling certainty that those living aboveground are only miserable longer in a world where they do not belong.

Is it worth cleaning up? I ask Virginia. Are you happier?

"Oh, yes," she replies with equal certainty. "I miss my people down there, my friends, and I want better for them. They were more my family than I ever had. My family gave up on me. They were the only people who cared whether I was alive. But then I was pregnant with Vicky and I knew I had to do right by her. She's what made me get out. I couldn't give her up. I miss them, but there'll be new friends someday, a full new life. We're halfway there. Please tell them they can do it, too. There are people for them up here, too. Not many, but we're here."

11

Bernard's Tunnel

"Behold! Human beings living in an underground den. . . . Like ourselves, they see only their own shadows, or the shadows of one another, which the fire throws on the opposite wall of the cave." —*Plato,* The Republic

FTER FIVE MINUTES THAT SEEM FOREVER, THE TUNNEL IS STILL impenetrably dark. It feels expansive in its own darkness. I have slipped through the grated emergency exit from the tunnel that stands flush in the steep hill overlooking the Hudson, then picked my way down a score of steep slate steps—some jagged, some broken and wobbly, and two missing—while holding tightly to the rusted pipe that serves as a banister. My flashlight helps, but its beam seems to fall short of the far wall and only dimly finds the single-track rail line. I switch it off and wait for my eyes to accustom themselves to the shadowless world. Subtle movements stir in the dirt.

I feel the chill of strange eyes on me before I become aware of the red glow of a fire in the distance. As I near, a thin figure separates itself slowly from the wall, and its shadow, the stretched form of an already tall and thin man with wild hair, glides toward me over the tracks and the weeping walls of the tunnel.

He crouches when he reaches me, like a wrestler preparing to lash out, and begins to circle me.

Bernard? I ask, extending my hand.

He continues to prowl, silently, until halfway around, my back to the fire, he stops and leans forward. The fire lights his face but I can barely discern its features. I think I have found a mole person and, panicked, I begin to look around for an escape.

Suddenly he takes my outstretched hand in a warm, firm shake.

"Don't be afraid," he says, standing erect now. "I just wanted to check you out, see who you are. Forgive me for being so rude. Please come in."

His welcoming words are in such contrast to his frightening pose a few seconds earlier that I am even more disoriented, but I follow him toward his home, one of a half-dozen cement-walled cubicles in this tunnel that once sheltered track maintenance crews. About forty-five men and women call this area home.

He offers me coffee or tea and soon, he says, some spaghetti that he dumps into water boiling on the campfire. I begin to relax as I listen to this intelligent and articulate black man. I'm embarrassed at how wrong I was in my first impression.

Bernard Isaacs is thirty-eight years old, has a slim six-foot-three-frame, and wears his hair reggae-style. He was once a model, he says, which is easy to believe. His high cheekbones and well-defined nose and lips were inherited, he says, from his Cherokee mother; his lithe frame came from his East African father.

"I'm pretty much what you see," he smiles expansively by the fire after I tell him of my terrified first impression. "The way I approached you back there, well, let me tell you, Jennifer, 'hello' is the most expensive word in the human language. Down here it can cost you your life. Or worse, your sanity."

"The only thing misleading about me is my name," he continues after stirring the spaghetti. "I'm no part Jewish. My father's family took the name of our family's slaveowners after they freed us."

Isaacs graduated from the University of Maryland in 1975,

he says, with a major in journalism and a minor in philosophy. He initially worked as an editorial assistant at CBS in New York for a short time, then went into modeling, and then into dealing drugs. He claims to be drug- and alcohol-free now, at least most of the time. Periodically, he admits, he slips back.

He stumbled into the tunnel one night after he broke up with a girl and has lived here for six years. "Found this place and never left, except to go back to my old place for a few things. But I never turned back. I don't blame her that I'm down here. She's a lawyer, beautiful girl, really beautiful. I definitely don't want her feeling responsible. I'm down here for me. People don't understand that."

In February 1990, *New York Daily News* reporter Samme Chitthum wrote about Bernard and his camp. Several former friends recognized Bernard and sent the article to his family. His brother, a successful Chicago lawyer, flew to New York and pleaded with Bernard to return aboveground. "He offered me $10,000," Bernard recalls, shaking his head. "He just didn't understand. This is where I want to be for now. Maybe not forever, but for now."

Freight and passenger trains once raced along this tunnel, which stretches underground more than four miles from 72nd Street to 122nd Street. Early on, local kids would crawl through grates to ride the trains for kicks, hiding from patrolmen who carried shotguns filled with salt pellets to sting rather than kill. When Bernard came to this spot, which is roughly under 96th Street, the tracks had been abandoned for years, and a ragtag collection of homeless people found shelter along its length.

The best feature of this tunnel was the fresh water. The "Tears of Allah," as Bernard named them, pulsed from a broken pipe twenty feet overhead and fell in one seamless curtain to the floor. The pipe went unrepaired for five years, during which time it provided an oasis for the tunnel dwellers.

Not long after he came, an incident occurred that made Bernard a legend among the underground and attracted the community that now surrounds him.

Hector, a thief and addict recently discharged from Riker's Island, moved into the northern entrance of the tunnel and with other men began extorting a "tariff" from homeless who passed. They beat those who refused or could not pay; sometimes they even beat those who paid. They challenged Bernard, who became incensed.

"You? You demand money from me?" he bellowed angrily as others peered out from their camps and coves.

"Do you know who I am?" he shouted, his voice echoing down the walls. "I am Bernard, Lord of the Tunnels!"

Hector and his friends, nonplused, allowed Bernard to pass without charge. From then on, Bernard was known as the Lord of the Tunnels.

"When I went to 'We Can' [a redemption center where discarded cans and bottles are turned in for cash], people would say to me, 'Yo, Lord of the Tunnels,' or point to me and whisper to each other like 'That's the Lord of the Tunnels.'" At first Bernard didn't like the title, but he has come to accept it as "them showing me respect."

Hector's bullying continued, but perhaps taking Bernard's cue, several of the tunnel dwellers "showed him disrespect." One night, to end the growing resistance, Hector and his friends attacked a camp about ten blocks north of Bernard's bunker, burning cardboard box homes and the primitive bedding and scattering pots and pans. They beat and raped a homeless woman named Sheila, whose husband Willie had been absent for some weeks, while most of the tunnel dwellers cowered on overhead pipes and in cubbyholes.

Bernard heard Sheila's screams even though he was outside of the tunnels at the time. He found her bleeding and nearly unconscious. Furious, he rallied about twenty-five homeless men and bats, pipes, and burning planks, and descended on Hector and his gang, surrounding them while one man went to get the police.

"It was a wild scene down there," says Chris Pape, a graffiti artist who happened to be watching through a grate. "All these people running around underground, yelling and waving these torches underground in the dark. It was surreal. That's about the only word for it." The organized strike against Hector was particularly surprising because the homeless in the Riverside Park tunnel are a passive group who go out of their way to avoid attention. They usually hide from visitors, says Pape, who paints murals in tunnels.

The police were reluctant to come with Bernard's messenger, Stash. The first patrolmen he found didn't believe him, he says, and the second pair went with him to the tunnel's entrance but refused to enter, fearing some kind of trap. Sheila finally went out to them, told her story and persuaded them to enter and arrest Hector and some of his men. Many of the tunnel dwellers went every day to Hector's trial, panhandling money for the subway fare, to testify against him. Hector went back to jail.

"After that," Bernard complains, "my haven of harmony became a haven of headaches." More people began to settle in the tunnel and look to Bernard for protection as well as food and advice. Although he professes "disdain for humanity," including other homeless, he is always willing to share what he has. "Who am I to deny someone in need?" he asks.

Several tunnel dwellers credit Bernard with saving their lives. One is Leon who came to the tunnel "stone drunk," in his words, on a bitter February night. "Bernard saw me laying up there in the street and wakes me up. 'Man,' he says, 'you can't stay here. You'll freeze to death.' 'Okay,' I says, 'then just let me die.' He says, 'Fuck,' and dragged me out of the draft, carried me two blocks over his shoulder, cursing all the way. Turns out I got frostbite bad that night. If Bernard hadn't helped me—and he gave me a blanket, too—I'd be dead and that ain't no lie."

Bernard pines for the days when he was alone, but he also remembers how dangerous such a life could be. One icy day, he slipped while carrying firewood down the steep stairs at the tunnel's entrance and fell about twenty feet to the tunnel's floor, breaking his hip. He crawled to his camp and attempted to heal himself by resting, but he ran out of wood for his fire and food for himself, and he caught a bad cold. "I couldn't even make my way out of the bunker, let alone the tunnel for help. I thought my time had come," he says now, "and I thought, well, if this is it, it's no big deal."

Another homeless man who lived farther up the tunnel came to his aid. The two had passed often but never spoken. Even now Bernard doesn't know his name. The man was aware that he hadn't seen Bernard for days, suspecting he had left, and came in hopes of scavenging anything useful that might be left behind. Rather than stealing, which he could easily have done in view of Bernard's weakness, he nursed Bernard back to health. Bernard never saw him again, but he tries to repay that care to others.

TODAY AMTRAK USES THE RAILROAD TRACKS AGAIN, BUT THE HOME-less continue to squat here. Most of them live in two areas: One consists of the bunkerlike concrete workstations like Bernard's, which occupants furnish and even decorate with carpeting and art-work, either graffitied murals or posters. The other campsite is at the southern end of the tunnel and less secure, where homeless like Seville live in more fragile quarters, usually makeshift tents and packing-crate homes. Between the two camps, and in fact along the entire length of the tunnel, are the most reclusive of the homeless, usually mentally ill, who sleep individually in small cubbyholes that have been hollowed out naturally or by man high up on the sheer walls of the tunnels. Some can be reached only by climbing metal rungs embedded in the walls.

Bernard's camp is the hub for these tunnel dwellers. His campfire lies directly under a grate that opens to the surface and carries out most of the smoke. Six chairs surround the fire. Food is shared, but many people also have their own private cache. Chores such as cooking and collecting firewood are also shared. One of the most burdensome chores, which came when the "Tears of Allah" dried up, is carrying five-gallon buckets of water to camp from a gas station more than a mile away. Most of the group eat at the same time, and there is always coffee on the grill for anyone stop-ping by. Anyone can use the grill anytime, but they are responsible for making sure the fire is out and the ashes completely gray when they leave.

Bernard spends more time at the fire than the others. His main source of income is collecting discarded cans and bottles from the trash. He prefers to do most of the cooking for the community, waking early to prepare breakfasts for those tunnel dwellers who have jobs to go to.

"People think food's the greatest problem down here," he says one morning over the grill with the flames snapping warmly in the dank air. "It's not. It's pride. They throw away the cream of the cream in New York, which makes scavenging relatively productive. I expect to find the Hope Diamond out there in the street some day. It's dignity that's hard to get."

Most members of this Riverside Park community are tunnel veterans. They have established communication networks that quickly pass around new information on where and when hot meals are being handed out. They know when a grocery store is throwing out slightly wilted produce or damaged cartons of macaroni. They know which restaurants and delicatessens give the days' leftovers to the homeless. They also know which restaurants throw ammonia on their garbage to keep the homeless away.

"Sometimes they do worse than that," says a tunnel dweller named Jesus. "Sometimes they put poison on it that you can't smell, can't taste, but you get sick after you eat it. My buddy, he died from rat poison they put in garbage. The doctor said it was rat poison, and he was so mad, he went to the manager of the restaurant to complain." Jesus just shrugs when I ask what effect it had.

Bernard complains about his loss of privacy, but he takes some pride in his particular community. "Everyone down here is settled. We have a base, and we function together. We don't have to deal with all the despair that goes on in the topside world," he says, sitting back on a discarded, purple recliner near his warm fire.

Near 79th Street off the West Side Highway, he says, is a homeless campsite aboveground composed of cardboard and other boxes covered with plastic sheets. "People are sleeping in there," Bernard says, wide-eyed. "I look at that and I say, 'Wow! That's incredible!' I mean, the weather so far this year has been unbelievably bad and I said to myself 'Man, you don't know how blessed you are.' I really think that's roughing it. My body has gone through a lot of changes; I'm beginning to feel my age based on the environment I'm living in. I wonder about some of these people. Down here, man, I'm lucky."

Still, he admits, his body has suffered physically from living underground, and he hints that his attitude has also changed. "Down here, man becomes an animal. Down here, the true animal in man comes out, evolves. His first instinct is to survive, and although he values his independence, he forms a community for support." He feels more sense of community now than he ever felt aboveground.

"I never voted in my life," he says, "never even registered to vote. I feel sure that everything up there is designed to work for those who have money. The politicians can talk about reforms, how they'll do this or that, but it's all bull." While he distrusts politicians in general, he distrusts homeless advocacy groups in particular.

"This Coalition for the Homeless is just bullshit," he says. "Red tape and litigation. They are procrastinators. They thrive on the homeless. Without us, they wouldn't have jobs, and they know it." Bernard is particularly affronted by the suspicious and condescending attitude of many employees of the Coalition and other such groups.

"A while ago, we were sitting up topside having some beers when this van from Project Reachout comes by," he recalls. "They ask if we want sandwiches and stuff. We weren't hungry, but we said, sure, why not? Then they said, 'Hey, you guys don't look homeless.' I said, 'What does a homeless person look like? We have to be in a certain attire and look dirty?' I said, 'Oh, man, keep your sandwiches.'

"Sure enough, two days later, same crew comes out giving out thermals [warm underwear]. Sure, I could use some thermals, but some guy sneaks around the back of the van with his camera to snap my picture taking the handout. They wanted pictures for their ads saying, 'Here are the poor homeless, aid the homeless.'"

A homeless agency offered Bernard an apartment, but after visiting it, he declined. "They lied about it. No one could have lived in that rat hole, not even a rat," he says, looking deeply into the fire as if revisiting the scene.

"It's all bullshit! These people can't play straight with God. And the way they talk about how the homeless problem should be solved, hell, they got it all wrong. A lot of work has to be done, sure—counseling, schooling, but most of all, treating us like the equals we are. I don't pity us and they shouldn't either. Everyone is responsible for his own life."

Bernard prefers the railroad tunnels to subway tunnels because they are safer. "The whole subway scene is dangerous now because all these gangs of hoodlums marauding around and preying on the homeless." Otherwise he doesn't fear the underground. "You draw vibrations to you by being afraid. Down here people are more afraid of the dark than anything else. I've seen real tough men freak out over rats they hear in the darkness, these big men carrying big pieces [guns] and knives and they shit, they freak over rats and ghosts."

If you aren't scared, he points out, you notice that it is never totally black in his tunnel during daylight hours. Grates allow light through, always enough to see something, as I now realize.

"And there's peace in the dark," he says. "I sit here at night at the fire with a pot of tea and just the solitude of the tunnel. I think what I've discovered down here is that what one really seeks in life is peace of mind."

You're happy down here, then? I ask.

"Sure," he says. "Whatever happy is. I understand that I can't change anything from the way it is, except for my mind. I accept things as they are and hey, that means I got to cover my necessities like food and shelter and that's it. And I have to keep some sort of sanity down here."

Bob

BERNARD AND OTHER MEMBERS OF THE COMMUNITY HAVE MADE IT clear that overt drug users are unwelcome in their tunnel, but they appear to make an exception for Bob. A fifty-one-year-old white man from Chicago, Bob brags that he was once New York's fastest short-order cook.

"I could handle eight pans and not burn an egg," he says. "But it cost me $100 a day to work, because I was paying $50 for a gram of coke and $50 for my amphetamines."

Bob is Bernard's best friend. He is also, according to underground artist Chris Pape, "the only one down here who has no illusions about himself. He knows he's a drug fiend and doesn't apologize or say he wants to change."

Bob is a burly man with a mountain man's gray beard and almost detached, cool blue eyes. He says matter-of-factly that he has chosen the life of an addict, wants no help to overcome it, and works only to support his habit. Bob is proud that he has never taken money from the government. He rises early to hunt for cans to redeem, and he picks up odd jobs on the street, such as helping unload produce from delivery trucks into grocery stores and fruit stands.

He is well known for his skill at working scams. He can con even his best friends, who are alert and wary. Once he scammed Pape, who he considers a friend, out of $20 on a VCR deal, and disappeared for a week on a speed binge. Bernard made Bob apologize, but of course the money was gone. "Sorry," Bob said with a shrug, "but, hey, that's the way it is. I just had to do it." Bernard offered the little money he had to Pape on Bob's behalf, but Chris refused Bernard's money.

Pape shrugs, too, about his loss. It's impossible to stay angry with Bob, he says. He is childlike, totally passive most of the time. Raised in a middle-class Chicago neighborhood and trained as an engineer, his eyes are flat and unfocused, although they can be frightening because they are so expressionless and because, under the calm veneer, Bob has shown sudden anger and violence. He blames the chemicals in his system, or the lack of them. "It's the drugs," he says a day after exploding angrily because he had no place to sit. "Nothing I can do about it," Bob says unapologetically. People avoid him on rainy days when he gets particularly depressed. Like most homeless, Bob's moods are very much affected by the weather.

Bob is as unashamed of his scamming habits as well as his addiction. He talks freely about both. "Listen, kid," he tells me out of earshot of the others, "don't trust anyone down here. No one. Never!" His eyes are intense now as we walk out of the tunnel. I expect he is setting me up for a touch, but in the months I knew him, Bob never asked me for money. Instead, he always acted protectively—he'd scold me for even coming into the tunnels alone—and then offer advice on how to behave during my journeys underground.

Like Bernard, Bob earns what little money he needs by "busting," or returning discarded cans and bottles to redemption centers. For 600 empties, they can receive $30, or a nickel each. A major problem is finding groceries to redeem the trash, however. Despite the law requiring stores to take up to 250 empties from any one person, storekeepers often refuse in an effort to discourage the homeless from entering their premises. A few nonprofit redemption centers exist, notably "We Can" at 12th Avenue and 52nd Street, which was begun by Guy Polhemus when he overheard homeless at a soup kitchen complain about their difficulty. However, these centers tend to be inconvenient and very crowded, with long lines and long waits.

This has led to the rise of middlemen, also called two-for-oners although they should be one-for-twoers. They buy two empties for a nickel, half the price at regular redemption centers, but offer "no waiting, no sorting, no hassle," as Bob says. Some middlemen have become full-blown entrepreneurs, like Chris Jeffers, a twenty-year-old who was sleeping in Riverside Park just two years earlier but now makes $70,000 a year. He rents an empty theater at Eighth Avenue and 50th Street and keeps it open around the clock for the homeless to bring their cans and bottles; it pays half the price, but it's convenient. Jeffers, who says he took some college courses in finance in Tampa, Florida, resells the empties to "We Can" for the full redemption price, earning thousands of dollars a day.

Most of the collectors go through the trash at night when they are less visible to the public. Many are addicts of one kind or another, Jeffers says, and often want to redeem their cans after hours to feed their night needs. "I know some people will say I'm exploiting those with alcohol and drug problems," Jeffers admitted to a *New York Times* reporter. "But tell me, how is what I'm doing any different from what commodity traders do when they buy crops at low prices from farmers in distress?"

Scavenging, panhandling, and scams provide some income for the homeless, but surviving underground is a full-time job. "Living here takes a lot of planning," Bob says as he contemplates the fire outside his bunker. "You have to prepare yourself in the summer for the winter, get your stuff washed and collect food." His bunker is one of the most elaborate. Last year, he says, he spent $200 to insulate his underground room, put in wall-to-wall carpeting, a queen-size mattress, a kerosene lamp, a table, and two chairs.

He takes his privacy seriously. "People like to inject chaos into their lives," he says. "I don't need that; that's why I live here. In all the time I've been down here, I've never had company in my room. When I go into my room, don't bother me," he warns. "Don't call me, and don't come in," he warns emphatically. "Bernard's the only one allowed in my room."

Bob has bad days when the weather is sour. He becomes irritable, edgy, and depressed because, he says, he can't get out to gather cans or do volunteer work at soup kitchens. "I hate doing nothing; I always have to be doing something," he explains, but ever since he left his wife and daughter—his wife always nagged him, he says, which is why he set off in his car one day for the grocery store and ended up in New York—he has never considered keeping a steady job.

"I like the way my life is now. I'm independent and do what I want. It's not that I'm lazy or don't want to work. I walk all the way around the city most days to collect cans. This is the life I want. I don't take government handouts because I don't pay taxes." Sometimes Bob will be gone for weeks, but Bernard keeps his bunker safe from scavengers and Bob has always returned. He lives by what he calls the Homeless Credo: "Do what you have to do today. Tomorrow will come. And if it doesn't, you won't have to deal with it."

Don

SOME OF THE HOMELESS IN BERNARD'S TUNNEL ARE LESS ATTACHED to the community, like Don, a large, clean-cut, smiling black man in his early thirties. He left his wife and children to go underground and straighten out his life, he says. He misses his family, but he promised his mother he would not return until he was free of drugs. He maintains ties with his mother, and even takes Bernard to Thanksgiving dinner at her house in Brooklyn. Although he has gone through detoxification centers several times, he is back on drugs.

He works regularly and hard. He wakes around 5:30 A.M. to get to a construction job at 7 A.M., and on weekends he usually has an odd job painting. He says he sends most of his money to his family. He is more frightened of underground life than most tunnel dwellers.

"The most dangerous animal on earth is man," he says often. "I like to think about things when it doesn't interfere with my safety, which isn't often. Thinking too much is dangerous, because it gets in the way of the basic instinct of survival. You think too much, you find yourself caring too much about other people, or you feel sorry for yourself, and both are dangerous. When you live down here, you have always got to be on the edge. If you think too much, you are dead. No matter how well you think you know someone, you never do. And down here, you don't want to."

Reactions to danger can be unpredictable. Faced with a man with a knife, Don fell to his knees and begged not to be hurt, even though the knife-wielder was four inches shorter and much skinnier than Don. When confronted by a taller man who pulled a gun, Don just threw up his hands in exasperation and walked away. "It was the stupidest thing I've ever done," he laughs now. "I just didn't care. I was sick of that shit and decided to walk away and forget it and if I got shot, well, I would be walking and not just waiting for it."

One morning at around 7:30, I arrive at Bernard's camp to find him pacing angrily. Don is in the hospital with an overdose. Bernard found him the night before, sprawled across the tracks, unable to be roused. Trains are running through the tunnels again and Amtrak is looking for excuses to evict the homeless from the tunnels, Bernard says. He wasn't going to let Don be that excuse, so he called the Amtrak police to take Don to a hospital.

"If you're going to get bugged out, do it on top," Bernard repeats to himself as he paces, convincing himself that he acted correctly. Bob stays strictly in his bunker when doing drugs underground. Don was irresponsible with drugs in general, Bernard says, working himself up. He often failed to bring wood for the fire despite repeated warnings. "He knows the rules: no drugging down here. They didn't build this camp; they don't deserve this. Fuck them. I built it. They think I own this tunnel. I do. I built it."

Bernard pokes at the fire, quiet now. He will evict Don, with force if necessary. "He gets a week to get his shit out of here," says Bernard. He leans back in his recliner and wonders if he can really force Don out because Don is also large and strong. "It's been a long time since I had my ass kicked. Who knows, maybe I'll like it," he smiles broadly.

A week later, a homeless man passes me on the street. He tells me that Don says good-bye. Don's name is seldom heard again in Bernard's tunnel.

Tim

TIM IS THE ONLY OTHER MAN THAT HAS BEEN EJECTED FROM BERnard's camp. A wiry, meek white man, Tim often stops at Bernard's fire, seeking an invitation to sit, which seldom comes. Occasionally he is offered a cigarette, but is always kept at a distance.

One afternoon I find Bernard shouting at Tim as they stand toe-to-toe on the tracks. Tim has been caught stealing from another one of the tunnel homeless. Bernard is furious and very close to thrashing him, but in the end just orders him to leave the community.

"He didn't want to get violent because you're here," Pape tells me later with a smile. "Part of Bernard's archaic thinking about women."

Flip

LIKE TIM, FLIP IS NOT WELCOME AT BERNARD'S CAMPFIRE. FLIP doesn't care for himself, Bernard explains; he lacks direction and wants to rely on people, trying to make them take care of him. Bernard once showed Flip an empty bunker and told him that if he cleaned it out, Bernard would help him set it up as a place to live. Flip hasn't done a thing with the bunker, Bernard says dismissively. Lazy, he says.

Now Flip comes to the fire shyly once again. He stands hands buried in his trouser pockets, slouching on the tracks.

"It's raining," he says.

"So what?" Bernard answers.

Flip moves away, and later that afternoon, as Bernard walks me out of the tunnel, Flip's figure stands silhouetted at the entrance, alone and forlorn against a cold, gray winter sky.

Tony

SOME OF THE HOMELESS WHO ARE PART OF BERNARD'S CAMP LIVE removed from his fire, like Tony, who has set up his home alone farther along the tunnel. One of the most gentle and popular men of the group, Tony is a fifty-five-year-old white man with a pepper-streaked beard and dark, arched eyebrows like Sean Connery, all topped by a red knit hat.

I meet Tony on the grate above Bernard's fire one snowy day in January. Light smoke rises through the steel mesh, toying with powdery snow that the wind has swept up off the ice-covered Hudson. Red-faced New Yorkers walking their dogs in the park try to hurry them through the morning ritual, but a few pull their

masters briefly toward the welcoming scent of burning wood min-
gling in the crisp air. Tony is standing on the grate stomping his
boots to make sure the snow falls on the camp scene below.

Faint growls rise with the smoke and Tony, having gotten the
response he wants, allows a boyish smile to break his face. He and
I start carefully down the steep and icy path toward the tunnel's
entrance. In one hand he clasps a black garbage bag full of empty
cans, and in the other, a dull green garbage bag full of plastic
bottles. The superintendent of a nearby apartment house has saved
them for him to redeem.

At the tunnel entrance, a young man named Joey emerges
from between the iron rungs that once barred passage. He has a
young, soft face but a skinny, nervous body that is unable to stay
still. Tony pulls a wad of wrinkled and crushed dollar bills from
the pocket of his corduroy pants and passes one to Joey. They
exchange brief winks, and Tony permits himself a small smile that
exposes two missing front teeth.

"Hey, man," a beseeching voice comes through the grating
as Flip emerges. "Gimme some, too," he asks, almost shyly. For a
large man, Flip looks as vulnerable as he sounds.

He offers Tony his plastic bag. Tony skims its contents
quickly.

"Naw, man," he says, "I don't need any of that stuff."

"C'mon, man, it's cold," Flip whines, almost whimpering.

"Naw, I don't got that much," Tony says firmly. He pulls
out a crumpled pack of cigarettes and offers one to Flip. The
younger man takes three and walks off without even nodding
thanks.

Tony and I carefully descend the steps into the tunnel, wary
of used syringes and fresh ice. We reach the bottom and Tony sighs
heavily, as if he is home.

He is less afraid of falling, he says, than of getting struck by
the nine-foot-long icicles that now hang from the tunnel's ceiling.
One killed a man two years ago, he claims, in case I should doubt
the danger. Small precautions take on greater importance the longer
you live in the tunnels, he explains.

I wonder aloud about Joey, to whom Tony has given the money unasked. Tony explains simply that he and Joey live together in an abandoned bunker. Joey is eighteen years old, and Tony refers to him at times as his son, other times as his lover.

As much as the tunnel regulars like Tony, they despise Joey as a useless parasite on the older man. "Joey's young; he can do anything he wants," says Bernard. "He doesn't have to be down here, but Tony does. Tony does everything for that kid, even went to banks trying to borrow money to send him to college. Believe that! What money he did get, Joey spent on drugs, but he told Tony he was going to college."

Tony prides himself on his two "mouses," which are king-size rats that he trains to perform. Ralph and George, the "mouses," can leap from the ground to a food bag hung five feet overhead. Tony claims they also guard his bunker from other rats, even that they have chased away stray cats, which from their size is credible. They are huge creatures, Ralph perching on Tony's shoulder, George on the back of his wrinkled hand.

"I taught my niece to read," Tony tells me with a happy smile as we sit around the fire. "Now she's going to be a doctor and has to read the big words to me." However, he hasn't seen any of his family for seventeen years, not since he murdered a man and went to prison for fifteen years. The last two years he has lived in Bernard's tunnel with Joey.

South End

John

THE TUNNEL'S SOUTHERN END HOSTS A LOOSER AFFILIATION OF THE homeless. Individuals barely interact with each other. They behave more like silent, hostile neighbors who both envy and fear the person in the next bunker.

"We don't talk much, but we won't let anyone steal from anyone else's stuff in the tunnel either," says John, who was seriously

John and Mama in a tunnel bunker. *Photo by Margaret Morton*

John's home. *Photo by Margaret Morton*

injured four years ago by a roving gang of homeless. He rarely answers knocks on his door, which he keeps padlocked, and he keeps a bayonet and hatchet handy for protection.

At fifty years old, John is a four-year tunnel veteran. Small and thin, he says he was abandoned as a child and grew up in institutions. He has had menial, low-paying jobs, many working with animals. His small monthly welfare check goes for food for himself, his fifteen cats, and his dog, Mama. All of them were strays that he found while he and they vied for food in garbage bins. His bunker walls are decorated with posters of animals, and on the table and boxes stand small statues and artificial flowers from the trash. The room is lit with red candles. During the day he reads the Bible and drinks coffee and whiskey. He spends most of the time listening to the radio and talking to himself, he says.

He has no friends in the world, he volunteers. "I'm a little high-class for some of these people down here," he explains. "That's why I don't get along too well with everybody."

New York Times reporter John Tierney wrote two articles about John. As a result, he briefly had a woman pen pal and enrolled in a new program for the homeless consisting of work on an upstate farm for free board and meals and a modest wage. John was apprehensive about leaving the tunnel. He was particularly torn when he had to give away his cats and kittens, but he was allowed to take Mama and also eager to begin life again aboveground.

Bernard was happy for John, but sad, too. "He'll be back. You can't just leave the tunnel. This is his home now. He doesn't know how to live in the topside world." Bernard sounds plaintive, as if he is speaking for all of the underground people, including himself.

John soon rebelled against the discipline of regular work, however, and says that he longed for the privacy and freedom of the tunnels. Within six months he is back in his tunnel bunker.

Tom

TOM IS FROM NORTH CAROLINA, A SEVENTEEN-YEAR-OLD WHITE MAN who lives with a couple, Butch and Brenda, in a large green tent upon the slope of the Riverside Park tunnel. He came to Manhattan eight months earlier with his girlfriend and their child. His parents had died in a car accident, and his two sisters were taken by godparents, but he was too old to be cared for by relatives. His girlfriend wanted to live in New York, but they broke up soon after they arrived. She took the car and all his money. He lived for a time in the Fort Washington shelter until he caught a man stealing from his locker.

"I asked him what he was doing, and he just said he was taking my stuff," Tom says evenly, his blond hair shyly tumbling over his trusting eyes. "He had no right." They fought and the thief was thrown out the window several floors above the street.

"He just lay there on his face, so still," Tom recalls, his blue eyes soberingly open. "They said I killed him, but the police took me aside and told me not to worry about it. I would have done it all over again, though," Tom says with a shake of his head. "I mean I didn't want to kill him, but he was taking the only stuff I had left."

Tom decided he was safer on the streets, where he met Butch and Brenda. Butch is a large black man with an angry attitude and very protective toward both Brenda and Tom. Brenda, whose story will be told later (see chapter 22, "Women"), is completely subservient to him. Butch refuses to talk about himself but he prowls, almost lurches, around Tom as he talks, listening to his words carefully as if ready to heed any order to attack.

The couple took Tom to live in the tunnels with them, but he found a job bartending on Amsterdam Avenue and with his earnings, bought the tent. A temporary measure until he can afford an apartment, he says, where his sisters can also come to live. "They keep asking me if they can come here," he says, "but I don't want them until we can live properly. I don't know that New York is the right place for two girls."

Tom gets an apartment in a few months, and despite the roaches, one of which he woke to find crawling up his nose, he considers it a step above tunnels and tents. He gives the tent to Butch and Brenda.

THE SURPRISING WONDER OF BERNARD'S TUNNEL IS LESS THAT PEOPLE can survive in such an environment than that they can work together and even care, sometimes intensely, for each other. Many would expect love and care to be the first emotions sacrificed in such a desolate environment, but Bernard would argue that emotions are more sincere underground. Unlike our society, the underground dwellers do not judge each other on their pasts or any element of how they live, except how they treat one another. Respect for privacy and property is critical. They lie to each other at times, usually about their pretunnel existences, but, even when these sound unlikely at best, no one challenges them. They can invent a past with which they can live while they get on with surviving the present.

The most important truth about underground people, Bernard also advises, is that there is no single truth about them. "They tell many stories and there is truth in all their stories. You just have to find it."

"We had one guy down here who was sometimes an ex–Navy Seal, sometimes a Green Beret, sometimes the king of an island, sometimes a pastry chef," one homeless man recalls. "All I know he was a decent man who used to share everything. When the police asked if I knew this guy, and showed me his picture and told me a name, I didn't have to lie. I said no, I don't know that guy. I don't care what he done. He's a good guy and if he wants to start over down here, he can. That's the beauty of the tunnels."

Bernard. *Photo by Margaret Morton*

12

Tunnel Art

"THESE PIECES, THEY'RE NOT JUST GRAFFITI," BERNARD EXPLAINS as his arm sweeps toward the mural covering the outside wall of his tunnel bunker. "They're works of art, and they mean a lot to us. We got food down here, some warmth, and we got art. What more could we ask for?"

"Pieces" to the tunnel homeless and to those who paint them is short for "masterpieces," works that are sometimes especially done for them by graffiti writers (sometimes called "artists"). Chris Pape, who "tags" or signs his work "Freedom"; Roger Smith, who is known as "Smith"; and David Smith, his brother, whose tag was "Sane"; are all graffiti writers who paint the tunnels.

"David and Roger did some of these for me and for my people down here. Chris was first to start doing them in this tunnel, but he didn't know he was doing them just for me," Bernard laughs.

"This piece makes me smile every time I look at it," says Bernard as he surveys the jagged, zany mural by Sane that decorates his fifteen-by-ten-foot wall. Sane got the idea for it one night sitting by the fire, sharing herbal tea with Bernard who was framed by the huge concrete wall. He returned late that night to spray-paint the piece before Bernard woke the next morning.

In a sharp-edged technique, chaotic lines and bright colors intersect and complement each other to create what Bernard considers to be a mural that best captures life below the ground—a

Self-portrait by Chris Pape (Freedom). *Photo by Margaret Morton*

mysterious truth amid complete craziness. The clothes, stone and metal rubble, and rubbish piled before it add to the sense of disorder it conveys.

"It's for me and it's all about me," says Bernard. "It's about the chaos in the topside world and the peace down here."

Above the piece are scrawled Bernard's words the night before; sharing herbal tea by the campfire, Sane scrawled in jaunty black letters: "Freedom, aw. Modern society is guilty of intellectual terrorism." It was Sane's last piece, which enhances its meaning and value for Bernard and others. Sane died two years after completing it, either in an accident, which often befalls graffiti artists because of the dangerous places in which they work, or by suicide. He was eighteen years old.

Sane was found drowned in the calm waters of Flushing Bay. Because he was a good swimmer, some believe he took his own life. Others say he fell into the water from a bridge while graffiting on it, perhaps while being chased by cops.

"Sane was the best," several of his fellow graffiti artists say, and after his death several pieces appeared in the tunnels spray-painted in his honor by mourning colleagues. Some are tribute pieces, with Sane's name highly stylized by the writers' own techniques. Others are messages in dark colors among spray-painted tears: "Sane Ruled" and "Sane never forgotten." Smith keeps his brother's legacy alive by painting Sane's tag as well as his own on his works.

"When we started, we always put our tags together: SANE SMITH. The 'word' was that we were some big black writer from Brooklyn," Smith smiles briefly through his neat, short beard under gentle eyes.

Speaking of Sane, one sixteen-year-old graffiti writer tells me, "Everything he touched burned. He was the greatest. Why would he want to kill himself?"

An older writer suggests Sane "burned out."

"He had reached the top and he knew it," he suggests. "He couldn't go any further. I think he felt that and didn't know what to do next. Maybe he felt empty like I did when I realized how many years of my life I've lost to graffiti, to the tunnels." He pauses for a minute, remembering Sane. "He was a pest back then when he was twelve and starting. He would run up to me all the time to ask for my autograph and I'd tell him to go away. I didn't associate with 'toys.' He was just a toy back then. But there was always something different about him, a real nice kid, eyes always friendly and laughing."

Sane and Smith were being sued for $3 million by the City of New York for graffiting the top level of the Brooklyn Bridge—the largest suit ever brought against graffiti writers anywhere. The city pressed the suit as a lesson to writers, to punish them for what many consider vandalizing public property and to discourage younger writers from the particularly dangerous locales like the heights of bridges. The police also wanted help in identifying other graffiti writers, which Sane and Smith refused to provide. The city dropped the case after Sane's death, but no one believes the suit could have caused Sane's suicide.

He did suffer from depression occasionally. If there was a flaw in Sane, it was that he cared too much, as another writer says. Just a week before his death, he did a piece in the tunnel to commemorate a four-year-old boy who had been struck and killed by a subway train. "He used to bring things to the homeless kids in tunnels and sit by the fires and have coffee and when he'd talk about them later to me, he'd sometimes get real sad about them. I mean real sad," the man recalls.

Sane did not go to college but his older brother, Smith, received a computer science degree from Fordham University. After Sane's death, Smith quit his job and spends most of his time in the tunnels now. Older writers encourage him to get out and find a job, but Smith refuses to consider becoming a conventional artist. That, to him, would be "selling out," he says. He recently spoke of training to become a subway train conductor.

"I've always liked the tunnels," Smith says. He particularly likes a huge, open underground cavern called the "playground" that is carved out of Manhattan's rock foundations about a half-hour walk from Grand Central Station along narrow tunnel ledges that parallel the tracks. Graffiti writers often congregate there, running about on catwalks and pipes, scribbling messages, and even, on occasion, playing baseball. "It's a nice open space," Smith says. "You don't get space like this up here, miles of space with no people."

While Sane and Smith retain the tragic mystique of tunnel graffiti writers, Freedom—Chris Pape—made the tunnels into his own personal studio. Now thirty years old, Chris has virtually left the underground graffiti scene but not before he almost made it to the Museum of Modern Art. He still ventures into the tunnels to do murals for Bernard and other tunnel dwellers.

My favorite image of Chris is his huge self-portrait sprayed on a tunnel wall, standing with the head of a spray-paint can tilted down inquiringly at a white rabbit sitting near Chris's Reeboked feet. His shoulders slouch inside a leather bomber jacket, Holden Caulfield–like; his hands are shoved deep into the front pockets of his well-worn jeans. His stance is typical of many street kids who want to proclaim that nothing can surprise or frighten them, and that any attack will be absorbed rather than avoided, shrugged off rather than replied to in kind. The autumn's dusty sunlight falls into the tunnel through overhead grates and with it comes a leaf about to alight near the rabbit, who prepares to scamper off as the spray-can head watches. The scene remains frozen on the soot-blackened wall; the only movement in the mural is Chris's sharp, scrawling tag, *Freedom,* beside his untied shoelace.

Chris's larger-than-life portrait suspended on the tunnel wall invites curiosity, but a specific blend of it very much like his own—subtle, unaggressive, and always accepting. Like the portrait, Chris invites curiosity. He was a runaway teenager, he says, a high school dropout from the West Side of Manhattan who lived for a time in a pool hall on the Upper West Side, eating poorly and occasionally. He is both intrigued by the tunnels and frightened of them.

"I used to look into subway tunnels on my way home from school and imagine dragons," he says. "Sometimes I'd see faces in them, wizards and monsters. I had to explore them, but I had this horror of them. I still hate the tunnels.

"When I go down there, I can't wait to come back up. I keep promising myself that the next mural will be my last. I hate the danger, I hate risking my life each time for something so stupid. But I get an idea in my head for a piece and I can't get rid of it, and I have to do it because, if I don't, no one else will."

More than a decade ago, when trains wore graffiti, Chris gave designs to graffiti gangs eager to prove their daring by executing them. He was far less interested in braving the dangers than in seeing his concept completed and appreciated.

One spring day, as he and I are watching a group of boys play baseball in Riverside Park, a long ball comes our way and stops next to a grating. The fielder rushes after it, and as he bends down to retrieve it, something through the grate catches his eye.

"Whoa, look at this!" he shouts to the other players, and they, ignoring the runners, come to see.

"Wow, it's Ted Williams," says a teammate, crouching down.

Chris smiles. They are viewing his tunnel portrait of the one-time baseball star painted much like he appears on the baseball cards that occupy much of Chris's aboveground life.

"That's what it's all about," Chris says quietly, wearing a broad, proud grin as he watches the discovery of his work.

Chris in his early years often spent his few dollars on paints rather than dinner. One winter he came down with bronchitis, which became pneumonia and mononucleosis, but he continued to crawl down into the tunnels to satisfy what he now regards as his obsession. He was in the Riverside Park tunnel before Bernard arrived, and when Bernard appeared, Chris ignored him, preferring to stay as anonymous as possible. He was also doing graffiti on subway cars at the time—"a chameleon," as he says. Bernard finally persuaded Chris to have a cup of tea at his fire and frightened him badly, much as he once did me.

Bernard had been talking about the discoveries that can be made in trash and refuse, then abruptly turned his tall frame from the fire to reach into his shirt and bring out a long, glistening butcher's knife. "Like this," he said, fingering the sharp edges. Chris reached for his spray can, ready to fire it into Bernard's face, but Bernard put the weapon away and the two resumed talking about art. They laugh about the incident now.

Bernard claims he did not know Chris was afraid of him. "I only thought you were very quiet, a little weird."

Sometimes, Bernard recalls, the homeless found Chris lying by a mural because he was very weak, or breathing heavily. He tried to convince Chris to give up graffiti writing in the tunnels, at least until he recovered his health. Often he brought blankets to throw over Chris's shoulders. Once Chris passed out and Bernard carried him to the fire.

While Sane and Smith created sporadically on the tunnel walls, Chris used most of the available wall space along thirty underground blocks of the Riverside Park tunnel walls as his personal gallery. As with the portrait of Ted Williams, he cleverly capitalizes on whatever sunlight penetrates to the underground and incorporates it into his works along with the natural breaks and textures of the walls themselves. Much of his work is derivative—Dali-esque melting watches that ooze down from catwalks and rafters and through grates in the ceiling, for example—although he believes it also asserts that time is running out on the lives of underground homeless. In another mural, a bizarre cherub with an automatic rifle floats above a green man with a ragged scar across his face. Another, titled *History of Graffiti,* chronicles graffiti on a sweeping train, each car a tribute to great "writers" and their styles. Yet another portrays a silver-black Madonna, face aglow with golden light, peacefully regarding the denizens of the tunnel who pass. The most romantic of his murals portrays an exotic woman with dark hair swept back to reveal features more blunt than flattering and mysterious but solicitous eyes. The treatment suggests he once loved her.

Perhaps his most famous work is the mural that took up the side of an entire subway car, a photograph of which almost got to the Museum of Modern Art as part of its "High and Low: Modern Art and Popular Culture" show. The exhibit featured great masters, their impact on street art, and in turn, street art's impact on them. Freedom's work was a version of Michelangelo's *Creation,* an ephemeral hand reaching down from a white cloud to touch fingertips with another from below. Across the bottom he scrawled the words "What is Art. Why is art." The photograph of the car with the mural was incorporated into the sixty-page catalog, but in the end the museum chose not to display the picture for fear it would alienate trustees and donors who might interpret it as an endorsement of graffiti.

WHEN CHRIS IS WORKING ON HIS TUNNEL ART HE IS FREEDOM. Recently, he and Smith have agreed to collaborate, but they are not agreed on the subject. Freedom wants to do Picasso's *Guernica,* but Smith argues for Goya's *Third of May.* Freedom agrees, recalling the sense of violence and terrorism in the original, which he wants to transfer onto the tunnel wall in an attempt to dramatize his fear and horror of that world. The campfire will illuminate the stinging colors, he explains, and the homeless around it will live with the scene even as they are part of it.

A twenty-foot ladder is trundled several miles along the tracks to Bernard's camp. Next come cartons of spray-paint cans. The work begins one morning before sunup. By the firelight, Freedom and Smith—and now the wakened Bernard—whitewash a thirty-foot-long, sixteen-foot-high section of wall.

It will be the largest piece in the tunnel, they say, and as they work, determined and intense, tunnel dwellers passing by only whisper lest they disturb the effort. Holding a picture of the original, Freedom outlines the scene with light blue paint. Neither he, with baseball cap under hooded sweatshirt, nor Smith, in green army jacket and heavy boots, talk much. From across the tracks, Bernard hands over old clothes for rags.

A train approaches and everyone freezes, melting against the tunnel's gray walls to escape sight. When it passes, the ladder is erected again and the work continues. Smith moves smoothly from side to side while Freedom, on the ladder, nearly falls several times.

Smith becomes impatient. He usually completes his murals within hours. Freedom is slower and more critical. When a figure looks wrong to him, he repaints it, despite Smith's objections. However, at the end of the first day, when they step back to regard their work, they agree it will be great. It will be big, big.

The word had reached the homeless on the surface by the next morning. "They're doing something big," one man says as I begin down the slope toward the tunnel's entrance. "Real big. For us."

Another man cautions me against going into the tunnels alone, and he comes with me. As we watch the second day begin, he says "Everyone down here knows about it. This is going to be the biggest thing in our tunnel. Too bad, though. A lot of people will want to come down here now to settle."

Bernard is not happy. As the mural takes shape, he sees the blood and gore and begins to reconsider his permission for the work right there across from his campfire. For the sake of friendship, he says, he shrugs off his doubts and Freedom and Smith continue to fill in the figures they have sketched and add lines that bring the figures to life. Smith completes the top of the cathedral and sprays the misty blue sky that symbolizes hope above the violent execution scene.

A man and woman who live in the tunnel pass by. "I think we should put this piece in our den," the man jokes.

"Do you think they'll eat sandwiches if we bring some?" the woman asks. "They're outsiders and I just don't want to intrude," she explains to me.

"We'll have to visit Bernard more often now," says another man to a group as they watch briefly. "It's civil here."

Toward the end of the day, Bernard tells Smith to walk me to the exit, but Smith is impatient to finish. He resists until Bernard orders him, almost threatening. "It's the law of the tunnel," he says, probably inventing a new law for the occasion, "that a woman visitor doesn't leave here alone. And you're in a tunnel."

Icy rain and bitter cold weather prevent Freedom and Smith from completing the work the next day. They wear light layers of clothes, Smith in an army jacket and Freedom in his bomber jacket, to allow flexible movement. Nothing can protect their hands and fingers spraying the paint, though. Even on a warm day, I can only spurt the paint for a few minutes at a time. Graffiti writers spend hours at a time.

The piece is completed a few days later. It spreads large and wide and intricately. The gruesome scene is alarming, just the effect Freedom wanted. The misty cathedral promises detail from afar, but up close turns out to be only an image—a sign of Smith's mastery of his material. Smith hands the signing paint can to Freedom. At first he refuses, for some reason I do not understand. Then he writes his tag. So does Smith. And he adds Sane's tag.

As I leave, the day seems more sweet than others despite the brisk chill blowing off the river. I feel I have witnessed something remarkable being created underground, a bit of wonder, if not beauty, for homeless underground people to appreciate and call their own.

"I like the place," Tony tells me. "It gets damp, but it's safe enough, and there's OK people down here, and I like the art," he says, almost embarrassed to use the word. "It makes me feel human, you know. And underground, believe me, you can feel like the animal they think you are upstairs."

The May Third Mural by Chris Pape and Roger Smith. *Photo by Thomas Bornemann*

13

Graffiti

IT WAS THE CHRISTMAS SEASON IN NEW YORK IN 1978. THE lights were still on in the Brooklyn train lay-up and Lee didn't like it.

"Let's go home," he told Mono.

"Yo, you crazy, man?" Mono was in his face. "We racked up all this paint," he yelled at the suitcases full of spray-paint cans they had stolen over several weeks and carried on subway trains, through stations, and finally into the tunnel. Their goal was to "do"—to cover with graffiti—the side of an entire ten-car train, which had never been done before.

The two men, along with a third, Slave, belong to the Fabulous Five, New York's most notorious graffiti gang. They crouched at the end of the tunnel before it opens into the train yard, or lay-up. They refused to allow Doc to take part because he was wasted on alcohol, and Dirty Slug, the fifth member, seldom joined them anymore.

"Ah, fuck it, man, let's do it," Lee agreed. The Transit Authority was cracking down on graffiti writers, increasing its police force to 4,300 in an effort to stop the "vandalism" that constituted "pollution of the eye and mind," as officials put it, and the gang might not get this close to sleeping subway trains again.

They apportioned the paint among the cars, donned gloves, and got to work. Lee had studied the train for two nights. He would do the first car—cascade green and faded blue—then Mono would do the next, Slave the third, then another by Mono, then a car with a Mickey Mouse and the Fabulous Five tag, then two holiday-festooned cars that would say "Merry Christmas, New York," and so on.

"When we started piecing, I did my first car in less than an hour," Lee recalls. "I was bombing. The colors were coming and it burned."*

About two hundred paint cans were empty, and eight of the ten cars were finished when the cops arrived. "Move, move!" shouted Mono as he waved toward a cluster of big flashlights coming down the tracks. "Cops, man, cops!"

Mono began running, fell, got up, and raced off. Slave had disappeared. Lee failed to see another train arriving on the next track before it sideswiped him, knocking him under the graffitied cars. He saw shiny, black shoes approaching.

"We got you now, c'mon out!" one voice called out loudly, but from a distance, so he bolted for the tunnel's mouth, stopping just inside for breath. Mono came out of the darkness, and they crouched in near panic near the spot where their evening adventure had begun.

Suddenly, both were caught in a flashlight beam. "Freeze!" the voice ordered.

Again they ran, across tracks and up a flight of stairs, clawing and scrambling toward an exit grate they knew. It was stuck, and they had to jump up in unison and push the grating free before they emerged onto the street. "There were people waiting for a bus. Dunno what they thought when they saw us coming out of the sidewalk, all dirty with our hands bleeding," Lee laughs now, "and these voices yelling up from the tunnels, and we just ran. Bang! We were out of there."

They walked around Brooklyn until the adrenaline wore off

---

*Graffiti writers have their own jargon, part of, but different from, other examples of hip-hop culture. "To bomb" is to accomplish a lot in a short time. A "burner" is superior work, so are pieces that are "nasty," "the death," "vicious," "bad," "dirty," or "snap." "Down by law" means having high status.

and Mono persuaded Lee to return to the tunnel to complete the work. To leave it unfinished would tell other graffiti writers that they had run and "lost the game," as he said. So they went back and painted the final two cars that same night, without any more interruptions.

The next morning at about 7 A.M., Lee went to the Brooklyn Bridge Station. It was the accepted time and place, amid the early morning commuter rush, for graffiti writers to gather and view each other's work from the previous night before the Transit Authority could pull the trains out of service for an acid bath to erase the paint.

"Oh, man! Oh man!" someone shouted at Lee. "I've seen it! A whole train! It's bad style, Lee," he yelled approvingly. He had seen it on another line, so Lee had to ride one train after another much of the day until he saw it. Even Lee was stunned. "The first cars came in like a roaring horse," he remembers. "You could barely see the side of it, all the colors flashing out of the windows we'd blanketed with paint."

He boarded the train and watched others on the platforms looking in amazement as it passed. "It was like crazy, like you could see the reflection in their eyes." Some viewers applauded. Even the "Wall Street Journals," as he calls businessmen with briefcases, were awed. A short, red-haired cop, watching the train unfold back to the fir-treed Merry Christmas cars, shook his head in admiration and smiled.

Inside, "people were looking at each other in confusion, like they were in church with stained glass windows, and talking about it. Some positive, some negative. But I knew they would talk about it at home," he says proudly, "and that's what New York is all about. It's giving to people with nothing in return."

GRAFFITI COMES FROM THE ITALIAN WORD, *GRAFFIO,* WHICH MEANS TO scratch. It is used to describe many different kinds of wall writings, and dates back at least to ancient Egypt. In ancient Rome, an inscription on private property asked people not to scribble on the walls. New York graffitists take credit for beginning, in the late sixties, the wave of contemporary graffiti writings not only in the United States but in Europe as well. A *New York Times* reporter tracked down a Washington Heights teenager named Demetrius, who signed his nickname and his street name, "Taki 183," on hundreds of walls, stoops, monuments, and subways. "Not for the girls," he said, "they don't care. You do it for yourself." Most of his successors were boys, but a few were girls, like Lady Pink.

Much of the rationale for New York's graffiti is explained in Lee's words—the need for self-assertion, particularly among urban youth whose creativity is stifled by an overbearing city; the need to be remembered; the need to define themselves differently than society has; and the need to feel in control, in some small way, of surroundings they deeply fear.

Chris Pape says graffiti writing was "just something to do. If we had Little League where I grew up, I probably would have put my energy into baseball and now I'd be with the Yankees." He pauses and then smiles, "Well, maybe not the Yankees."

Whatever the motivation, Lee, whose full name is Jorge Lee Quinones, contends that the public appreciated both the graffiti art and the artists when they were at their peak nearly two decades ago. "The art captured a movement which New Yorkers understood, a message of color on darkness, individuality, continuity, and survival," he says. They also respected the artists beyond the art, for the danger they ran to paint the subway cars, bringing the trains to life with color and imagination amid the dark and crumbling city.

"I was always scared shitless down there in the tunnels," Lee recalls, although also always intrigued by the subway system. "We were poor and didn't travel much, so as a kid I would get excited whenever my mother took me on a subway train. I was almost infatuated with the construction, the speed of the machinery, its power, the darkness and mystery of the tunnels. It was like a big monster: neglected, derelict, desolate, dark, and dreary like the city itself. Each gray car looked like a sad clone."

Lee began graffiti writing in the subways when he was fourteen and "saw graffiti as an actual thinking and physically challenging process. I saw the meditation and discipline it took. I thought, wow, I can express myself in the same heroic, anonymous way. People could see it and say 'Yo, that kid was daring; he worked through the night to do that, while I slept.' I wanted to be respected, whether they liked what I did or not. I could turn out color and change the way people looked at the system. I had control of the subway.

"We dared to put art right out front," he says. "The media put us down as vandals, but Picasso used spray paint, too. There's continuity there, man." He complains that the Transit Authority is committing "artistic genocide by showering off graffiti with acid rains and operating graffiti-proof trains."

One graffiti writer actually wrote a poetic lament to his fading craft suitably in black ink:

> There once was a time when the Lexington Line was a beautiful line
> When Children of the ghetto expressed with art, not with crime.
> But then as evolution past,
> The transits buffing did it blast,
> And now the trains look like rusted trash.
>
> Now we wonder if graffiti will ever last ?????*

THE FABULOUS FIVE STOPPED PAINTING LONG AGO. "WE GREW UP," says Lee. Mono became a policeman. Slave is a drag racer down South. Doc is an electrician. Dirty Slug, who went to college, has disappeared.

Lee, now thirty-two years old, is a successful artist on canvas. "My studio is not a subway tunnel anymore, but when I paint, I'm in the tunnel again, where things are clear-cut and dope. And my message is the same. I still capture movement, survival. It has to do with struggling in New York. The tunnels make artists strong

---

*Captured in a photo by Henry Chalfant, who recorded much of New York's graffiti with his camera.

within themselves. Behind my stuff is a story; it's life. I want it to live." *The New Yorker* magazine called Lee Quinones "a sort of Jasper Johns figure . . . stylistically speaking."

"Lee was the best, king of the lines," says Ace, a thirteen-year-old "toy" who aspires to Lee's fame, but a "toy" like him has a "wacky style," which in graffiti jargon means he has no talent yet. He "bites" or steals other styles, and he fails to "get up," which means leave his mark, or to "tag" around town widely enough to be noticed. "Taggers" must leave their calling cards hundreds of times, often on the pieces of established graffiti writers, to win recognition. Worst of all, Ace's tags drip, which is the most obvious sign that a writer has not yet mastered his paint can.

With subway train graffiti a vanished art form, some of its would-be practitioners have moved into the tunnels themselves, but the dangers are terrifying—a third rail pulsing with electricity, criminals, drug addicts, rats, and rushing trains that often leave insufficient clearance with walls for a standing man.

Many, particularly the young taggers, do it just for thrills. "Like jumping gorges," explained one recently arrived young boy from upper New York City, "or jumping off bridges." Another likened it to mountain climbing and leaving a flag at the peak.

Tracy 168, an established writer, made it sound natural: "We were like moles [as kids]," he told Craig Castleman, author of *Getting Up: Subway Graffiti in New York*. "If anyone chased us, we ran into the nearest subway station and we'd be gone [into the tunnels]. No one would follow us down there."

14

Runaways

"We're not like the other people down here. We have the future." —Frederick (1972–1991)

I N 1988, TWO HOMELESS BOYS FOUND A LOOSE GRATE AT THE northern end of Riverside Park on Manhattan's West Side. They lifted the metal grid and slipped into the underground for a safe night's rest. They called it their hole. Over the next few years, other homeless boys and some girls, most of them runaways also looking for a place to rest, joined to create a community of about twenty teenagers in the hole.

One of the two founders was Frederick, a light-complexioned black youth with curly hair and a wide-eyed look. Born in New York, he had been on the streets since his mother became too addicted to alcohol and heroin to care for him or maintain an apartment. When he was twelve, one of his mother's boyfriends raped him. After that he felt more comfortable away from their flat. He mostly hung around Penn Station, asking for handouts. He came to know the homeless men who lived there, and when his mother lost their apartment and moved in with her supplier, Frederick began to live with various homeless men in the cardboard shacks that lined the outsides of the station. He was thirteen years old.

"They took care of me," Frederick says. "Sometimes I'd be laying next to them and I'd feel them getting hard but they didn't make me do nothing," he shrugs.

A social worker persuaded him to enter a foster home. "One night I was in bed and I hear my foster dad come up to my room. 'Whatcha want?' I say. I knew it would be bad cuz he didn't turn on the lights. He just wanted to say good night, he says, but then he starts kissing me and put his hand over my mouth and raped me. I left after that bullshit!" he spits out with unusual anger.

"I think I became gay after that," he adds, reverting to his passive manner.

After a few more months on the street, he registered himself at the Covenant House, a shelter in Manhattan for runaway and homeless youths.

"Too many rules there," he complains. "When to eat, when to sleep, what you had to do if you wanted to stay."

By age fourteen, Frederick was profoundly cynical toward anyone who wasn't living on the streets. "On the streets you know what people want," he explains. "Sex, drugs, food, warm clothes. You know what they're after. People who got homes, I don't know what they want. I never been like them. They say they just want to help you for nothing, but no one wants to do anything for nothing. Everyone wants something. I can't figure what they want but a good fuck."

Back at Penn Station, he lived with several different men. "They started giving me money and I figure I could keep getting fucked for nothing or I could get money for getting fucked. It stopped bothering me. I took money."

On a cold spring day, he remembers, he met David at the station. A runaway from a foster home in Illinois, David is a skinny, red-haired boy. He was "just sittin' there on his hot dog [duffel bag] like this," Frederick hunches over with his head hung miserably in his hands, "and he doesn't move so I go up to him because he was my age and I thought I could help him. I said 'you want a donut or something?' He was like a puppy. I had to take care of him. Turns out he was gay, too, molested and all by his stepfather when he was only seven."

If David resembles a puppy, he looks like an incorrigible one—playful, soft, and vulnerable. He is also annoying, unable to stay with a conversation for more than a few minutes, and a habitual liar.

"He's a congenital liar," Chris Pape says. "One day he'll tell you he's dying of cancer and the next day it's tuberculosis. He even lies about things that aren't important, like what he had for dinner."

Tunnel people become irate at his stories at times. He was one of a group of underground homeless who appeared on Sally Jesse Raphael's talk show about mole people. The story of his life that he related there was totally different from the one he told me just two months earlier. Bernard was part of the audience and became so furious during the show that he rose and challenged David.

"I don't know where he was coming from with all those stories about how horrible we got it in our tunnel," Bernard says. "He always said he loved our tunnel. All those stories about how bad it is in our tunnel were made up. It's pitiful," he says disgustedly.

David often goes into a bookstore with young boys for whom he buys comics. Pape often sees him there and, because David is so unscrupulous, he suspected David intended to take the boys into the tunnels for sex. But he didn't. "I've followed him several times, and I've never seen him touch any of the boys," says Pape. "I think he just likes their company. He relates to them better than adults or even teenagers. Mentally, he is very young."

Frederick and David began turning tricks in their hole on the Upper West Side with homeless men in the tunnels as well as working men from the streets. They were joined by Carlos and Dameon, teenagers whom they found homeless in the park.

"I don't usually like it," Frederick said of the sex when I last saw him. "But I don't care much. I know I'm gay." That summer he had huge dark rings under his sad eyes and was frighteningly thin. He swore he was well, "just stomach flu I can't get rid of," he insisted in a hollow voice.

"Anyway, it can't be AIDS cause you can't get it until you're at least twenty. A doctor who came down here for a quick one told me that."

Frederick died of AIDS-related pneumonia the fall of 1991. Dameon died a few months later.

David now wanders the tunnels and has withdrawn even further from truth. "After Frederick died, David turned to all lies," says Carlos. "He don't even admit he's gay anymore."

Frederick had brought into the hole two young runaway girls from Iowa, Monica and Felicia, "to shelter them from the men up top," says Carlos, who has accepted the responsibility for them. "Frederick told me I was gonna hafta take care of the girls until they found their way. I don't know how to, but I'll try." He worries about leaving them in the hole while he is away because homeless men still go there seeking the boys and might rape the girls.

"Frederick was always looking out for me." Carlos continues as he explains his debt to the older boy. "He took all the bad ones [men] who came down to the hole and refused to pay for it. They scared me. They'd hurt you.

"One time I told Frederick that I didn't know if I was really gay, and he told me to stop doing tricks, that I didn't need to; he'd take care of me. So I did stop, and I felt better. After he died, I was walking the park, all sad and stuff, and it was like Frederick entered my head. I decided never to get screwed by any guy again. I didn't need to, and I decided to stand up for myself and take care of the others like Frederick did."

Carlos, who is seventeen, decided that the community would move deeper into the tunnel, away from the entrance that was so well known, but more accessible to the surface at a different spot. "It's a good place because the girls can just walk out and sneak into the back door of a welfare hotel and take showers and stuff," he says proudly. "They've never been bothered."

"We let other kids, real young ones, live with us and we sort of set up camp for them. We think of Frederick a lot and the things he used to say to us. Sometimes I miss him, but I'm not sad for him. Because he can't be anywhere worse than where he was here.

"Sometimes I wish he could see all we done. We made it much better than it was, and I think he'd be proud," he says sheepishly. "We've changed everything but the name. We can't call it home. We still call it the hole."

However, the rules have changed. "No sex in the hole," Carlos says flatly. "No drugs, either. We do that for the girls," he confides, "because they don't do no drugs, usually."

No dating among those who live in the hole either?

"Hadn't thought about that." After a pause he says, "We're like brothers and sisters. Who'd wanna date?"

A FAIRLY SIMPLE TAPPING CODE ON THE TRAPDOOR GAINS ENTRY TO the runaways' hole. The faces are all young. Some are open and trusting, others tough and closed. Their short personal histories vary, but most come from foster homes, group homes, or orphanages. A few left close families to ease the strain on their impoverished parents. Their anger and depression are understandable. The surprise is the amount of hope and caring among them.

Monica and Felicia

"I SEE PEOPLE IN SOUP KITCHENS SOMETIMES WHO HAVE LOST HOPE," says Felicia, a bright-eyed, fifteen-year-old white girl. "Like a man the other day who just stared at his plate. I couldn't get him to eat. I saw a teardrop fall into it, but he didn't move the whole time. I cried all day after that. That's the only thing we got, is hope. All of us are gonna make it someday. That's what keeps us going."

Felicia's sister Monica is two years older. They ran away from their Iowa home a year earlier, after their stepfather molested Felicia. Monica called the police, but they did not arrest the man. Their mother seemed to believe the girls, but, says Monica plaintively, "she wanted him more." So they packed up and headed for New York City.

"I figured it was far enough away from them," Monica says, "and we can make it here, we can." The two never considered entering Covenant House or another shelter for fear they'd be separated or sent back to the parents.

Monica lied about her age to get a job as a waitress in a seedy bar. "If I get really good at it, I can go work as a hostess at a really nice place and meet a really rich man and marry him, and we'll be set for life," she smiles, hope still alive in her rich brown eyes.

Felicia, who looks so young she couldn't lie about her age, works at a Mister Donut on after-school hours. "Soon enough we'll be able to get an apartment and I'll be able to go back to school," she says brightly. "We love the kids down here. They've helped us tons. But we've got plans."

"Whatever happens," Felicia smiles at her sister, "we'll always be together."

Carlos

CARLOS, THE ELDEST OF NINE CHILDREN, HAS HAD "A DRINKING problem," as he puts it, since he was thirteen. "There was a lot of violence in our family," he says matter-of-factly as he picks the bark off a twig. "My parents were always fighting each other and beating us up. They did lots of drugs and drank a lot. My father went to jail and we had no money for the apartment, so we had to sleep outside. My mother went to jail, too, for dealing [drugs]. When they came for her, the government took the little ones into foster care or something. They were all crying, but I was hiding behind boxes."

He found odd jobs like sweeping storefronts, cleaning windows, and sorting fruit for grocers, and when his mother returned from prison, she and Carlos lived with another family. "One night I come back with some wine for her and our room was empty. There was a note that says she went back to Puerto Rico and I should come as soon as I make enough money. But I'm going to find the little ones first and bring them with me," he says. "I hope she's OK," he adds quietly, looking up with gentle, brown eyes.

Carlos continues to work at the margins, sometimes at jobs that are illegal. He's had enough money at times to find a cheap apartment, but he says he can't leave "until the rest of the kids here are OK."

"Shit, man," interjects Frank, who has been listening. "You gotta do things for yourself, not for nobody else. We don't want you around here anyway," he says, trying to push Carlos up out of the hole.

"Carlos is the greatest guy in the world," Frank says. "He'd give you every cent in his pocket. That's the way he is. But he isn't gonna make it long, because he don't look out for himself over all the others, like the rest of us."

Carlos doesn't answer, but as he walks me out of the park, he admits that moving back aboveground would be difficult. "I'm afraid of being lonely, not having somewhere to go, scared to find no one there. I know I'm living down there partly because I'm afraid of going to an empty room and being by myself."

Frank

CARLOS AND FRANK MET IN A POOL HALL WHERE FRANK, WHO IS A large eighteen-year-old from New Jersey, was hustling. He lost more money than he had, and Carlos helped him escape out the bathroom window. Since he had no place to sleep, Carlos took him to the hole. Frank has lived there three weeks, and each day announces that he does not intend to "live in this shit hole for another fucking day."

He is filled with violent anger and prone to fits of rage. Once he broke his hand when he slammed his fist into a concrete wall. He refuses to speak much about his family except that as often as the subject comes up, he declares with bravado that "I couldn't give a damn whether they all die and go to hell." His father had a nasty temper and knocked the children around. "That toughened me up for the real world," he says. His bottom line is "Everything has always been bad for me."

He hated school, where he was a slow learner and rebellious. "I liked to keep my hair long and greasy," he says, peering out from behind the scraggly hanks that he wears over his face. "My school, see, was Catholic. They didn't go for the hair or the leather jacket. I don't do well with authority."

In fact, he got into trouble well before he grew his hair long, he admits. At five, he tried to choke another boy. At seven, he was in reform school for having beaten up several boys. By the time he was eight years old, he had learned how to break and enter. "I was also into arson and petty theft," he says casually, throwing out the criminal charges precisely. The Catholic school took him in, long hair and all, until a boy called his brother ugly and Frank broke the boy's jaw with a baseball bat. The baseball coach who tried to interfere was knocked unconscious in the melee.

Back in reform school, Frank learned how to pick locks, rob stores, and make and use various drugs. He was freed at fourteen to attend public school where he was more comfortable, he says, "because everyone carried knives." He quit at sixteen though, and his father kicked him out as a bad influence on his younger brother and sister. His mother and sister sneaked him into the basement to sleep during the cold months, however.

"She's a pistol," he says of his nine-year-old sister, smiling at the recollection. "A real beautiful little girl. Always was. She wanted me to take her wherever I go, but I had to stop going there because she would start crying every time I saw her." That's when he took a bus to New York City, but without any experience, the best work he could find was pumping gas.

Teddy

AT A SOUP KITCHEN ONE NIGHT, FRANK MET TEDDY, A SOFT-LOOK-ing young man of seventeen with glasses and sad eyes, and took him to the hole. Teddy is quiet and articulate, with clean-cut, almost preppy features. His father was killed in a car accident on Christmas Day when he was three years old, and his mother, he says, died "a violent death" two years ago.

"He's never told us how she died exactly," Frank says. "But I think it had to do with some boyfriend. I think Teddy saw it all, too."

During the day, Teddy walks the streets, sometimes selling books and magazines for homeless entrepreneurs who use the operation as a front for dealing drugs. Teddy, himself, is very honest. "The only scam he'll run is telling a storeowner that the soda machine took his money," says Frank.

"I usually get something for that," Teddy admits with a shy smile. "It's an advantage I have, being white and looking the way I do. People tend to believe me. But I don't want to abuse that too often, only when I really need some money. Once I went up to a lady on the street and told her I was new to the city and someone had stolen my money, and I was trying to get enough together to get back home. She gave me fifty bucks. She wanted to give me more, but I couldn't let her. I spent most of the money on myself and felt rotten to the core, so I gave the rest away. I just couldn't do that again," he says contritely.

Teddy did well in school. "I was what they called a 'gifted child,' which of course means worthless on the streets. What makes you smart in school has nothing to do with the outside. I never realized how dumb I was until I met these guys," he nods meekly toward the other boys in the hole. "Someday I'd like to go to college, though. I've been trying, but I can't seem to save money. I need someone to keep it for me, not give it to me."

Most of the community are undisciplined in keeping schedules. After waking with the others, Teddy leaves to buy coffee and, if he has enough money, a piece of pizza as well. He wanders for the rest of the day, looking for odd jobs and each day foraging a bit farther out, but by dusk, at least so far, he's back in the hole.

"We have to stick together at night," he says, clearly frightened at the prospect of not returning in time. "Anything can happen when you're alone."

The veterans in the hole community are protective of Teddy. "He wouldn't leave for days when he first got here," Felicia remembers. "We had to bring him food, but he wouldn't eat. He'd just sit there," she points to a corner, "and he'd cry. He'd stare at the wall and the light coming down and just stare and stare. It was the saddest thing I ever saw. Frank finally just carried him out, took

him for pizza. I remember he said: 'You haven't lived until you've
had New York pizza.'

"I didn't think he should do that, pick him up and all. I mean
he's fully grown. After that, Teddy goes out most every day. He's
always back about sunset. But every so often he still stares at the
walls for hours, like before."

Teddy is upstairs in the park, staring vacantly at autumn's
changing leaves. "I dream a lot," he says. "It's like thinking for
me."

Jimmy

"TEDDY WILL TOUGHEN UP," JIMMY ASSURES FRANK. JIMMY'S A TRUE
street kid and proud of it. He frequently spends the night in the
runaway hole, but will often disappear for weeks.

"I know everything there is to know about this city," he
boasts, hands on hips.

Which is the Empire State Building and which is the Chrysler
Building?

"Everything important," he amends, undeterred. "Everything important about surviving in the city. All the scams, drugs,
people. You wouldn't believe the people I know. I won't tell you,
but they're big stars," he smiles as if excited at the thought of really
knowing the rich and famous.

Whatever his contacts, he has more energy than any two or
three other homeless kids here. He wakes early, buys a cup of coffee
and some candy bars, and leaves the area to "visit friends," as he
puts it, on the streets in other areas of the city. When he runs low
on cash, he says, he visits tourist spots where he can pick pockets.
Times Square was once his favorite. "It's no good there now," he
says, "too many plain clothes cops." So he prowls Penn Station.

"I like to steal, too," he volunteers boldly. "It makes me feel
productive."

Jimmy's story is a poignant variation of the others. At four-teen, he "took off" from a home where there were six children "and more on the way," he says. "My father drinks more than he works. Comes home just to lay my mother. I was another mouth to feed, and there wasn't much money, so I left. I still go home sometimes to visit, you know. I usually bring a turkey home for Thanksgiving." He gives a bright, lively laugh. "Now that's hard, stealing a turkey, and one big enough to feed all of us."

Dolly

DOLLY CAME TO THE COMMUNITY WITH MONICA. MONICA HAD JUST finished work and found Dolly on the streets at 2 A.M., wandering around, a disoriented fourteen-year-old. She still becomes disoriented, and sometimes Monica wishes she'd leave.

"She's full of herself sometimes," Monica says. "Always talks about how men can't stop touching her, and how she hates men. Then you see her on a park bench all over some guy. I told her if she doesn't talk to them, they won't come after her. She just says she's too pretty; they'd come after her anyway."

Dolly paints her huge, doll-like eyes with heavy black eyeliner and mascara. Her face is round, as if she still has baby fat, but her small body is shapely, and she wears tight jeans and a too-small T-shirt that accentuates her figure. She worries almost as much about her hair and makeup as she does about men.

"I tried to kill myself when I was ten," she says, showing her scarred wrists. "I fell in love with my stepfather and he raped me. I've been drugged, raped, molested, and abused so many times by men at parties that I want a sex change operation so men will leave me alone." She hates sex, she says. "But men love me for it. That's what I got."

Dolly was the only member of the community who agreed to go with me to Covenant House. Others encouraged her, and we set a date and place to meet, but she never showed up. She hasn't returned to the community.*

EACH UNDERGROUND COMMUNITY IS DIFFERENT, BUT ANGER, SAD-ness, and often hopelessness pervade most of them. The runaway community is unique, with its mutual caring and the atmosphere of hope that the future will be better. Like any family, they fight among themselves, but they also protect each other. When a regular customer at the Mister Donut began to harass Felicia, Frank and Jimmy showed up for a few words with him.

"I could have lost my job!" Felicia remembers, wide-eyed. "They took him out behind the restaurant and threatened him. They said they didn't care if I got fired, at least I wouldn't get hurt." Carlos or Frank also usually meet Monica on her way back from work late at night so she will avoid trouble on the way to the hole.

Being runaways themselves, the community is particularly sympathetic to younger kids on the run. "The best people to help runaways are those like us," says Freddy, "and the best way to help is to be yourself. We know the emotions and we know how to make our way. We have the independence we couldn't have at Covenant House or in a group home, and we've got real support from each other, not for just an hour from some social worker, but from people who really care and understand."

These teenagers, for all their experiences, are frighteningly vulnerable. Hardly ever do I suspect they are exaggerating their histories, and their emotions are always ready to break the surface. Like the children they are, they cry one moment and laugh the next. Their wounds are still raw, and the pain is still fresh. They want more than to just survive. They aren't living to die, and they

---

*The runaways brought me into their group as a peer rather than as an adult. They were perhaps the most trusting and open community I met in the tunnels. There were no status lines to break through. They saw that I was like them, only they were on their way to doing what they wanted to do, and I was half a step ahead in doing it. I never had the "adult authority" to take them anywhere.

don't want pity. They aren't looking for understanding, but they aren't afraid to be understood.

"You ask me if it bothers me to talk about all this," says Jeff, a seventeen-year-old recent arrival after he described his family and his own route to this place. "I dunno. I don't think so, because I don't see how anything you write could hurt me. They're just words. My parents and I hurt each other pretty bad, far worse than any words. So, no, it doesn't bother me if you write about me, because maybe it will help someone sometime. I dunno how, though, because we're all so different. We all left home for different reasons. Me, because of the authority thing. I hate my stepmother. But maybe some kid out there won't make the same mistake, won't be so quick to take off, if you write about me. I hope so. Who knows, maybe one day I'll pick up what you write and understand what's going on here with me now."

With encouragement from others, Jeff subsequently returned home after "patching things up" with his father and stepmother, I'm told.

Depression is a malady that hits all of the members of the community at one time or another, and shows up in different ways. Some cry; others are silently despondent. "The best way to deal with it is to help others," says Felicia over a breakfast of Coca-Cola and last night's leftover donuts from her job.

"Or to just keep busy," adds Jimmy through the remnants of two chocolate-covered cream donuts he has just snarfed down.

"It's my fear of death that pulls me out and keeps me going," says Teddy, staring at a glazed donut that Felicia has just placed in his hand.

"I don't know," Jimmy muses, almost to himself. "I never let myself get that far down. I just gotta laugh when they hit me. I laugh all the time."

"I still daydream," replies Teddy, looking a bit embarrassed as Jimmy rolls his eyes. "And that helps. When things don't look good, I can still dream and I feel good."

Sometimes the depression can also become anger and take a suicidal or violent turn.

"I don't know why," says Frank, "but sometimes I feel like climbing the Brooklyn Bridge and jumping off, or getting a gun and going into a grocery store and blowing everyone away." He has found himself walking toward the bridge in a melancholy daze, only to wake and go for his gun. "One of these days I'm gonna do something bad. I can feel it. Sometimes I hope they get me before I get them."

One evening as the sun is setting we climb to a rooftop. Frank passes around a bottle of Johnny Walker Red. Within an hour, as darkness arrives, the group is pensive.

If you had one wish, what would it be? I ask them.

"I wish my mother would come back," Teddy says immediately.

"I'd change the world so there would be a place for us," Carlos answers. "A good place where we would have real freedom and not live in a hole."

"I'd like to blow my head off," says Frank, looking down between his knees.

Others object, and Frank is persuaded to revise his wish. "I'd change things in myself if I could. You go to prison and you get this 'fuck you' attitude, and it stays with you all the time. You resent every fucking thing in the establishment. You forget how it is not to be angry all the time."

Someone points out that Frank has never been to prison.

"You ever been to reform school?" he demands. "That's prison."

Jeff joins the wishers. "I'd want to go back to when I was nine, and know the things I know now, so I wouldn't make the same mistakes," he says.

And I remember what Dolly once said: "I wish I'd never been born."

Rather than leave it there, I ask them what's the best thing about being on the streets?

"The freedom," says Jimmy.

"Just being alive," says Monica.

"Hope," says Carlos, who after a moment tries to explain.

"Sometimes I get on this depression-suicide trip like Frank. But then I think there's a person I'm gonna miss if I leave now. There's a place I should see that I wouldn't see. There's too much I want to do before I go. There's someone I want to meet."

THE RUNAWAY COMMUNITY DISBANDED SOON AFTER THAT. I DON'T know why. I found a handwritten note from Teddy under a rock, but the smudged penciling is illegible. The only other remnant was a tube of forgotten lipstick under an old chair. I went back to the rooftop where we had all watched the sunset, and I dreamed that they were all finding that someone or someplace or something better that they all hoped for.

15

Tunnel Outreach

IN SEPTEMBER 1990, THE METROPOLITAN TRANSIT AUTHORITY authorized funds for a program to provide outreach and referral services to homeless people living in and around subway tunnels and train tunnels. Among other things, the aim was to obtain information about the homeless in the transportation system of New York, and to improve the safety and cleanliness of the system. Preliminary estimates showed that 80 to 85 percent of the homeless were substance abusers, so the Metropolitan Transit Authority hired ADAPT (Association for Drug Abuse Prevention and Treatment), a nonprofit organization partially funded by the New York Health Department, to provide outreach in the tunnels of the Grand Central and Penn stations. After almost a year, ADAPT counted 6,031 homeless in the system, far more than any authority had anticipated, with one-third to one-half of them living directly under the Penn and Grand Central stations.

The following year, however, the Metropolitan Transit Authority went a different route in an effort to cope with the growing tunnel homeless problem. Instead of ADAPT, it contracted with the controversial Homeless Emergency Liaison Project (HELP), a mobile outreach organization that provides crisis psychiatric services to the mentally ill. Some studies have found anywhere between 25 and 60 percent of the aboveground homeless to be mentally impaired, but the ADAPT project reported that only 10 to 15 percent of those they encountered had mental problems. The Metropolitan Transit Authority's choice of Project HELP (rather than continue with ADAPT) surprised many in the field until it was recognized that Project HELP offers a service no other outreach unit could provide. It has authority to physically incarcerate a mentally ill person if he or she is considered "imminently at risk to himself or others." Those people can be taken to hospital emergency wards for psychiatric evaluation and held without their permission for as long as a team of psychiatric workers deems necessary.

Put bluntly, only Project HELP can forcibly eject the homeless from the tunnels on grounds of mental illness and commit them to hospitals. "And that was the MTA's primary goal," says Michael Bethea, ADAPT's outreach director. "Subway and train ridership was down, and the Metropolitan Transit Authority didn't want commuters to see these homeless people, to smell them, to feel threatened by them. In addition, the Democratic Convention was coming to town in a few months, with all the national press, so the Metropolitan Transit Authority did what it had to do.

"In fairness, MTA also has a responsibility to the homeless people in the tunnels who were getting hit by trains," he says. Almost a hundred such victims were counted the year before. In addition, more than eighty fires had occurred in the tunnels in connection with homeless living along the tracks, endangering commuters, workers, and firefighters. Sometimes their campfires would get out of control; other times sparks from the third rail would ignite their flimsy clothes and bedding near the tracks.*

However, ADAPT workers complain that the Metropolitan Transit Authority's strategy of using Project HELP risks lumping all homeless individuals, including those who are not mentally ill, into the same category and permits even those who are not mentally

---

*In 1991, seventy-nine homeless persons died on or near the tracks, according to New York City's Metropolitan Transit Authority. Most were struck by trains or electrocuted when they rolled in their sleep onto the third rail. That same year, forty-nine fires were reported in tunnels, most of them set for cooking or for warmth, but some lit by a spark from the third rail falling on the cardboard houses or other flammable debris that the homeless bring to tunnel camps.

ill to be rounded up. Moreover, it neglects the larger needs of this destitute community.

"Our fear is that they [Project HELP] are going to mistakenly perceive someone strung out from crack or heroin as being mentally sick and commit him or her. Then, that person is lost," complains Bethea. "We found that they do have difficulties making that distinction." In addition to the addicts, there are also physically ill people with tuberculosis, HIV, and AIDS in the tunnels, "and there's just plain people who are homeless. All of these have to be dealt with separately, not approached through mental illness," he says.

"MTA wants quick fixes," adds ADAPT's executive director Yolanda Serrano. "What underground homeless need is time to develop relationships with outreach workers down there, so, when the homeless come up from the tunnels, they come up for good, not just for a few days in a hospital, after which they run back down to a new tunnel." ADAPT's tracking statistics find that almost all tunnel dwellers who go through detoxification programs, which usually last five to seven days, go back down underground afterward.

"The attitudes and behavior that took them into the tunnels don't change overnight," she continues. "Sometimes they don't change even after residential treatment programs that last two years. It takes time and acceptance. Even a 'normal' person has to quit smoking five or six or more times before it sticks. And here we're talking about some people who have used mind-altering substances for five to ten years."

Project HELP is well aware of its strong-arm image. "We've got the nasty reputation on the homeless grapevine," admits Dr. Sam Tsemberis, a young but seasoned psychologist and the new director of Project HELP. Tsemberis has a more liberal tinge and announces to me early on that, when he came to interview for the job, he told his interviewers up front that he was not sure he believed in the very premise of Project HELP. He looks forward to changing its image, though it has existed since Project HELP's founding. However, as he sees the homeless situation in light of his new position, he better understands where Project HELP comes from and is not so quick to make changes.

"We're always the last people they want to see, the bad guys who come and take people away. People see our van and run. Other units that can't handle certain homeless persons call us to do their dirty work. I didn't like that at first, but, after seeing some of the things I've seen out there with Project HELP, I recognize that there is a need for this type of organization," Tsemberis says, looking concerned.

Project HELP was created about a decade earlier after the celebrated case in January 1982, when Joyce (aka Billy) Boggs, a sixty-one-year-old homeless woman living in a cardboard box on the street died of hypothermia after refusing help several times. She had been a psychiatric patient who was on the street for eight months, since her public assistance benefits were revoked for "failure to appear for recertification." She died, despite last-minute efforts by medical personnel, just a few hours before authorities secured a court order to permit authorities to take her to a hospital against her will.

Only the so-called "STIPSO" statute applied at the time. An acronym for short-term involuntary protective services order, it required that a physician must certify that the person would die within seventy-two hours if not hospitalized, find a judge to declare the person incompetent, and then return to locate the homeless person, who usually had moved on.

The Boggs case, coming amid signs of a rising homeless population on the streets that seemed made up overwhelmingly of mentally ill people, pushed New York to establish Project HELP under New York State's Mental Hygiene law. The statute states that Project HELP may provide services that are voluntary or involuntary for the patient. The criteria for involuntary provision of services is that the person be mentally ill and a danger to himself or others.

"At first I didn't believe in Project HELP," says Tsemberis. "I thought it was a fascistic, Koch [former Mayor Ed Koch] program to get people off the street involuntarily, using psychiatry for social control, but I've concluded there is a need to take people off the streets when they are really in a bad way." He admits that homeless people who are not mentally ill may be taken to Bellevue Hospital. He contends that, even when an error is made, the homeless are helped by the basic care they get at the hospital.

Mental illness deals with idiosyncratic behaviors that may or may not be indigenous to the individual, he says, but there is a great difficulty separating what is innate to that individual and what comes from the underground life they have been living.

"These people we take to the hospital, you wouldn't believe what they look like," Tsemberis says. "Some have toilet paper wrapped around their heads because they don't want their ideas flying out or new ideas flying in. And after a week in Bellevue, eating and sleeping four or five nights, they go before a judge and they say, 'I don't know why I was brought here, your honor. I just want to get out and get a job.'"

Tsemberis is also frustrated, like others who work with the homeless, by lack of resources. He believes that the most effective outreach program would include three types of medical specialists—one for physical health, one for mental health, and one for addiction. More crucial is the lack of programs to keep homeless off the streets and out of the tunnels after treatment. This would primarily require housing—after detoxification, rehabilitation, and psychiatric counseling—to allow time for attacking the root causes that drove the homeless individuals underground in the first place.

As it is now, says ADAPT's Bethea, fewer than 15 percent of the underground homeless make it back aboveground to a relatively normal life.

Bureaucratic provisions, particularly those requiring children to be taken from addicted parents, keep many of the homeless from seeking help. Bethea recalls a woman who lived in the tunnels with her daughter and wanted drug counseling but feared the authorities would take the child. ADAPT encouraged her to enter a rehabilitation program and promised to do their best to help her keep her daughter. "But the child is in a foster home," says Bethea, shaking his head. "The mother has finished rehab and is doing fine, but they still won't give the child back to her."

ADAPT has sought to cut other red tape that hinders aid to the homeless. "Many people we deal with have no identification," Bethea says. "But in order to access a treatment program or apply for social services or welfare, they need at least two forms of ID, plus a place of residence. We had to learn where we could get a quick, temporary form of ID that is valid, or at least accepted by the social services." ADAPT workers often shelled out $10 or $15 from their own pockets to get the less-than-legal IDs when the project lacked funds.

ADAPT complains that not only did the Metropolitan Transit Authority shift to the mental health focus of Project HELP, it also rejected ADAPT's statistics on the homeless population. "They didn't want to scare the public, while we didn't worry about that aspect of it," says Bethea. The Metropolitan Transit Authority authorities changed the definition of homeless to reduce the population figures, says Bethea. "They decided that a person is not homeless if he or she is not lying down or sitting outside of a designated sitting area. If a person is standing, even with garbage bags, they are not in violation (by that definition) and so not counted, overlooked. Our numbers were always higher than the Long Island Rail Road police would have liked, for example, although we have very good relations with the police. It was just that once they sat in a board room, things started to look different. The homeless population just became a political game of numbers."

From their very first trips into the tunnels, ADAPT's workers were shocked not only by the number of homeless they found, but also by the sometimes elaborate living quarters and "conveniences" underground. There were dwellings with wallpaper, pictures, and posters hanging from walls. Running water, showers, heat, electricity, and even a microwave oven helped make life in the tunnels a bit more bearable.

"Seven stories under Grand Central," says Bethea, eyes still widening at the memory, "we found families. Mother, child, and a male. We brought up two pregnant women our first month. One had her baby and went back down without the baby. The baby's in foster care now."

Tunnel people always amaze outsiders at how well they hide. "We walked the tunnels along tracks, trains coming back and forth, 600 volts in the third rail, and we would walk right past people no more than four feet away and sometimes never see them 'til they called out," recalls Bethea. "We found people living above the tracks, on gratings, who we'd never see if we didn't happen to look up.

"I remember climbing a ladder, going into a little crawl space, and my eyes caught the eyes of someone watching me. I could feel his eyes at first, then I could see his eyes, and I thought, 'I'm outta here!' And I kept going. I don't know if I scared him, but he surely scared me. Then I said, 'Oh, shit. I gotta go see this guy.' And I did. We kept contact with him and eventually got him out of the tunnel, for a while."

On the upper levels of the underground are mostly crack users who distrust everyone, Bethea says, and who essentially want to be alone. "Crack is a selfish type of drug, as opposed to heroin, which is a little more communal. Its users want to be with others.

"But there were lots of people who weren't doing drugs, who weren't crazy. We ran across working people, people who could not afford an apartment but were making too much money for social service supplements. So they chose to live in the tunnels and work rather than take public assistance," he says.

ADAPT's final report, never published but made available to me, states that "a significant proportion of the homeless (in the subway system) work for pay at least occasionally. Most homeless men have substantial work histories."

Bethea and his group found that many of the homeless, rather than preferring to stay in the depths, want to get back to life aboveground.

"Despite the perceived notion that they are suicidal because they live along the tracks and do drugs," he says, "those people don't want to die. They still know they're human beings. One woman refused to see a doctor for no obvious reason until we found out why: she was embarrassed because she hadn't washed for several weeks. They know that they didn't come from that environment originally, that problems brought them down. And you can get them to believe, because they already do, that they can get back to their 'normal' lives aboveground.

"They don't want to die. You can see it in the way they live. They haven't given up living. They may not have much self-esteem. We have to give them empowerment counseling, but like those guys under the Waldorf-Astoria, the homosexual community, we found condoms all around that place. They practice safe sex. They don't want to die of AIDS."

ADAPT was very successful in finding homeless in large part because of the diligence and dedication of the staff. At least two workers had to be ordered out of the tunnels when Bethea feared they were overworked. "They were down there everyday for four months," he says. "I was afraid they would burn out, that they were going to get hurt. They were so involved they didn't worry about their own safety and it's very dangerous down there."

One of those men is Harold Deamues, a smiling, good-humored, dark-skinned man in his mid-thirties. He wears a short, well-groomed beard and closely trimmed hair. He believes he can help because he once used drugs himself.

"I know what's out there. I know what I've been through. I know what it's like for people to give up on you, and you lose your spirit. I knew I could break out, with help," Deamues says, and he wants to repay those who helped him by helping others. "You can't help everyone; you got to accept that not everyone wants help. But there are some you can help."

Deamues grew up in East Harlem and thought he knew just about every way a person could be down and out in New York, but he didn't know about tunnel people. "I thought talk about people living underground was just handing out a story; I couldn't believe it," he says. "Who would go down there? Why? What's down there? When I saw it with my own eyes, I was amazed, truly amazed.

"They call them the mole people, and you can catch them sleeping, having sex, eating. But strange. One older gentleman, fifty-something, with this ashen look, his feet were matted together at the toes like they were all one part. All you could see was the shape of the top of his toes. He was barefooted, and he lived way down there, three levels. Said he hasn't been up in three years. I asked him if he ate rats and stuff down there. He smiled. Didn't want to give me no definite answer. But he smiled like, you know, what else is there for me to eat sometimes.

"His eyes had that dullish gray, you know, like he might have drank a lot for years. But it's hard to say he was crazy. He was able to speak fluently, answer any questions without any problem. Sometimes when we saw him he was buck-naked and running around, quick. He was alone, but I imagine there were other people down there, that area called Burma's Road in the lowest tunnel levels under Grand Central.

"I found a gentleman on pipes one time, steam pipes. They got big steam pipes down there. I said, 'Peace, I'm coming up,' because the worst thing you can do is scare someone down there. That's when it's dangerous, when you surprise someone. But he was cool. He had his food heating up on the pipes and he lay on them, reading a newspaper."

Deamues says he's even found people singing in their shower underground, using water from fire extinguisher sprinklers. Some homeless use the bathrooms that the Metropolitan Transit Authority workers leave open for them.

A social network of sorts has been developed among the homeless, according to Tsemberis. Food, drugs, and medicine are often shared, as is gossip and stories of the underground.

Within this network, he says, "the mole people have taken on mythological proportions. They are supposed to be somehow different, unique. They've lived underground for years. They may even look different, like they are from a different planet. I run a men's group in the drop-in center on 44th Street and these guys talk about how scary the mole people are, about faces showing up and skinny heads, and since they smoke crack, I don't know if they are high or out of their minds." The stories, he says, demonize the mole people.

ADAPT headquarters is an old synagogue on 111th Street in Harlem, the only intact building in a drug-zoned block. Drive-by shootings are commonplace in the neighborhood. Riders at the nearest subway station are hard-pressed to explain the safest route to the building, ending by telling the visitor to be "very careful however you go." ADAPT staffers are unfazed by dangers near their office, but even they say the dangers underground are of a whole different proportion.

"You know that down there, besides the trains and the third rail, you have people who are afraid. Afraid of being attacked by others, scared crazy by coke. When we're scared and they're scared, it's really dangerous for everyone. But there is one area down there that is particularly scary for me: an abandoned tunnel that was once used to store or transport coal, for the old trains, I guess. Very, very scary, like if someone wants to do something to you there, you lost without knowing something started," Deamues says.

"There you can feel the eyes. That's the eeriest feeling, sensing eyes but seeing no body. I have confidence in myself that once I make contact with them, I'll be OK, able to do something for them, whatever. But, man, you feel their eyes and you start to wonder about the stories about cannibalism," he laughs self-consciously. "They seem to live in the asbestos insulation around steam pipes, and they got rats so big they look like they lift weights. You think they want your clothes because they are cold, or your boots, and there's all them glass vials and needles and shit on the floor. And you can't call for help, the police walkie-talkie radios don't carry upstairs. If something happens down there and you call upstairs, you get nothing.

"I used to tell the others, 'Don't get fat because, if you get hurt, I'm gonna have to carry your ass out of there.' You couldn't leave anyone alone in those tunnels."

On top of the various diseases, filth, mental illness, and addiction, homeless living underground also have gotten mauled by subway track workers, according to ADAPT. Sometimes a homeless person steals tools from the workers, and the workers take it out on the next homeless person they find. Hangman's nooses have been left dangling from overhead pipes to intimidate the homeless.

Subway workers have also reported being "piped"—struck over the head with a steel pipe—by homeless who want their clothes, shoes, and tools. "Workers get piped down here all the time," says Daniel Crump, a steward for the Transit Workers and Mechanics Union who was one of the first knowledgeable people to talk openly to me about the underground homeless and has been frustrated by the Metropolitan Transit Authority and city inaction. "I get calls all the time from workers afraid to go into the tunnels because they say, 'mole people are all around.'"

Most mole stories come up from the very bowels of Grand Central, seven levels down. "Down there," says Deamues, "there are no trains. It's quiet. There are old tracks, and electricity in some parts. Big areas. I'm waiting for someone to swing down like Tarzan. The deeper and deeper you go, the quieter it gets. But there's still those eyes. It's always like, 'Where are they?'"

The homeless feel safer the deeper down they go, ADAPT workers believe. "They get that sense of security down there," Deamues says. "To go further back in the tunnels, or deeper, says 'I don't want to bother nobody. I don't want nobody bothering me. I'm where nothing should go wrong. I don't want to deal with nobody. I won't cause problems; just let me stay here; I'll keep this place in order. Outside it's crazy, but at least down here I can close my eyes.'

"When I come up and I smell of those places, people think they need to take antibiotics just to come near me. In tunnels closer to the surface, the homeless mainly need a place to stay. The shelter system is too dangerous. They feel they can't close their eyes in the shelters, fearing rape or beating or getting killed. People yelling and stealing their clothes. And they're treated like they're subhuman there, like dogs," he says.

The irony is that, as Deamues sees it, "they feel much more human underground, safer, freer to move around. Tranquil, even serene to some of them, despite the trains running by.

"But worst, most heartbreaking, is when you find people who say, 'Hey, I don't want to be here, but I have no choice. I can't take another shelter and I can't go home.'"

One of the greatest difficulties that underground people have in trying to "go home"—back to the surface—is believing in themselves again. ADAPT found in its report that the tunnel dwellers "exhibit a paradoxical mix of self-sufficiency and dependency—they survive under the most difficult of circumstances, but they have lost faith in their ability to change their lives."

Outreach workers claim that tunnel dwellers never lose the basic tools they need to succeed aboveground and they even develop greater incentives to succeed in general. "It's like their instinct for caring and love is as basic as their instinct for survival," Deamues says. "Like making a bad situation seem less bad. I see this guy down under Grand Central laughing, sitting there reading books. You put yourself down there and you'd probably drive yourself crazy, but they create an environment, build up a core inside and say, 'This is happening, but this ain't the worstest thing in life.'"

Aren't some of them beyond repair? I ask.

He looks confused and angry, shaking his head. "No. That's something a normal person might think, but once you know a little about them, you can't give up on them. Some of us, like me, are living proof that no matter what you've been through, you can be someone again in the future. You can't give up on them. That's all they got. They're still human. They can still have a life."

Director Michael Bethea is just as persistent as Deamues but in a more objective, less personal way.

"If they can make it down there as well as they do, they can make it up here," Bethea says earnestly. "You go down there and see how they take care of each other, and not just that, but how they rig things like water and electricity. Some of these are very bright individuals who could have been engineers or something. We just got to find the one thing, or things, that are stopping them. Like drug addiction—it's just a problem that they *can* overcome. If they can deal with the underground, they can certainly make it up here. That's what we've got to convince them. We know it. We've seen it. We just got to make them see it in themselves, and that comes with consistent outreach and trust."

Whatever one might think about the optimism of Bethea, Deamues, and the other outreach workers in the tunnels, there is something heroic in their efforts. As Dr. Tsemberis put it, "They were touching and handling people that no one else would go near. You see really awful things down there: infected legs, faces half eaten away by cancer sores. There is a whole aura around the people who worked there . . . like they were doing God's work."

16

Dark Angel

"**I** CAN'T HURT YOU, LOST ANGEL."

The words come out of the tunnel's blackness without warning when I stumble into a cavelike recess.

"But I can hurt those you care about," he says silkily. In the dusty tunnel light, I feel eyes to my left and turn to find him facing me, hands on his hips in a bold and graceful stance. He is barely four feet from me.

I stare, stunned.

"Some of me is within you," he says, shielding his eyes with his left forearm as though there is a flood of light that I don't see. "Not enough for me to hurt you. But enough for me to hurt others close to you. You have a fascination with the darkness of my tunnels. The evil within it. And it is evil," he says with cool force, a fine layer from fury. "Everything down here is pure evil."

Unwittingly I step back, shaking. He has appeared suddenly to me out of darkness, and his words chill my spine. He calls himself the Dark Angel. He has mastered the greatest weapon anyone has in the tunnels, the fear and discomfort that the environment inherently provides.

Tunnel homeless, welfare workers, and police officers have all met this devil-like figure. All of them come away scared, not of the supernatural powers he claims, but of the man himself.

He lives under Grand Central, like many other tunnel people, but he is entirely unlike any other. None have set up camps any-where near his. He hisses, spits, and screams. He is unforgettable, in part, because of his words and his forceful delivery.

He is neither large nor small, about five foot seven, with a slim frame. He is white with slicked-back brown hair. His power-ful eyes are always a bloodshot, fiery red, recalls Jamall, a veteran of the tunnels who had given me sketchy directions to "Satan's den."

"Madness is the most powerful evil," Jamall warned. Jamall does not believe the Dark Angel is really the devil, but he does believe that the man is mad, and from his madness he derives evil powers.

He is mad. But most who have met this self-proclaimed Angel of Death, including the police, are at least slightly afraid of him because he believes he is the devil, and, in his black tunnel, he has an edge.

Tunnel people steer clear of his den.

"It's the vibes he gives off," another homeless man explains. "The guy can look at you and he knows what will scare you. Maybe it's the way he stares; maybe it's what he says. And if he can't scare you, he threatens voodoo on people you know. Weird-ass guy. Everyone laughs but no one wants to get near him."

"Satan's den" is simple: a bed of stacked cardboard on which blankets are neatly laid, scattered books and magazines, and rats the size of cats. The rodents often walk up unafraid to visitors in his den and sniff, but they stay away from Satan.

"Down here," he declares, "I am the law. I keep the order."

He refuses to go upstairs for prolonged periods of time be-cause, he says, he belongs underground.

However, he has been seen aboveground. Sergeant Bryan Henry, the first and, for a long time, only officer charged with policing the tunnels, acknowledges the sense of power he projects.

"Upstairs he looked at me as if saying, this is your turf, cool," recalls Henry, "but I get you on my turf, down below, it's you and me and you are mine. I'll take you." Henry, a hulking cop, rolls his shoulders as if suddenly cold at the memory. "He is a dangerous individual," he says. "Very dangerous."

Satan uses the fear he incites to live better. Runners, mostly young homeless men, bring him food—not for reward but for what they believe is their own safety.

"I do it cuz the man scares the shit out of me," says Rico, who is six foot three and 240 pounds. "It would be unlucky for me to leave him without food. When I run stuff down, he tells me 'it's about time' and that he was going to 'make things get nasty' for me.

"One time I thought, 'This is shit, man. I'm not afraid of this hot dog,'" Rico goes on after a pause. "I didn't go down with food that day. Next day I broke my leg climbing a fence I climb hundreds of times. Crazy," he shakes his head.

Even before the cast was dried, Rico made his penance trip to Satan. "I swear I never knew such pain! And he was waiting for me. He knew! He said, 'That's what happens when you don't serve me. Next time it will be worse. Much worse.' I believe him, man," Rico said, wide-eyed.

A young transit cop in Penn Station says he doesn't mind seeing "Satan" in the terminal aboveground, but he makes sure he wears a cross when going into the tunnel where he might encounter the Dark Angel.

"It's like, up here he knows better than to do anything," the cop says. "But under there, he thinks the turf is his and he can do anything. And a guy like that, he's capable of anything."

Police walkie-talkies don't extend deep into the tunnels, "so you're all alone," the officer says. "You got no back-up. It's strange but the radios carry right up to his camp, but, as soon as you reach his area, they go dead."

Harold Deamues of ADAPT had one of the most striking encounters with the Dark Angel.

"We were walking along looking for people and suddenly it felt all weird like, quiet or something. Me and my partner were looking straight ahead and suddenly this guy, arms crossed over his chest, rises out of a coffin-shaped box. I almost started screaming. Me and my partner, we thought this was the real Dracula," Deamues now roars with laughter at the memory, but adds, "I mean under there, anything is possible, you know what I'm saying?"

Deamues, who has the best rapport with "Satan" of anyone who has encountered him, does not believe the man takes drugs because he always speaks fluently and coherently. Rico has never seen him even light a cigarette.

"But his eyes are red, always red and glowing," says Rico, wondering why.

I notice this striking redness as the Dark Angel paces about his den, talking on and on. Each of my questions is lost to his monologue. He seems hardly aware of me, but it can only be me to whom he is speaking. I am glad he is not staring at me as he speaks. Instead he focuses on his tirade.

"You have left the world of fairness and good. Goodness can no longer reach you down here. You are no longer safe," he says, now looking at the ground. Then he hisses. "Leave, little lost angel, before the tunnels swallow you and you are one of mine."

I do leave, almost as quickly as he has appeared to me. My back feels cold, as though he has changed his mind and his hand will reach my shoulder and stop me. But it doesn't. I turn to watch him swing a cloth robe across his back, fashioning a cape. Then he vanishes into his own darkness.

Rather than visiting him again, I press others for information about him.

Jamall responds decisively, "All you need to know about that guy is to avoid him."

17

The Underground in History, Literature, and Culture

"You do not know me if you think I am afraid, or that I build my burrow simply out of fear."
—*Franz Kafka, "The Burrow"*

THE SELF-PROCLAIMED DARK ANGEL PERSONIFIES MANY VISCERAL fears ordinary people have of the underground and the creatures that exist there. Frightening philosophical and psychological notions of the underground, which have been passed from one generation to the next in our culture, color our perception of the region and the people who live there. For centuries, the depths have been depicted in literature and history as a nurturing environment for evil and madness. It is the perfect dark, unknown, and foreboding terrain on which imaginations avidly feed.

From those images, the subterranean environment in Western culture has evolved metaphorically as a mental landscape, a social environment, and an ideological map. The underground has been portrayed as a threatening underside of aboveground society.

169

Although the symbolic significance has changed dramatically over the centuries, recurring metaphors in social and literary history have spawned widespread and enduring connotations, damaging prejudices, and a simple but deep fear of the dark—all resulting in serious obstacles to helping the underground homeless. Fortunately, scholars are recognizing and exposing this cultural inheritance—the first steps toward ridding ourselves of its pernicious effects.

The underground in literature is seldom portrayed as an Eden. One of the few exceptions is the ancient legend of Agharthi, which promises a 900-mile tunnel to a fantastically rich and sophisticated civilization. Several modern-day writers have tried to move Agharthi from the dark underground to the sublime mountains of Tibet, as in Hollywood's Shangri-la, and into the vast oceans of Atlantis. However, adherers to the Agharthi legend still place it in the heart of the underground, some even claiming that the tunnel system under Central Park is part of the Agharthi network.

Mostly, the underground has long been synonymous with hell, in the Bible and in its interpretations. Dante's rings descend downward, for example. In the nineteenth century, writers used the underground as a metaphor for a people who lived on the surface but were doomed by crime and mutilating poverty. Today's criminal world is the "underworld" in popular terms.

In her book *Notes on the Underground,* historian Rosalind Williams explains that the underground was not always feared. She contends that subterranean iconography is based on historical and literary interpretations of underworlds as technological environments. Fear of the underground emerged historically, at the same time as fear of technological progress.

In prehistoric times, the underground was a comforting refuge from natural dangers aboveground. Humanity's earliest constructions were burrows rather than buildings, "representing the wish to return to the dark, enclosed safety of the womb, which is so primitive as to be premythic," Williams writes. Until the scientific revolution, the general image of the earth was that of a nurturing mother. "It was a sacred entity," according to Williams. "To delve into the earth was akin to rape. Mining was therefore an enterprise of dubious morality, comparable to mutilation and violation." Through the end of the Middle Ages in Europe, sinking a mine was a ritual operation and religious ceremonies were held before entering the sacred underground.

In the Renaissance, however, the oral and sacred epic tradition of the journey to the underworld was transformed into narratives that were written and secular. In these narratives, an adventurous, mad, or unlucky traveler discovers an underworld, which he enters and from which he sometimes fails to reemerge.

In some of these narratives the imprint of the earlier sacred tradition is still evident. William Beckford's *Vathek* (1787) tells how the caliph Vathek, a haughty monarch of portentous powers and appetites, enters into a pact with Eblis, the Oriental Satan. After renouncing his religion and God, the caliph is allowed to enter Eblis's Palace of Subterranean Fire, which lies below the ruins of an ancient city and holds treasure and talismans. When Vathek and his lover approach the ruined city, a rock platform opens before them and a polished marble staircase leads them downward to the realm of Eblis: " . . . they found themselves in a place which, although vaulted, was so spacious and lofty that at first they took it for a great plain. Eventually, their eyes became accustomed to the great size of surrounding objects, they discovered rows of columns and arcades running off in diminishing perspective until they concentrated in a radiant spot like the setting sun painting the sea with his last rays." They see an immense hall lined with pale specters, some shrieking, others silent, all with glimmering eyes and with their right hands covering their hearts being consumed by fire. Vathek and his lover begin to burn with hatred and are condemned to eternal despair.

In the introduction to *Vathek,* Jorge Luis Borges praised it as "the first truly atrocious hell in literature." Beckford set a precedent for a demonic underground that continues into contemporary works such as Jean-Paul Sartre's *No Exit*.

Technology provided new images of the underground, and some literature began to depict the depths as a source of knowledge and philosophical truth. In particular, a new type of intellectual inquiry called natural science—now called science—emerged in the late Renaissance and depended on mining images to explain its principles and methods. Using excavation of the earth as a metaphor, Francis Bacon suggested researchers should dig "further and further into the mine of natural knowledge." For deep within the earth "the truth of nature lies hid in certain deep mines and caves" (in Williams, *Notes on the Underground*).

Throughout the eighteenth century and into the next, social and philosophical thinkers used the underground as a metaphor to dig into the rich truth. *Les Miserables,* Victor Hugo's 1862 book on the underclass uprising in France, is a prime example of a narrative exploring the underground, metaphorically and literally. Crucial events are set in the sewers under Paris.

Hugo explained why he journeyed metaphorically into the depths:

> The historian of moral and ideas has a mission no less austere than that of the historian of events. The latter has the surface of civilization, the struggles of the crowns, the births of princes, the marriages of kings, the battles, the assemblies, the great public men, the revolutions in the sunlight, all the exterior; the other historian has the interior, the foundation, the people who work, who suffer, and who wait, overburdened woman, agonizing childhood, the secret wars of man against man, the obscure ferocities, the prejudices, the established iniquities, the subterranean reactions of the law, the secret evolutions of souls, the vague shudderings of the multitudes, the starvation, the barefoot, the bare-armed, the disinherited, the orphans, the unfortunate and the infamous, all the specters that wander in darkness. . . . Is the underworld of civilization, because it is deeper and gloomier, less important than the upper? Do we really know the mountain when we do not know the cavern?

Historians have responded to Hugo's challenge for a century and a half, says Williams, digging beneath the surface manifestations to unearth submerged groups (homosexuals, criminals, and women), submerged evidence (dreams, sexual customs, and mental constructs), and submerged forces (economic, technological, and ecological).

Much of nineteenth century realism also incorporated the theme that a journey into the underground was a quest. "The pilgrim descends into the social depths in search of social truth," as Williams explains. "The descent is always metaphorical, but in view of the living conditions of the poor, it may be literal as well."

England's mid-Victorian realists in particular, like Charles Dickens, William Thackeray, and George Eliot, were praised for their realistic descriptions of the social life of the "underground." George Gissing's 1889 novel, *The Nether World,* was eerily prescient in describing the plight of many of today's underground homeless, although in his book, the people striving to survive and maintain a modicum of dignity have been trapped physically beneath the surface rather than trapped by social circumstances.

It was Hugo who most effectively used the idea of a dark underworld to threaten the mighty and the wealthy. His subterranean world is not only poor but also ominous to French society. "Men heard beneath their feet the obscure course of a muffled sound, when some mysterious uprising of molehills appeared on the surface of civilization, when the earth fissured, the mouths of caverns opened, and men saw monstrous heads spring suddenly from the earth." Again, from "an enormous black hole . . . the gloomy voice of the people was heard dimly growling. A fearful sacred voice, composed of the roaring brute and speech of God . . . which comes at the same time from below like the voice of the lion and from above like the voice of thunder."

Although Hugo exposes the reader to the brutality of underground life, he also dramatizes the unbreakable ties between societies above and below ground, as in the climactic chase scene in which Jean Valjean carries Marius through the sewers. His message is that society underground is part of society as a whole and therefore can be rescued from its misery.

Marx and Freud depended so much on underground imagery

that it is now virtually impossible to read a text about the underworld without filtering it through a Marxist or Freudian interpreta-
tion, Williams claims.

More literally, the underground basis of modern industry began between the late 1700s and the late 1800s with the building
of a transportation network of canals and railroads. The construction of sewers, water mains, steam pipes, subways, telephone lines,
and electrical cables followed, requiring interaction and coordina-
tion of the city aboveground with its vital innards below.

As new material foundations of industrial and urban life were
laid, so were new social foundations. Excavation projects were
metaphors for profound changes being made in existing society and
even for the abstract progress of civilization. Established neighborhoods and communities were uprooted for the construction of subway lines. Daily traffic patterns and workplaces were changing
because of the rapid transit subways offered. With such advances
came anxiety about the new order. In the nineteenth century another type of underground story appeared: The underworld became
a place where people not only visited but actually lived.

In Jules Verne's 1864 *A Journey to the Center of the Earth,*
human life underground is completely independent of the surface
world. This idea of permanently living below the surface of the
earth coincided with the development of modern science and technology. In the middle of the eighteenth century, the possibility
that the earth was hollow and habitable still had some respectable
advocates. As scientific knowledge advanced, the idea of discovering a hidden inner world became less and less credible. However,
with the march of technology, the idea of building an inner world
became more and more legitimate.

The technological possibility of building an underground society brought concerns of social engineering, and with them, a profound fear that technology was growing beyond society's control.
While technology progressed, H. G. Wells complained that its
uncontrolled growth and society's uncritical faith in growth for its
own sake might lead to a degenerative society that abused the
working class. Wells's narrator of the *Time Machine* explains to his

readers of the 1890s that, although the evolution of an underground species might seem grotesque, "even now there are existing circumstances to point that way."

"There is a tendency to utilize underground space for the less ornamental purposes of civilization; there is the Metropolitan Railway in London, for instance, there are new electric railways, there are subways, there are underground workrooms and restaurants, and they increase and multiply," Wells wrote. "Evidently, I thought, this tendency has increased till Industry had gradually lost its birthright in the sky. I mean that it had gone deeper and deeper into larger and ever larger underground factories, spending a still-increasing amount of its time therein, till, in the end—! Even now, does an East-End worker live in such artificial conditions as practically to be cut off from the natural surface of the earth?"

In exploring the implications of underground technological growth in the future, Wells touched on a past truth: underground laborers throughout history have been considered a lower form of life. Slaves of Egypt and Rome were forced to live and work in their mines. After the Middle Ages, subterranean life was experienced only by those at the bottom of the social ladder; the underground lost its "nurturing mother" mystique.

Most underground laborers were serfs, slaves, criminals, or prisoners of war. Mining was often a form of punishment. In almost all cases, their working conditions were morbidly inhumane. In the United States, convicts, prisoners of war, and slaves worked the underground until the Industrial Revolution when such labor, particularly mining, was reserved for immigrants—the newest segment of the population and the one most desperate for money. The social degradation of underground laborers helps explain why the underworld came to be dreaded as a region of sorrow and death.

In the nineteenth century for the first time, railway and subway tunnels allowed the middle and even upper classes to taste the underground. The experience of being disconnected from nature and immersed in an artificial environment was no longer limited to lower classes and social outcasts. The more known and utilized for society's benefit, the less frightening and ugly the underground became. Gradually, with the advent of technology as an ideal—particularly with the advent of electricity to light the lower regions—the underworld came to be perceived as remote but also magical and sublime.

Some writers came forward in rebellion against the underground and technology, seeing it as a threat to society's future. H. G. Wells consciously used his stories to consider the relationship between technological progress and human degeneration. In the *Time Machine,* he displays fear that workers will become increasingly brutalized as their labor becomes more mechanized and repetitive, with the individual disappearing into a hostile collective force underground. He warns of "people calmly developing, in regions excluded from our sight and deemed uninhabitable by our sages, power surpassing our most disciplined modes of force."

"The ages may yet elapse," wrote Wells, "before there emerge into sunlight our inevitable destroyers."

In today's world, the word *underground* carries a mosaic of contemporary social and political images, such as revolution, avant-garde newspapers, organized crime, left-wing terrorism, and drug trafficking. There is also the concept in literature of the "underground man," who is the ultimate dissident from the modern world. Literary critic Edward F. Abood, while acknowledging that his *Underground Man* is a twentieth-century creature, guides us back to Fyodor Dostoyevsky's *Notes from Underground.*

"Dostoyevsky's classic literary figure, an immortal neurotic, speaks to more kindred souls today than he did in 1864," Abood writes.* According to Abood, the underground man is a rebel against prevailing norms of the society he lives in and the forces that perpetuate them. His action (if he is capable of action) is always essentially personal. Even when he joins a group, his com-

---

*While many of his attributes and qualities are centuries old, their synthesis into the underground man is a modern development. He is essentially a reaction to forces of the past century. Hemingway's Jake Barnes, Kafka's clerks, Hesse's Steppenwolf were underground men, as were Sartre's lonely existentialist, Camus's absurd man, Ellison's invisible man, and Koestler's Rubashove, betrayed by the communist gods of his own creation. Despite their radical differences, all of them possessed pronounced features of the underground man.

mitment is subjective, and he is thus ultimately isolated. He denies other codes of conduct, particularly the values by which the majority of his contemporaries live. Consequently he exists in a constant state of tension and anxiety, aggravated by what is perhaps his most distinguishing quality—a keen and often morbid sensibility.

This underground human is far from a romantic hero, primarily because his self is his main cause of agony. He is isolated, not because he chooses isolation, but because it is his burden and his fate.

Most characteristic of the underground man is his extreme withdrawal and isolation. He is a self-declared exile from human society, with which he maintains only as much contact as is necessary for survival. He has rejected the world outside, but, at the same time, he harbors an elementary fear that he will be forgotten in his "mousehole," as Dostoyevsky's hero referred to his home. Though he has chosen his own exile, he finds society's indifference of him intolerable. His apartment is not a retreat but is more like a jail. Ultimately, he has nothing to believe in. He experiences anguish, estrangement, heightened consciousness turning in upon itself, and impotent rage at being reduced, misunderstood, and finally, forgotten.

The best amalgamation of the metaphorical and literal underground man is Ralph Ellison's *Invisible Man*. He comes closest to telling it the way many tunnel dwellers see their situation—that they have been pushed underground by a society that considers them lost, without identities. In Ellison's terms, they are "invisible."

Ellison's protagonist is an African-American man who explains that he is invisible in New York's racist society of the fifties "simply because people refuse to see me." He struggles to survive aboveground, but, in the end, he is literally chased by a mob into an abandoned coal pit under the streets of Harlem. White men cover the top with a heavy iron lid, imprisoning him.

"You ache with the need to convince yourself that you do exist in the real world," he says, "that you're a part of all the sound and anguish, and you strike out with your fists, you curse and you swear to make them recognize you. And, alas, it's seldom successful."

He returns aboveground but decides he really belongs in a "hole" because it more honestly and correctly expresses his invisibility. "I did not become alive until I discovered my invisibility," he explains. Invisible and underground, he sets up a home, siphons off electricity, and lives. From there, he seeks retribution for society's poor sight. He wages his own independent fight against society and its institutions in his own terms, such as stealing the electricity of Monopolated Light & Power.

"They suspect that power is being drained off, but they don't know where. . . . Several years ago I went through the routine process of buying service and paying their outrageous rates. But no more. I gave up all that, along with my apartment and my old way of life. That was based on the fallacious assumption that I, like other men, was visible. Now, aware of my invisibility, I live rent-free [under] a building rented strictly to whites, in a section . . . that was shut off and forgotten during the nineteenth century."

Is he abdicating his responsibility to humankind?

"Irresponsibility is part of my invisibility; anyway you face it, it is denial," he admits. "But to whom can I be responsible, and why should I be, when you refuse to see me? and wait until I reveal how truly irresponsible I am. Responsibility rests on recognition, and recognition is a form of agreement."

In a passage that resonates in the tunnels of today's underground homeless, for it articulates their reasons for taking peace underground, Ellison's invisible man insists that he has not run into the earth because of fear or self-pity.

"I found a home—or a hole in the ground, as you will. Now don't jump to the conclusion that because I call my home a hole, it is damp and cold like a grave. There are cold holes and warm holes. Mine is a warm hole. . . . My hole is warm and full of light. Yes *full* of light. I doubt if there is a brighter spot in all of New York than this hole of mine, and I do not exclude Broadway. Or the Empire State Building on a photographer's dream night. But that is taking advantage of you. Those two spots are among the darkest of our civilization."

Ellison ends his book with the invisible man deciding to stay underground until he is chased out. "Here, at least, I could try to think things out in peace, or, if not in peace, in quiet. I would take up residence underground. The end was in the beginning."

18

Wanderers

NEAR THE ENTRANCES TO SOME TUNNELS THERE ARE WANDER-
ers, those who meander, drift, and almost seep unknow-
ingly and unintentionally toward the underground. They
are usually exhausted, mentally ill, or drugged. Some are simply
looking for shelter from the weather or for a place that promises
uninterrupted sleep. Some seek a place to shoot, snort, smoke, or
drink drugs. Others look to submerge their depression in solitude.

The underground is a dangerous place for wanderers. Most are
unaware of the electrified third rail, of tracks that can trap unwary
feet, and of the speed of oncoming trains and the disorienting effect
of their blinding headlights.

However, the most feared by wanderers are the gangs of
youths, primarily in their early to mid-teens, who roam tunnels for
helpless prey.

"Yeah, sure, we're looking for violence if you wanna put it
that way," says a boy who calls himself "Stealth." He is fourteen
years old, and, at about five foot seven, the largest of a gang of four
boys who enter a tunnel near Riverside Park one afternoon while
playing hookey from school. They are excited and edgy as they walk
dangerously close to discovering some underground homeless they
seek. One swings a wooden plank at the air, another is mesmerized
by the leaping flame of his lighter. Their eyes are wide and disbe-
lieving of the underground, and they keep close to each other, none
willing to trail too far behind.

"These people down here ain't people," says Stealth as he approaches, uneasy at first but more confident as he tries to show leadership. "They're mole people." His head goes back in a laugh meant to be tough. One of the other kids giggles, another crinkles his nose and squeezes his eyes together to mime an ugly rodent face.

"They're moles," Stealth repeats. "No one cares what happens to them anyway."

They have no parents? or family?

Stealth pauses. He looks toward his twelve-year-old cousin, but Little Man, as he's called, is bewildered by the question.

"C'mon," he orders the others with a sharp jerk of his head back toward the entrance. "This is bullshit. I don't care who they are. They're ugly." As he saunters out, he looks back at me and says, "Anyway, we're doing you a favor, getting rid of these moles. The police would do it if they were allowed. You should thank us."

Real criminals, who not much older than Stealth and his gang, use the tunnels as meeting sites, hideouts, places to cache stolen goods including money and sometimes drugs—although the dampness damages dry powders. Even huge, five-gallon containers of flammable chemicals used to convert some drugs into more potent or more transportable forms are hidden underground.

Drug dealers and gangs of older males are less inclined to search out wanderers for senseless killing. "We got bigger things on our mind than outtin' a mole," one says, but they are no less violent toward underground homeless who may anger them.

"Killin' down here ain't like on the streets," says Slam, a beefy twenty-two-year-old whose scarred face displays a record of his battles. "It's harder to kill a dog on the streets than it is to do someone down here." Fewer eyes, he indicates.

Slam explains that the tunnels are also convenient for disposing of people murdered on the surface because they are hardly policed and contain may niches into which bodies can be hidden to decay beyond recognition.

"The tunnels are right for crime," Slam says, chillingly calm. "Look at them; they made for it."

19

Harlem Gang

"In a world where you have to struggle to survive, I don't know how much 'goodness' is worth."
— *Walter Mosley (mystery writer)*

UNDERGROUND CRIMINALS BRAG THAT THEY DO NOT THINK twice about killing someone who happens across them at the wrong time. One of these gangs meets near the IRT (Interborough Rapid Transit) subway tunnels around 125th Street in Harlem, as I discover accidentally.

Blade, who says he was once a tunnel dweller and now still frequents the tunnels as a graffiti writer, is walking the underground with me when we stumble across the gang. It is growing late in the afternoon, and the air, even in the tunnels, has cooled. Light through the grates is fading. We have come miles north of where we entered, and I am tired. Blade says I look pale, and begins to lead me on a "shortcut" to the surface.

We climb a few levels higher, but the air thickens with fumes and, feeling nauseated, I ask Blade for a quick exit to air. He knows of none.

"Besides," he smiles, "we're in the middle of Harlem. You're safer down here."

As we walk, the megaphone voices of the New Alliance Party

carry down through the grates, pounding on about "white geno-cide," "pigs," "anarchy," and "black nationalism." So rather than going up, we go on.

The tunnel turns gently and Blade takes my hand in warning. We step over a rusted barbed wire at shin level, and I wonder what we are entering. Blade leans forward, also curious, and the black-ness is suddenly shattered by a blinding flash of light. I recoil but resist the instinct to turn my back; "It's easier for someone to 'do you' when your back's turned," Blade has told me.

Blade moves in front of me, protectively, and I bend around him to see a dark figure thinly outlined by the backscatter of his powerful flashlight.

"Yo, Moe!" he calls out. "That you, Moe?"

I begin to laugh at the alienlike figure who resembles E.T., but Blade sweeps his arm angrily back, hitting my ribs. I keep silent.

"Moe, that you man?" the figure calls again.

Blade moves us closer to the tunnel wall. "Go back to where we were," he whispers. "Stay along the wall."

I start to protest, but he shoves me hard. "Go!" he orders, in the breathy whisper of tunnel people. "I've had enough of you. Do what I say. Go!"

I stumble a few yards back and wait, still watching the bizarre scene in stark black-and-white.

"Stop messin', Moe man," the figure says loudly. "Ain't funny no more."

Another figure moves behind the voice. A mumbled exchange of words is followed by a metal click that echoes against the walls as the figure raises an arm.

"Come on out," the figure orders. "I got a nine here, man. If that you, Moe, you better stop this shit!"

Blade remains silent. I realize that Blade can only be dimly seen, and I'm probably beyond the reach of their light.

"You ain't Moe, and I'm comin' for you, cause I ain't gonna be made no fool!" the voice declares, rising in anger.

"Go!" Blade whispers to me again, louder and more urgently, and steps forward with his hands raised.

"Yo," he says. "Don't mean nothin'. Jus' passin' through, man. Didn't know this was your tunnel."

I stay put, and find a rock to wield as a weapon, feeling stupid.

"I should blow you right now," the gunman says as he comes toward us. "What you mean, pretending to be Moe."

"Look, man," Blade says with a twinge of impatience, "I don't know Moe, jus' happened to be passin' by, like I said. Don't know your gig, and don't care to know, neither. I'm gonna just turn around and be outta here. Right?"

"Hold it!" the gunman orders confidently. "Ain't through with you yet."

"Look, man," says Blade, angrily now. "I tol' you I don't mean nothin'. Let it be, man. I leavin'."

Blade turns his back on the light and walks past me.

"I'm going to tell him that I'm behind him when he passes," I whisper, "and that I'll shoot him if he shoots you." My voice sounds like thunder in my ears. I fear I've spoken too loudly.

"You say somethin'?" the gunman asks Blade.

"Jus' that I'm goin'," Blade recovers. In his throaty whisper aside, he tells me, "That's the stupidest thing I ever heard!" He shakes his head. "Don't you know he can hear where your voice come from? Fool!"

"You got someone down there with you?" demands the gunman."

"Yeah," I answer, trembling. "I'm a reporter."

Blade shakes his head again, exasperated. He twists his hands at his thighs as though wishing he had snapped my neck like a chicken. The two of us move back toward the light.

We must look cowed and helpless because the gunman laughs in relief. I introduce myself, explaining that I'm collecting material on tunnel people.

"Good thing," he says importantly. "Don' want to waste no lead. Don' have lead to waste."

His fear and hostility have largely disappeared. "How about me interviewing you?" I ask.

"Don' see it as no problem," he replies, "long as we know where to find you."

You won't know, I tell him, but soften it by offering to withhold names and descriptions. "I'm writing a book, and in a book you'll live forever," I say.

That seems persuasive. "I'll have to clear it with Doc," he says.

I can see him more clearly now as we move forward—a tall, slim man, perhaps in his twenties, but looking much older. We turn a sharp corner that seems flooded with grate light to find Doc, their leader, a short, heavyset man with dark glasses.

He likes the idea of being part of a book. He also trusts my guide.

"She's with Blade," he says, "it's cool."

Surprised, I look questioningly at Blade. He just nods to Doc and ignores me.

New arrivals entering the tunnel also appear to know Blade. I ask him directly where he met them. "Can't remember," he shrugs, brushing me off.

The new arrivals have slipped down through a manhole on one of Harlem's less trafficked streets, I'm told. Children playing there have grown accustomed to men struggling to remove the heavy manhole cover and disappearing.

"Yeah," says Bingo, young and eager to talk about his exploits, "sometimes kids see us. But the kids don't count. No one watches cuz they know it ain't good for them. The young ones think we're workers, I guess, and the bigger ones know not to follow.

"We got it good down here; we know the place. Anyone who comes down here be lost and bingo." His face lights up. "We get them before they see what's coming at them."

Doc leans back on a wobbly metal chair, eyes drooping coolly, while Bingo talks. Like the others, I'm invited to call him Doc but perhaps for a different reason. "You call me Doc for doctor, because I'm gonna teach you," he says.

"The group, it ain't like those gangs like Bloods and Crips or the kid gangs out here," he begins. "We's small, mostly just brothers. We hang together. If we see someone doing something we don't like, if someone 'disses' [shows disrespect to] us, we take him out. That's how we operate. Either we do it, or someone asks us to do it."

The gang hires itself out for money, threatening and assaulting in the pay and at the direction of others, usually adult criminals. They will kill for a price, Doc says, sometimes for as little as $20. "It depends on how much they got on them, and how much we want cash."

The last man to slip into the tunnel is smaller than the others, and quieter. He leans against a wall, arms folded, distrustful.

"What are you gonna call him?" Doc asks, pointing the silver tip of his switchblade at the newcomer.

"Depend on what he says," Blade answers for me with a touch of pride. The book seems almost as much his project as mine.

"He don't say much," Doc laughs. "Do you X?" he asks. "Don't say much at all."

"Don't like talk," the man replies, mouth curling importantly with the attention. "I like action."

"Small Talk," I say, "that will be your name."

Everyone waited in an uneasy pause to learn the response.

"That's cool," he says in a low voice and comes forward with a pleased smile. Doc breaks into loud laughter. Others join in.

"We's all like action," says Dart, another new arrival. "That's why we're with these brothers. It ain't that we got nothin' better to do. We talk mostly about who to take out next. It's our work.

"We's respected for our work," he continues hurriedly. "We's not afraid of nothin' and up there, see," he points to the surface, "they know it. Look at this, see." He pulls his shirt open to expose a well-muscled shoulder. An almost circular scar shines smoothly. "That's from a bullet these punks . . ."

Dart explains the knife scar that runs the width of his forehead, which came from a fight with a Chinatown gang, and he is starting on a scar on his calf when Blade turns to me.

"You better call this one Diarrhea Mouth," Blade says in an aside, "cuz he's got it bad." I smile.

Dart stops, sensing the unkind interruption.

"You say somethin', man?" he asks.

"Naw, ain't nothin'. Jus' sort of a joke," Blade says.

"What was it? We want to hear it," Dart stands provocatively, shaking down the leg of his jeans where the scar was exposed.

"It was nothin'," Blade says, raising his voice to meet the anger in Dart's move. "Nothin' you want to hear."

The two men gravitate slowly toward each other until they are face-to-face, Blade towering over the younger man. A fight seems just one word away, but Doc intervenes.

"He was talkin' to the girl, Dart," Doc says, barely looking up. "Sit down." He adds politely to me, "Excuse me, Jennifer."

Blade raises his hands to his shoulders, palms forward, to indicate an end to the confrontation, but Dart remains poised to strike, his chest inflated and tense.

Doc glares at Dart. "Blade would remove your ass," he says sharply. "Give it up, man."

"You'll have to excuse Dart, Jennifer," Doc continues, more easily now. "He don' know how to turn it off."

Dart sits down, pouting. However, within seconds, he is showing me more scars.

When he finishes, he shouts to another man. "Slim, show her the one on your neck," he says. Slim complies, and then exposes a fresh welt, red and raised, just above his ankle.

"Fucking Chinks," he says, "they use chains to fight."

"Naw," laughs Dart, "that's from that pussy you took."

"The bitch in leather," Bingo throws in. Slim just shakes his head.

Before the gang completes showing me their battle scars, Small Talk begins cleaning a gun with a cloth.

I ignore him, but Bingo plays along. "Whatcha got?" he asks.

"A mac," Small Talk replies, not looking up.

"Lemme see," Bingo says. "Nice piece."

"It got lead," Small Talk warns.

Bingo handles the weapon roughly to show disdain for the danger. "How much did you give for it?" he asks.

"It was a present," Small Talk says, head tilted to look up, slowly chewing gum. He tongues the gum into his front teeth as Bingo smiles, knowingly.

"Nice," Bingo says. He points the gun at Dart and various other targets. "Nice," he says again.

Slim pulls out some crack.

"Ah man," says Jamaica, a skinny little newcomer with dreadlocks and a strong lilting accent, "I thought you were going to bring ecstasy [a hallucinogenic]."

"We gotta do the Frog first," Slim says, passing the crack.

"I gonna do it, man, you be backup," Jamaica says.

"Naw, I'm gonna do it," Dart interrupts. "I was backup last time. I wanna be the trigger man," he pleads.

"I done nine," boasts Slim. "You only done four."

"Yeah, but mine were clean [kills]," Dart says. Slim seems not to care.

"Aw, man," whines Dart, sucking air through his teeth.

"Yeah, but we only seen the three," says Jamaica, exhaling thin blue smoke.

"I tol' you, they took him away before the police got there," Dart insists to defend his claim. Status is evidently based on the number of murders.

"It's our thing," Doc explains when he sees me puzzling it out. "That's what we do. We do it to survive, to live, to succeed. It's what we know how to do. We know how to do it well," he emphasizes, leaning forward with hard eyes.

He is boasting, I know, but only a little. He is trying to frighten me, I know, and he succeeds.

"We gonna talk about Frog?" Doc is asked.

"Not until she leaves," Doc nods at me. "You understand," he says, again politely. "We don't want your involvement."

I don't understand his words precisely, but I do get the meaning.

"Time to leave," I say brightly to Blade.

"It was time to leave ten minutes ago," he hisses at me when we are safely out of earshot. "Those are fucking bad men. You don't want them saying hi to you on the street. You don't want them to remember ever seeing you. They ain't messin' with you. They kill for fun."

And so do you, Blade, as I later discover.

20

J.C.'s Community

J.C. HAS AN UNIMPOSING BUILD. HE STANDS FIVE foot seven or eight and is slim. He usually wears jeans, a T-shirt, and sneakers, and carries a boom box. He is neater than most of the station's homeless and blends easily into the Grand Central scene, except for his very angry eyes. He is a paradox, living now aboveground and working as a janitor and as a volunteer with the Parks Department's street kids program, but passionately defending those who choose to live where he once did, underground. He defends underground life fiercely, sometimes belligerently, in part as a vehicle for attacking society that lives on the surface, but in part also because of his strong attachment and protectiveness toward his "multicultural community" of about two hundred men, women, and children who live under Grand Central Station. He is, he says, their "spokesman."

He initially refuses to take me down to visit the community unless I promise to remain underground for a week and wear my hair in braids. All women in the community have braids, he says, to keep their hair clean. I refuse. A month later, he offers a visit on the condition that I not write about it. Again I refuse. Later still, he tells me that against his advice, the leader of the community—its elected "mayor," he says—has ordered him to bring me down.

"I wanted someone from the outside to see us," the mayor

191

explains to me later. "I want you to write that we're better off down here without the perversions of the world upstairs. I need no man to validate me or my existence. I did this only to let you know how sick the upstairs is."

J.C. wants to impose a final condition, that I wear a blindfold. I refuse, but agree to use no description that will precisely locate the community. So we finally set off.

We descend through Grand Central Station, which is spread over forty-eight acres, making it the largest train station in the world. It also goes down six levels beneath the subway tracks. There is no complete blueprint of the tunnels and tracks under the station. Many tunnels were begun but abandoned. Some were built but forgotten. Some were sealed off, but underground homeless people have broken through, either directly by hacking a hole through the wall or by circuitous routes, to inhabit them now.

One of the largest disused tunnels starts out in a northwest direction, taking it under Central Park, before turning southwest toward Penn Station across town. This tunnel can be entered from either station, as well as at various places in the park itself. "There are hundreds, maybe even a thousand people living in that tunnel," I was told by Zack, a member of J.C.'s community. "The utilities are still working there and everything."

The homeless in the station distinguish between "track people" and "mole people" by the level at which they live. Track people usually live under the train and subway platforms, a first stop for many who later move deeper into the tunnels. Mole people live at least a level deeper. At each deeper level, the communities are said to be more established and cohesive, and members go to the surface less frequently, living as well as sleeping underground. In the deeper tunnels, it is not uncommon to find homeless who have gone a week or more without seeing sunlight.

We enter the tunnels through the subway in Grand Central, passing first along a platform with a scattering of commuters and onto the subway tracks. We carry no flashlights and wear no reflective clothing. I wear black, as J.C. advised me, but I doubt than any color would be discernible in the darkness.

We snake along various tracks for what seems a frightening eternity as subway trains thunder out of the dark. As they approach with blazing white lights, J.C. moves agilely to the side and I quickly follow. We bow our heads to avoid the glare of the headlights and the motorman's eyes and stand totally still. When the train has passed, we move on. Soon we leave the main track to pass through cavernous rooms, one after another, each with grated doors that are locked but easily circumvented.

Sleeping bags and a few mattresses, evidence of "track people," remain from the night before and prepare for the night to come. Each room is slightly different and yet the same, but the signs of the "camps" at each level increase as we go farther.

Now we begin to go deeper, down a set of rusty stairs, to another level, still an operating subway tunnel, and move along tracks until finally J.C. stops and points to a wall of slate gray cement. "That's the main entrance," he announces. "Find it or I won't take you down further." I know he is teasing, but I touch the wall, which looks solid and impregnable, as if nothing could get through it.

I bend over to search more carefully, and find below waist level a hole, about as large as the entrance to a good-sized dog house. Nervous and unsteady, I stick my head through and see a light on the other side and about thirty feet below us. We crawl inside a broad ridge. A cable hangs close enough to reach. A train passes, and we turn our backs, waiting for darkness to return before J.C. clambers down the cable, hand over hand, feet against the rock wall. Once down, he scavenges for a long wooden plank, which he props against the side for me. Using the cable and the plank, I back down the steep incline and feel level ground once again.

The floor is covered with black garbage bags taken from Sanitation Department workers. Each is filled with clothes or balled up newspapers to disguise the place and hide various items, including the plank, stolen tool boxes, and other implements, from any intruder who might look through the entrance hole above.

On this level, at least three down from the subway platform, J.C. is more comfortable and relaxed. At higher levels, he is always on guard, eyes darting, movements quick. Now he walks more loosely, freer. He laughs more often. He still speaks in a hushed whisper, a lower register, and he never shouts to compete with tunnel noise. Yet his words carry distinctly over intrusive tunnel sounds, even those of distant trains.

Now, as we pick our way on planks and catwalks, worrying more about our footing than transit cops, he becomes almost talkative.

"You can see now why no one wanders onto our community," he says. "You have to be invited down."

In fact, he admits that two homeless once did stumble into the area. "One of them never left," he says. "The other we blindfolded and walked around all day so he couldn't find his way back. We left him near the IRT subway track so a [maintenance] crew would find him. Or a train."

We follow a narrow tunnel with steep steps down one more level, where it is much warmer. The hiss of escaping steam explains why. J.C. stops and taps on a thick pipe with a heavy stick lying nearby, and we wait for a moment until answering taps arrive before moving forward again.

The pipes begin to clatter with new tapping, and more tapping, until it sounds like a tin cavalry. "That's Junior," J.C. laughs. "He thinks he can bang out real messages on the pipes."

The din stops before we arrive at the camp where a dozen people sit around a bright gas lantern. They watch silently as we approach. Two women interrupt hanging laundry to stare, while a boy and a girl who had been playing on the overhead pipes quiet their dangling feet to peer down on us.

J.C. touches my arm. "Wait here," he says, and keeps walking into the camp. "If they try to eat you, run," he calls back with a smile, and for a change, I welcome his sarcasm and even begin to feel less awkward. My watch says it has been an hour since we started out.

The boy of about seven climbs down from the pipes and walks curiously toward me before a man comes out of the darkness to pull him back. I smile but get no answering smiles. I wait.

A black man in his early forties comes from the tent J.C. had entered. An unkempt curly beard streaked with professorial gray surrounds his huge welcoming smile, which is full of large white teeth.

"Jennifer," he says, extending his hand and whispering in the manner of the tunnel people, "I'm Ali M. I'm the elected mayor of this community. You can just call me Mayor. Everyone else does," he adds confidently.

"I hope you enjoy visiting us. I'm sure you'll find it interesting. You probably won't be able to see things the way we see them because of your conditioning, but we'll work on that. Take care to open your mind as much as possible and recognize that your eyes physically can't see what we see. It takes weeks for eyes to adjust to the darkness.

"My eyes won't take the light upstairs anymore. Most people's down here won't. Even the weakest light can be blinding when you've lived down here. A few months ago I went up just to see what things were like. Someone said a man needed help just inside the tunnel near the tracks, so I went to get him. I couldn't stand the light there. I take it as a sign," he says and winks, as if to ease his words, "a sign that I'm meant to be right here for the rest of my life."

The camp begins to move and make small sounds. I hear sweeping with a broom but beyond six feet I can barely see shadows, fleeting and evasive figures like those I sometimes glimpsed in the higher tunnels but dismissed as imaginary. I struggle to focus on the shapes but it is a strain to see, and I begin to develop a sharp headache. I give up trying to take notes in the dark, particularly after the mayor threatens to confiscate my notebook.

"We don't want you giving any names or too many details that might lead them to us," he says. "What you remember will have to be enough."

The boy and girl, each about five years old, come closer and I give them the fresh notebook and pen. They shriek and giggle over the gifts, and we play a variety of tag as I'm led around. They crawl into a hole and emerge on the pipes, waving at me. They get ahead unseen and surprise me from crevices and small tunnels.

"You see," the mayor tells me, "this is a child's dream. They run free and are not hindered by people who would hurt them."

Who are they? I ask. Who are their parents?

"They are all of ours," he replies. "We take all the children here as our own."

How many children live here?

He refused to answer. "If I told you," he says finally, "there'd be a witch hunt for us. Better leave that unanswered. We don't lie down here."

The mayor introduces me to a woman who he describes as the community's school teacher. She says she is certified by the City of New York. Along with math, science, English, and some social sciences, she says, she teaches ethics, morals, and philosophy to children underground.

"That's our greatest gift down here," she claims, eyes wide in an effort to convey her convictions, "that I can teach what's important. The best teachers do that, teach what's important in their particular environment. Here it is ethics, the basis of our 'human religion.'"

I look puzzled at the phrase, which other tunnel dwellers have used but never explained. "It's based on caring and protecting our brothers and sisters, on communication and love," she says, much as the others did. "It's what sets this race above all others." By race, she explains, she means all the homeless who live in underground communities like this, not black, brown, or white.

"Color?" she asks. "God, no! We have no color down here. Look, can you tell if I'm black or Hispanic?"

I guess a mixture of the two. She laughs. "I'm as white as you are. I think it's the lack of sunlight and the soot in the tunnel that turns us all a shade of gray."

Don't the children need sunlight?

"We go to a little room two levels up, where there is bright warm sunlight coming through grates," she says. "That's where I do most of my teaching. One of the runners [who bring food and other necessities to the community from aboveground] brought us a blackboard to use. We hide it when we come back down so no one who might get into that room can break it."

Next I meet the community's nurse, who says she is registered in the State of New York. She is a large, older woman with thick black hair locked in a firm braid that hangs well down her back. A gray streak runs along each side of her head. She has a gentle smile. When the mayor leaves us for a moment, she admits that she often thinks of "going back up."

"I have a daughter who maybe I could stay with. I write her often and she writes back. She sends my mail to an apartment complex and one of the runners is able to get into the mail room through a tunnel and look through the mail before they are distributed. Many of us have our mail and government checks sent to that address. Different communities use other addresses," she says, "but they get mail the same way."

"I've thought about leaving," she continues after a while. "But then someone gets hurt, or I think someone might get hurt. These people need me. And frankly, that's what I want most, to be needed."

Her medical kit includes bandages, neck braces, codeine as well as aspirin, an antiseptic, needles and threads (which she calls sutures) for stitching cuts, and even a set of crutches. She insists that community members be taken to hospitals on the surface if they are too ill or injured for her to treat. "Often they refuse because they're hiding from the law," she says, "but I won't be responsible for killing someone by letting him stay if he's badly hurt. I just won't!" she insists as if the issue has arisen often in the past.

Chairs and a few tables are spotted around the chamber. Milk and other perishables are stored in a small refrigerator. The mayor directs me to put my hand inside to prove that it is cold but I can see no electric wire attachment. To cook food, the community uses a tunnel with the hottest steam pipes. Pans of water are rested on the pipes. In them are cooked rice, oatmeal, and Cream of Wheat, he says.

"You'll notice how none of us smell," the mayor says proudly and leads me to the "steam room." Clothes are spread out on the hot pipes outside to dry. Inside, men's voices, off-key and punctuated with laughter, are trying to sing. I see several figures showering with soap in the spray of hot water and steam from a leaking pipe.

"Shit, man!" yells a man inside, "you brought a woman here?" The singing stops.

"Brothers," says the mayor, "we are all human."

The figures recede deeper into the mist.

"Sorry, mayor," the complaining voice says, "I didn't know it was you."

The mayor smiles paternally. "This is men's time in the room," he explains. "Women have it earlier, in the morning with the children."

"We even have an exercise room," he says as we resume walking. We enter an area with many barlike pipes. A man is doing pull-ups from one, chinning himself at the top. Over another pipe hangs a wire, one end attached to weights and the other to an old set of bicycle handlebars.

Beyond is a laundry room where three women kneel over a basin of wet clothes, rubbing and chatting and laughing. Warm water sloshes from a pipe into the basin and out, running along a channel against the wall before it disappears.

We return to the mayor's tent, three walls of wood and cardboard and an overhead canopy made of a once-white sheet. Inside is a small round table, draped with a cloth. The mayor lights a fat blue candle sitting on it. I see two bookcases, filled mostly with sociology, psychology, and philosophy texts and a sprinkling of classics. A tightly made bed stands against one wall.

"It took me a long time to bring down everything I had," he says, indicating the room. "I did it over several months, but as you see, I set up a home. I built these bookshelves. I didn't expect any people to come with me to live here, but when I saw them suffering, up above, I invited them down."

J.C. had told me two hundred people live here, but I've seen only about fifty. I ask about the rest.

"Many of them are runners, either passing through or spending the day or even a week upstairs. Some are visiting other communities. It's hard to say," he offers vaguely.

He pours red wine into two tin cups.

"You see we are a clean and healthy community," he says expansively. "We don't allow drugs or hard liquor here. We're not crazy or insane. We're healthy individuals who have chose an alternative. We don't need their help."

Since my time with his people is so limited, the mayor "guides" me to members who will be the most helpful he says. He chooses the people to whom I speak. When I wonder if anyone in his community would prefer to return aboveground, he snaps, "No, of course not."

"That is another of those myths and undeserved rumors about us. Anyone is free to come and go as they please. If someone has his doubts, I don't encourage him to go because I firmly believe life is better here."

It is now mealtime and we watch the community eat. The staple is a bowl filled with oatmeal-like porridge. Several sandwiches are distributed. They resemble the sandwiches from Meals-on-Wheels, perhaps the leftovers.

"Sometimes they send dogs to find us," the mayor observes as we watch. "They don't go back."

You eat them? I ask, taken aback.

"Sometimes they're good meat," he answers with a little smile. I don't know if he is just trying to shock me. Either way, I'm upset as we return into his compartment where he tries to explain who he is and why he is so totally alienated from society.

THE MAYOR SAYS HE HAS STUDIED LITERATURE, PHILOSOPHY, AND writing. He has been a member of the working class, and he has experienced poverty.

His anger comes from being "left out of society." He has not rejected society, but it has rejected him, he says, cast him out because of his black skin. The black world on the surface has cast him out when he tried to fit into the white society. They both cast him out when he fought against both. He still suffers from the "conditioning" he received aboveground, conditioning that still causes him to doubt his self-worth and question his own "validity," he says.

All of the members of his community feel the same, he claims, as do all members of all the communities of underground homeless—the "Federation," as he calls it, which stretches along the East Side of Manhattan from Astor Place to 110th Street. All have been cast out and forced to find an alternative way of living.

The mayor left the surface five years ago, he says, but still feels insecure. "It's not enough to leave, they won't let you. Your past life above haunts you like a nightmare. That's why you sense anger here. Because they won't let us leave them completely. You always remember. You always hear those loud, ugly voices telling you you're doing something wrong because you're not doing it up there."

Often he wakes from sleep in a panic. "I only see darkness and I wonder, 'am I alive? What am I doing? How do I know that I exist?' I can't breathe, and I think that if I could take one breath into my lungs and fill my soul with air, I would be alive. If I could see some sort of light, I would be alive. If I was able to do something real, I'd be living.

"Yes, I've thought that if I go upstairs, I wouldn't always wake up in darkness. And I've thought about breathing real air and getting back into things up there . . .

"Maybe it is in the back of my mind that I'm not doing anything if it's not part of your society up there," he resumes. "But then I ask, 'Who am I up there? No one.' At least down here I can't be passed by or ignored. Here I am here. My job is to take care of these people."

He begins to rave. "Fuck the people on top! They want to exterminate us. We'll do anything to survive. Sure, we'd sacrifice them sons of bitches!" He quiets down directly after the outburst.

"This is home," he says more easily now. "This is where my conscious self meets reality. This is where my mind has been all my adult life. Underground."

As a child, he recalls, he thought he was from another planet. As an adult, he believed it. "All black men are looking in from the outside up there topside. But me, I was looking in at the black community from the outside, too. I was outside of outside. I was way, way out."

He grew up in a place like Harlem, which he wouldn't identify for fear his family would recognize him. "They would think this is a crazy life when, in reality, it's the only sane life for me and for everyone else down here."

In fact, it is better than just sane. "We may not have the comforts of living aboveground. But we are a superior people. We've purified ourselves. We don't allow just anyone to come and live with us. We allow only those who we can save, those who can believe in the human spirit above all else."

His favorite book is Claude Brown's *Manchild in the Promised Land*. "I read that book when it came out in the late sixties and I thought, 'That's me. How the hell did he know me? What is the message to me?' I also got shot that year, when I was thirteen. I even liked a girl with buckteeth. That's the first time I says to myself, 'Man, something just ain't right with you in this world.'"

He says he tried many routes to fit into society. He attended the City College of New York on a scholarship for a year. He joined a socialist group, then became part of the Revolutionary Communist Party, which was founded by one of the Black Panthers. He says he worked as a reporter, a youth counselor, a garbage collector, and even attempted to go to the police academy.

His passion throughout has been writing. "But I never want anyone on the outside to see my work, because they can't understand." He tries to explain, with metaphysical imagery. "When I tried to write before, no one cared what I went through, who I was. And writing, no matter what you're writing about, you're coming from the perspective of who you are. If you're invisible, your work means nothing. It has no soul to those who can't see you. It's transparent. I write from my soul, which is deeper than any man's out there. That's why it's invisible to them. It's beyond their simple understanding, their simple ways."

It was to explain all this, he says, that he invited me to visit his community despite the opposition of his advisers like J.C. He wanted someone "from the outside" to tell the world that he and his community are "better off" than those aboveground, those who are sick.

The mayor may see himself as Brown's "Manchild," but he is much more the "underground man" in Irving Howe's "Celine."

"A creature of the city, he has no fixed place among the social classes; he lives in holes and crevices, burrowing beneath the visible structure of society. . . . Even while tormenting himself with reflections upon his own insignificance, the underground man hates still more—hates more than his own hateful self—the world aboveground."

21

"City of Friends"

IN BROAD DAYLIGHT I SLIP BEHIND A GRAFFITIED BILLBOARD AND onto a rubble-strewn lot that hides from hurrying pedestrians along 34th Street, a block from Penn Station. I walk across the lot and into a small alleyway to a wooden door with a brass-colored handle, just as I've been told. The door opens smoothly into a very small room, almost an entryway, of a deserted building. In one corner, amid dusty brooms and discarded clothes, opens a jagged-edged hole that has been chopped through the concrete floor, and projecting up through the hole are two rungs of a rusted metal ladder. Another invitation to visit the underground.

As the door to the outside world closes, I pause and allow my eyes to adjust to the stagnant blackness that I sense at the bottom of the ladder. I am expecting a guide, who last night on a warm grate reluctantly promised to lead me to what he called "the camp" of about forty people in a disused tunnel here. He was supposed to meet me half an hour ago. He has given me some directions and I follow them now, thinking of how foolish I am to be doing this alone.

Down in the tunnel, the air is oppressive and it's even darker. I should be comforted by the absence of trains, but the dank emptiness increases my anxiety and sense of isolation. I wait motionless, hoping my mind will settle when my eyes adjust. Rhythmic water drops fall like deep drumbeats, and then the sound of tapping on

pipes begins, slow and dull at first, but then more erratic. Warnings of a trespasser.

My ankles twist and I struggle to keep my footing on the
gravel of the track bed. Sunlight occasionally filters down through
grates on the surface two or three stories above me. The light never
seems to reach the floor of the tunnel, yet suffuses the scene. My
senses are sharp, but my body seems to move in slow motion,
smoothly, almost automaton-like without conscious thought. It is
as if I've passed into a new dimension, but inwardly, into myself
rather than into the tunnel, and I am self-assured, impregnable.
Rats will not make me jump, or taps on pipes, or even as now, the
sudden blast of steam being released from a not-too-distant valve.

Eyes behind me, watching my back. I turn slowly, somehow
not surprised to see a man, about six feet tall, in a flannel shirt and
jeans, with long light-colored hair, beard, and mustache. He slowly
raises his arms as if holding a rifle, and soundlessly, he aims at me.
He squeezes the imaginary trigger once, then again, and again, his
thin body rippling with each evenly timed recoil. He looks directly
at me, coldly.

"It's OK," I hear myself saying soothingly. My heart seems
to have stopped. "It's OK," I repeat, "I'm just passing through."

The rifle follows me, firing again and again into my back, as
I move farther into the tunnel in search of the camp.

Again eyes seem to watch me. "Hello?" I finally ask, with a
shiver in my voice that sounds so foreign I think someone else is
speaking.

A laugh answers. "I see you met Rambo," it says. "His
mind's still stuck in 'Nam. Likes the tunnels cuz they remind him
of the jungle and he knows where he is," explains George, my
late-arriving guide, as he steps from the shadows. "He just can't
figure out who to fight."

"Brave girl," he says, trying to calm me. "I didn't think
you'd come."

I feel like he is breathing life back into me, and I'm so thankful that I want to hug him.

George holds a lantern, an old kerosene lamp, and leads me

to a side tunnel off the main tracks. Its shape is different from those I had visited before—smaller, with a low ceiling, more confining than subway tunnels and far more confining than spacious railroad tunnels. It is cool and damp, almost misty at parts, and lined with brick walls that are coated in soot.

I feel a sharp sting through my jeans at the knees, and fear rushes through my body as I begin to stumble.

"Watch your step!" George warns me too late. Someone catches me—a man but not George. He has been silently walking alongside me and keeps me from a bad fall over a sharp wire.

His name, he says, is Chud. It isn't, really, but a nickname he chose for me to call him after he read one of my newspaper articles on the underground homeless that interviewed some transit workers, as well as some homeless who live on the surface, who call underground homeless CHUDs, short for Cannibalistic Human Underground Dweller. The label is partly humorous, but in part, too, CHUDs are feared as subhuman feral dwellers of the netherworld.

"We don't eat people," he tells me immediately, while George laughs. "Those stories are wrong. We don't eat dogs neither. Sometimes, the 'runners' don't make it down with food, we eat 'track rabbits' [rats], but I ain't never ate no human. I ain't never sinned like that."

That's good to know, I say uncomfortably.

Chud shows me the wire I had tripped over. It stretches directly across the tracks, from one wall to the other, at shin height, and just beyond it shards of broken glass twinkle yellow in the light of George's lantern. He calls it a "Vietnam trap," intended to both frighten and impede any strangers and, at the same time, warn the community of the intruders. Small strips of white cloth mark the wire where it is nailed to the walls, alerting regular inhabitants to the trap.

After Chud's initial outburst, he becomes less talkative. Whenever I ask a question he does not like, he stays silent. So we don't talk much. George, on the other hand, can't stop talking, sometimes so fast that I lose the meaning of his words.

We enter a large, tile-walled chamber, with high ceiling, which could have been a waiting room at one time. Water drops sound different here, for some reason. The floor is firmer than in the tunnel, with less cushioning dirt and grime. I scrape an area with my shoe and the underlying surface, perhaps tile, reflects dully the lantern glow.

Against the far wall of the cavern leans a row of cardboard homes. Several dozen men and a few women sit sullenly around two fires in this underground shantytown, watching us enter.

"Hey, what's she doing here?" a man finally asks. "Why'd you bring her here?" A general disgruntled murmur seconds his disapproval.

"Yo, she found it on her own and came down alone," George lies. "I just saw her at the hanger. I couldn't let the CHUD people get her, now could I?" he asks, joking at my expense. After a second, a tinkling laughter breaks the tension.

"Hey, honey," says a lean, handsome black man, "you didn't let them scare you bad, did you?" He is called Fay and his wrist literally goes limp as he approaches. "Come have a seat by me and April," he reaches for my hand. "You look white as a ghost," he titters.

April looks up, the fire lighting her eyes. She looks as frightened and vulnerable as I feel.

"His name is Fay," a man named Slim says, "and he's a bit . . . you know," his voice trailing into a giggle.

"Now you better watch what you say, honey buns," Fay warns Slim, drawing his hands to his hips in an exaggerated pose. To me he says, "I do the cooking around here."

The community is well defined by duty, and the duties are allotted by the boss, Sam, whose title is mayor. I was introduced to each by name and by job.

Fay, as he said, is the community's cook. April is the nurse. Chud is in charge of security. He is helped by Beeper, a weasel-like little man, who got his name because he was always first to detect a stranger in the tunnel and alert the community. George is a runner, along with Slim and Rex. They collect food and other necessities from the surface, often running scams in Penn Station that run the gamut from begging to pickpocketing to selling drugs, sometimes "drugs" that are just sugar or another inert substitute.

"Most of these people are too scared to go back up," explains George. "Somebody's got to take care of them."

"And some people just need to be needed," says Sam, the mayor.

He is a small, white man in his early forties, with round wire-rim John Lennon glasses and a tie-dyed shirt, who likes to talk about the sixties. He was trained as a sociologist. He is also a frightening man, one of the most frightening I have ever met in the tunnels.

The community elected him mayor, and there is no doubt they consider him their leader. He takes care of them as if they are family, even children, young children. Even men older than he are treated as five-year-olds at times.

Sam's theory is that individuals remain stuck at the mental age at which they drop out of society: A thirty-five-year-old who got hooked on drugs at fifteen thinks that society only expects of him now what they did when he was fifteen. Those homeless people who live on the fringes of society, particularly those who live underground, have failed even to see—let alone experience—the development and socialization that is considered normal in people who live aboveground, he says. Sam also believes that most members of his community were pushed out of society at age five or six, as products of dysfunctional families, even though society may officially make them drop out at a much older age.

Sam's management style is much like a parent, sometimes shaming members who fail to complete a task by berating them before the group, sometimes threatening to expel them from the underground family. He decides who should do which chores, and when the community is rousted from one tunnel, he decides where they will settle next. One day he sends April for water from a broken pipe in a distant tunnel; another time he has her mend clothes and sew old cloth pieces into blankets. He directs George

to run a scam to get medicine. Whatever money is collected aboveground is put into a jar every night. Sam is its custodian. Only Sam
dispenses from the collective funds. No one can leave "the camp"
without his permission. He discourages members from trying to
resume lives aboveground.

When Sam lived aboveground, he was a social worker. In
1982 he began working with the tunnel homeless, and about the
same time he divorced his wife—for adultery, he says—and she has
custody of their only daughter. Not long afterward, he was fired
for what he terms "eccentricities."

"Tell her about the final hour," George says with a mischievous laugh.

In the final hour of his working life, Sam stripped down to
the nude in his office—to demonstrate, he says, "how vulnerable
people are in communicating." I ask him several times what that
means but never understand his explanation.

He refused psychiatric counseling after the incident, dismiss-
ing it as "a societal brainwashing ploy where they impose on me
their beliefs of who I should be," he says intensely, "so I would
just fit in and not disturb society, just like a robot." Instead, he
decided to come where he could be free, completely himself, he
says, to the tunnels that he found while working with their inhabitants.

What drove him underground, he explains, was "red tape.
All that fucking red tape," he begins, with voice rising and face
reddening. "How can you help anyone when there's that red tape?
Kids would get abused to death in foster care and you couldn't get
them out without that red tape. Two of them were killed before I
got through the red tape. How can you live with that?" he demands, angrily waving his arms.

"How can you live in a society like that?" he asks, more
quietly now. "The rules don't make sense. They're not based on
human needs or caring. The laws and the rules, and what they call
morals, are logical and warped. They are based on money, not right
or wrong. They might as well have come from a computer. No one
really cares up there. Down here this is basic survival. We make

our own laws. Our laws are based on what we feel, not preconceived notions of morality. We call it the 'human morality.' That's what we live by."

"Human morality" is similar to the phrase "human religion," which I have heard from the members of other underground communities. Neither has specific rules or ethics so far as I can learn. Adherents appear to equate the concept to honesty and caring.

I suppose, because he is white, I think I can understand Sam better, but he scares me with swings of mood that are extreme and change rapidly. At one moment we are discussing Woodstock, and suddenly he flares off on a tirade about where society is going wrong, so furious he seems close to violence. Beeper seems to be the only member of the community who attempts to calm Sam during these outbursts, and he pays for it. More than once Sam shows the strength of a man twice his size and actually throws the weaker man out of his way.

Why do you put up with it? I ask Beeper. Why does the community accept such behavior?

"He loves and he cares," says Beeper. "More than anyone else here in this world, he cares. It's not him who gets mad; it's them drugs he used to take."

Sam tells Dopey—so named because he is lazy and acts dumb—to get wood and water. Dopey refuses to get up from the floor. Sam pulls a knife and stands over him, threatening to throw him out and never let him back into the community. Beeper offers to do the chores in place of Dopey, but the mayor won't hear of it. The community stands back, watching. Sam won't back down. Eventually Dopey limps down the tunnel, disappearing from sight.

"Why'd you do that?" April asks. "Dopey wasn't feeling well."

"Because he's depressed, April," the mayor calmly explains. "Someone had to make him get up."

The following day I half expect to find out that Dopey has returned and killed Sam in the night. Instead, the two are talking cheerfully, Dopey clean and smiling brightly.

Rex is another remarkable figure here. He says he is rarely

underground and is not a member of the community, but they consider him part of the family.

He prefers to remain in Penn Station, begging, hustling, or running scams, including taking money from other homeless and promising to return with a radio or coat. He claims he makes a "good living" and that he recently was assigned an apartment by one of the homeless advocacy organizations.

"But other people need it more than me, so I gave it up," he says. "Don't regret it at all. I felt boxed in that place. No one around but me. I could hear myself thinking," he laughs almost shyly. "I guess it was good. Didn't have to worry about people sneaking up behind me when I was asleep. But it was weird, man. I couldn't sleep in the bed. Had to sleep on the floor. And then I just felt like I was crazy. I brought people [from the station] up to stay with me, but that felt even lonelier. It just wasn't natural, not like the tunnels where people come together."

Yet he insists he isn't a member of the tunnel community. He often comes down to meals, according to other members, although he says he rarely does. Whenever they need something from "up top," as they say, "Rex will find a way to get it." Sometimes it is medicine, sometimes blankets and coats, sometimes money.

"They took care of me once," he explains. "This guy knifed me in the station once because I sold him fake drugs. I couldn't go to the hospital because I was on probation and I would go back to jail." Somehow he found the tunnel's entrance, where he passed out. The next thing he remembered was Fay standing over him, laughing. The community nursed him back to health, and he repays them by helping when they need him.

Rex is not alone among the community for having had trouble with the law. Most of the members of the camp have been in jail. Beeper was in for hustling drugs, for example. "But I ain't dealt since joining the community," he says, "'cept of course the occasional vic." A "vic" is a person who is easily taken advantage of or victimized. The camp boasts it is drug- and alcohol-free.

After a while I stop visiting the camp. Sam is uncomfortable with me. He complains I'm too busy taking notes to listen.

"Truth isn't in words; it's in listening," he says. "If you listen to us, you can make the rest up and tell more of the truth than if you write down the cold facts.

"I'm doing what's best for each and every one of these people," he contends. "I know what these people need. I treat each of them differently, as I assume you've noticed. I treat April according to her needs, Rex according to his, Beeper for his, and so on. I am a trained counselor and I know each and every member of our community distinctly. Our little community down here is immune from the cruelty and horror of the topside world. We are growing into a city down here, and we are all friends, the definition of which you cannot learn without living with us, under my wing."

They tell me not to come down alone again, warning me that there are more Vietnam traps. If I wish to come again, I am to leave a note under a brick by the door and someone will come up for me. Several times I do this, but, after a month, I stop asking to visit. A couple of times I bring supplies and leave them at the brick.

I meet George on the street and when he asks why I haven't visited, I'm embarrassed. I say that my last conversation with Sam was very disturbing, but George believes I'm repelled by the physical environment.

"It got too much for you, didn't it?" he asks gently. "I know. It's OK though, kid. I wish you could understand how it is. It would be easier for you. See, no matter how ugly the camp seems to you, it don't matter to us, we don't see it that way because we're friends, and that matters more. For most of us, it's the first time we ever had a real friend."

He smiles brightly at the thought. "We're a city of friends. That's what Sam says." He winks at me and walks away without saying good-bye.

The phrase sounds familiar and I find it in Walt Whitman:

"I dream'd in a dream, I saw a city invincible to the attacks
  of the whole rest of the earth;
I dream'd that was the new City of Friends."

22

Women

"I LOVE THE LONELINESS OF THE TUNNELS," BRENDA SAYS SOFTLY. "It seeps through your ears and your skin. It's like a hug with nothing to hold you. It's an understanding."

Her mouth does not smile, but the frown lines in her young face smooth away.

"I guess it comforts me," she says, looking up from Central Park into the January sky. "Do you understand? It's like when the stars fill your eyes with their light, and they fill your emptiness. It's the same understanding, in a way. The same connection. That's what matters."

She speaks so softly that her words are almost lost to the night. She is mesmerized by the secure image of herself she has created with her words, living that idealization, almost forgetting that I am listening.

I have to strain to hear, and strain, too, to understand. I have questions, but I don't want to interrupt her. For the few hours we are together here, we could be old college roommates who have lost touch, and she is telling me about the few years since graduation.

Brenda is my age, twenty-four. She is a slight, light-complexioned black woman. She went to Dartmouth and majored in English literature, but she never finished. She stumbled into the tunnels four years ago with a man who was supplying her with drugs, and now she doesn't want to leave, because the tunnels comfort her.

What else comforts you? I ask.

"I'll tell you what doesn't comfort me," she says. She pulls her knees to her chest for warmth and then gives a rueful smile, exposing a missing tooth, which one of her boyfriends recently knocked out. "Touch doesn't comfort me. Men's touches don't comfort me anymore; they repulse me. When a man gets on top of me, I go completely numb, like I'm water miles away from shore.

"Talk doesn't comfort me, either. The tunnels comfort me, I guess, because they're mine. They know what's inside me and they feel the way I do. Always. Like, you know, when you bomb a test but it's sunny outside? Well, that doesn't happen in the tunnels," she laughs. "They're always dark inside, like me, but inside, I'm like the tunnel—dark, winding, and twisting."

Tonight Brenda has come back aboveground to the world she left almost four years ago. For several hours she is lucid and talkative, completely different from the evasive, almost shrunken young woman who, while not hostile, moved away whenever I approached her in the tunnels.

I FIRST SAW HER IN A TUNNEL ON THE UPPER WEST SIDE OF MANhattan. She was sitting on a small stool, wearing black stretch pants, as she scraped carrots and cut them into a large blackened iron pot on the grate over a campfire. An opened bag of potatoes waited their turn to go in with the pasta and tomato sauce and melting cheese. The odor, carried with the smoke from the fire toward the entrance of the tunnel, was sharp but pleasant, more appetizing than the sight. She smiled but when I neared, she looked down at her work. She said, please to excuse her, because she had to get lunch ready.

As she spoke, a large black man came to her side and scowled at me, hands on hips.

"She's a reporter doing a book," Brenda told him. "She wants to ask me some questions."

He looked me up and down scowling.

"She paying you?" he demanded, as if I weren't there, though he looked straight at me. Had she not been there, I would have felt in danger.

I waited for Brenda's reply. Instead, she looked nervously up at me from bowed head.

"No," I answered for her.

"Then you ain't gonna talk," he said flatly, still watching me.

She shrugged and bent back for another potato.

I began to speak to him, but he waved away my words. "Ain't gonna talk without money," he said. Brenda busied herself even more, as if increasingly uneasy at what could become a confrontation. So I said good-bye and turned to leave.

"Bring some money and I'll tell you stories you won't believe," he called to my back.

When I looked back, Brenda seemed embarrassed. "Hey," she said, "bring me some cigarettes next time."

"You get out of here now!" her man yelled at me. "And you shut up, bitch!" he shouted at Brenda.

She did, and I left quickly.

I bought cigarettes the next time I was near her tunnel, and was talking to a group of homeless in the Rotunda at West 79th Street in Riverside Park when she appeared. Most of the people greeted her, and one woman gave her a hug.

"Hey," she asked me loudly, "did you get my cigarettes?"

I tossed the pack to her over the heads of the group.

She seemed surprised as she caught it. "Thanks," she said as people rushed to share her gift. She gave all of the cigarettes away except for one, which she lit. Then she walked off.

TONIGHT IN CENTRAL PARK OCCURS BY ACCIDENT. WE HAPPEN INTO each other outside a movie theater, and on the spur of the moment decide to go inside to see the feature, *The Fisher King*. Brenda wants to see Robin Williams. I am interested in seeing a popular film that deals with homeless people.

Brenda immediately feels threatened, unused to a crowd in close quarters.

"Don't let anyone touch me," she almost pleads, her voice tight. "I can't stand it in here if anyone touches me." Brenda is generous with her hugs in the tunnels, but here her eyes dart and her body jumps at any movement close by. Half of the movie passes before I feel her relax. She even laughs at one point.

Afterwards, she invites me to go to the park and lie nude like Robin Williams and Jeff Bridges in the movie. Even if she could get me into the park at night, I say, I'm not much for lying in the buff, particularly in cold weather. She invites me to what she calls her "secret place" anyway. I often have nightmares of being in the tunnels at night, of glaring eyes and desperate faces, but I go with Brenda.

She leads me into a tunnel. It has a surreal calmness to it as we walk. White moonlight falling through grates lends a pale and glowing purity to the tunnel. Water drips from pipes soothingly. We could be walking through a nature trail. We seem to have gone miles.

Brenda has been silent for so long that I wonder if she has forgotten me. My old fears return as I worry about getting lost if she suddenly disappears. We emerge finally, next to Central Park, and we compromise: I will go into the park if she promises to get me out safely. And the clothes stay on. She laughs, but I am still very anxious. I covered the Central Park jogger trial several months earlier, and the graphic testimony of the gang rape and brutalization of the young woman victim are fresh in my mind.

"Look," Brenda says abruptly, "you don't have to do this."

I say I'll go on.

"Well then, get a grip, girl! Man!" she orders in an unexpectedly strong voice. I do, or at least I pretend to, and if you pretend long enough, it becomes real. That is one of the first lessons Brenda teaches me.

We eventually settle on grass off the path. "No pictures," she insists, meaning no details of her relatives or past that would identify her to her family.

"I stay with men so they can supply me, not because they

protect me," she volunteers. "I don't care what happens to me. The worst has happened. It can happen again and I won't care."

You've given up trying to be happy?

"No," she replies, "just given up fighting. It's not so bad being unhappy. It even becomes comforting. It's like that's the real me. I'm not afraid of anything, not even of fear. I'm not afraid to be afraid."

I'm about to suggest that she sounds like she wants to convince herself of that.

"Now, you, you're afraid," she says. "That's why some of the people laugh at you. They can see in your eyes that you're afraid to be like us, not because you might be cold or hurt but because you're afraid how you'd feel."

Well, people do talk to me anyway, I say defensively.

"Yeah, they know you're trying to be brave and they appreciate that," she says in a softer tone. "They also feel sorry for you."

I laugh, but I'm still stung. "Well, being afraid to feel something is better than feeling nothing at all," I insist.

"No matter what anyone says, you can't stop having feelings," she goes on. "Sometimes I'll sit there reading," she points toward a park bench on which two men lie bundled in sleep, "like the other day, I was reading a copy of the *Post* about Liz Taylor's wedding and suddenly my face was wet. I think I was crying, I don't know." She pauses and looks away, then asks, almost plaintively, "Why can't they just leave her alone?"

Why don't you leave the tunnels? You're smarter and could be more attractive than most women and could do very well, I say.

"Because I don't want that life, I don't want that pressure," she says. "I don't want to be fighting all the time, struggling to be someone. I'm sick of pretending I'm white, or that I'm a man. I hate pretending to be an insider in an insider's world when everything about me says 'outsider.'" Angry now, she pauses for a long minute, and I think she is moving to another subject when she turns toward me in almost slow motion.

"Furthermore," she declares firmly to emphasize an important point about herself, "I can't see past my next hit. That's all that matters to me. There's no greater pleasure or need. I can't imagine anything up here that can compete with my next high. I don't even want it to be different."

I peer at her, wondering if her revelation was only to prevent me from pitying her, but she meets my eyes without wavering. The moment has been too emotional, and we stand up.

"Now you can write anything you want about me," she says as we leave the park, "but I told you the truth. I don't want you to feel sorry for me, and you should not think you should have done something to help me. You can't. If I wind up face down one of these days, you should know you couldn't have done anything to prevent it. Don't think you're God."

Our mood lightens as she walks me to a subway. She wants me to take a cab home.

"You're such a kid," she laughs. "It's late, and it's dangerous for you."

She comes down onto the subway platform with me, easing her thin hips past a turnstile, and she hugs me and urges me to be careful as I enter the last car of the train. Out of the back window I watch as she first waves, then looks both ways before slipping off the platform and into the darkness along the tracks.

I see Brenda several times more, but we never talk again. Each time she is with a large man, never the same one. Usually she does not even say hello, although we always manage to share a small smile. Every one of her men makes it clear they distrust me, and she defers to them, even to asking permission with a glance before speaking.

This behavior is common among homeless women, particularly younger ones. Despite what Brenda said about herself, the women usually seek the man for protection, and in exchange, they allow the man to be totally dominant. The bargain is somewhat paradoxical because the women sacrifice the same autonomy and independence in the tunnels that they would relinquish in a homeless shelter, yet they refuse to enter a shelter program, they often say, in order to keep their freedom.

Homeless women also often allow themselves to be physically abused by their men. Again they compare the treatment in tunnels to what occurs in shelters. Brenda said the risks are the same, that women are as dangerous as men in this respect.

Still, Brenda may well have been addicted not only to crack but also to such men. "Maybe it's my punishment," she said half-seriously one time. "Maybe I'm meant to be with men like this because they're as bad as I am."

Brenda disappeared abruptly from the West Side tunnels. No one has seen her for a while. Many stories are offered: A boyfriend killed her when he suspected she was cheating on him. Her father found her and took her home. She killed herself. She just decided on her own to go aboveground and try to make it there after all. Or, one person told me, she has gone deeper underground, to live with a community that will not allow her to return.

FEW TUNNEL WOMEN ARE LIKE BRENDA. DEMOGRAPHICALLY, THE tunnels reflect the homeless population aboveground, except for fewer elderly people underground. An estimated 40 percent of the underground homeless are females, with the number having risen rapidly in recent years. An increasing number are white.

Most women go underground initially with a man and occasionally, with a woman. Many are addicted, or were at one time. Many have families who would care for them, they say, but they refuse to give up their drugs or their autonomy.

Michelle

MICHELLE HAD LIVED WITH TWO MEN ON A CATWALK IN THE TUNNELS under Grand Central, "but that was when I was pretty messed up," she explains. Now she lives in a rehabilitation center for women. She is one of Sergeant Henry's success stories. He persuaded her to enter the rehabilitation center where she is waiting for an apartment whose rent, she says, her father will provide.

She is more than petite, she is tiny, barely four foot four inches and fine as a bird. She could pass as a teenager with her Walkman wired into her ears, bobbed hair, jeans, a soft brown leather coat, and white sneakers. She defines her brown Italian eyes with thick, steady lines of an eye pencil. But when she speaks, her mouth sinks without teeth, and suddenly she looks far older than her thirty-five years. She has been clean of drugs for almost a year, she says.

Michelle is eager to tell her story, though she rambles, frequently repeating herself, and trails off into silence in mid-sentence at times.

"I was stupid," she says. Through a numb smile, she tells how she gave birth to a baby in the tunnels, when she first settled there. That was five years ago she thinks, or longer—she's not sure; the drugs have thinned her memory. She went into the tunnels with a man she no longer remembers to escape confessing to her family that she was pregnant, she says.

She believes the baby was born alive, a boy, but she doesn't know what happened to him.

"I'd like to know what I did with him," she says matter-of-factly, without a hint of emotion. "Who took him?"

Some tunnel homeless found Michelle underground, severely overdosing, and carried her up to Sergeant Henry. In rehab, she had to learn everything again, including her name and how to tie her shoes.

"I thank God every day I wake up and I'm alive," she says dimly, as if in a dream.

Then she wanders off, talking to herself and saying hello to every passerby. Some men raise their eyebrows speculatively, but after a few words, they pass on. She meanders down the broad marble halls of the station waving her hands at strangers. It's difficult to see how she, who remembers very little of her past and seems to have virtually no future, is a success story. But then, she once roamed the tunnels in bare feet, eating roaches and garbage to survive and turning tricks for the drugs that have almost destroyed her.

Gwen

UNLIKE MICHELLE, GWEN HAS CONTROL. SHE VISITS HER MOTHER at an Amsterdam Avenue apartment on the Upper West Side twice a week and stays overnight there. She chooses not to live there, however, because of "the stress" in relations between the women. Her mother does not know Gwen lives on the streets and below them most of the week.

Gwen, who says her full name is Gwendolyn Scott, is twenty-nine years old, a healthy-looking black woman with a ready smile. She has lived on the streets or in tunnels for five years, at first in the 72nd Street tunnel with two men, Jess and Stone, who kept her safe. There is less hassle underground than on park benches, she says, and no one robs you. As more and more people came into that underground area, garbage and makeshift sleeping quarters accumulated and police moved in regularly to clear out the homeless. Gwen gave up on tunnel life, she says, when she realized she did not want to go aboveground anymore. "I didn't want to become like the mole people," she says.

Now she is part of the Rotunda Gang of about forty homeless who sleep in the Rotunda in the park at 79th Street. They are docile, but park workers have orders to disperse any cluster of homeless people that might frighten citizens using the park in the daytime. Several public toilets stand near the stone structure, their gagging smells of urine and feces at times drifting up into the vault areas.

It's early on a rainy November morning when I hurry to the Rotunda to meet Gwen and her current man, Rick, whose full name is Roderick van Hollar, she says. Everything is a shade of gray, including the calm, slate-hued Hudson. A mist across the river blurs the tops of some buildings. Most of the homeless have left or are packing up for a day of trudging the city, before returning at night, but a number still remain. Papa, so named because he is the community's eldest, is still asleep, snug within cardboard walls and surrounded by garbage bags full of clothes and other possessions. His coat hangs on an outside hook in the stone wall as I pass quietly.

Gwen calls out a welcome from a balcony overlooking the river, which stops the hostile looks and clicking teeth of a group of men. Her man is still in bed, watching me skeptically as I approach, and she pulls her house robe together more tightly. A gray Yankee baseball cap, its peak turned backward, holds her hair until she exchanges it for a black turban. She pulls on hefty hiking boots and proudly shows me a Ziplock bag of Elizabeth Arden jewelry that Rick found in a trash can.

She is on the street because of alcohol and drugs, she says. She is trying to change, but she has been to most of the city-run detoxification centers. Her last detox visit was six months ago, which was where she met Rick. Detox only works for seven days, she explains, and you are out on the street. Not enough time to kick the habit. She and Rick have applied for admission to another center, one that would keep them from drugs for six to eight weeks, but the waiting list is long. Meanwhile they live in the Rotunda community where no overt use of drugs or alcohol is permitted. In part this is because the Parks Department would close the camp if it saw such abuse, but in part, too, because most of the homeless here are trying to stay straight, says Gwen.

According to her, breaking the drug habit is more difficult underground. "You get afraid to go up and be seen by people," she says, "but then you get more depressed and lonely in the tunnels, so you do drugs again."

Both she and Rick want to work. She has had many jobs, including home care for elderly couples, which she wants to do again. Rick has just passed the sanitation workers exam and is waiting to be called at a drop-in center. Until something comes up, the two visit museums and libraries, Gwen says, to stay away from temptation. The Egyptian room at the Museum of Natural History is their favorite.

"I'm just a rookie," Rick says, out of bed now and willing to talk as Gwen feeds some regular pigeon visitors. "I've only been without housing for two and a half years, but Gwen, she's a veteran. Right, hon?" he calls out.

She laughs. "Yeah, veteran of the homeless life. Seen it all and lived just about everywhere, and the worst is the tunnels. They trick you. You think you're safe because no one can see you and you can't see yourself in the darkness. But you can't see beyond yourself, either," she says.

Dericka

DERICKA IS THE OPPOSITE OF GWEN. RATHER THAN STRONG AND self-possessed, she is so shy that she often hides her face in her hands, sitting for hours at a time, rocking back and forth. She doesn't cry; she withdraws and seeks to erase her memories.

She was physically abused by her boyfriend of four years, who whipped her with a belt. The relationship was born of sorrow after her brother died of a drug overdose. She had cared for her brother, six years her junior, as if he were her son, and she feels overwhelming guilt that she did not insist that he get help to end his addiction.

Another underground homeless woman, Sheila, found Dericka sleeping on a park bench and brought her into the tunnels. Now the tunnels are an effort to mask the shame she has built around herself.

"I live down here because there are no mirrors," she says. "I can't look at myself anymore." She believes she deserves the dirt and darkness. "I hope my children never know me. I hope they never know the scars I carry inside my heart."

The fear of seeing their reflections, perhaps when passing a store window aboveground or in some other way, runs through the comments of many homeless women who live or have lived underground. Men often admit they hide in the tunnels in shame that they cannot provide for their families, but none of the men ever told me they wanted to avoid seeing their physical image. Women, aside from being more aware of appearances, sometimes hint that they can even see their inner selves in the reflections that strike them unaware when they are on the streets.

Sheila and Willie

SHEILA HELPS HERSELF BY HELPING DERICKA. SHE IS A MOTHER FIG-
ure, in her early thirties, who thrives on responsibility for weaker
sisters and brothers, children and parents. In Bernard's tunnel, she
is the den mother, making rounds on colder winter days with
blankets and coaxing food down men who are barely conscious after
exhausting their drugs and whiskey. She has a natural energy that
is paced, not frenetic.

Sheila seldom uses drugs, but sometimes drinks herself into
oblivion. She is only sober and clean when I visit, a blue bandanna
tying back her hair and a generous smile of welcome. Her smile
warms the entire tunnel, one man says.

She came into the tunnel with Willie, her common-law husband fifteen years her senior. They met in the Douglas Housing
Project, which rises tens of stories between 100th and 105th
streets, between Amsterdam and Manhattan avenues on the Upper
West Side. Sheila had moved into the project with her family. At
the time, Willie worked for the city, but he is a drug addict who
recognizes that he will die soon.

Willie does not blame society. He accepts responsibility for
his own fate. He does not delude himself, as many addicts do, by
insisting he is not addicted and that come next month, he'll be
clean. He only regrets Sheila, that she came into the tunnels with
him but deserves better; he promises that one day he will get her
out.

She moved in with him at Douglas, but he missed a few days
of work, as she tells it, and got fired. One day they found their
apartment padlocked against them, with their belongings on the
roof. So they lived on the roof of the twenty-story apartment house
for months before moving into the public bath and toilet facility
at 104th Street in Riverside Park. When they were locked out of
the bathroom, they moved into the tunnels.

As Willie's health worsens, Sheila seems to get stronger, as if
responding to the increasing responsibility toward him. She has
never held a job, and the idea of looking for work makes no sense

to her. Willie spends any of the money she makes on drugs, she explains simply. Their dilemma is obvious: Willie does not want to give up drugs, and Sheila does not want to give up Willie. To the extent that an outsider can judge, they love each other.

One day in early spring Willie disappeared. Talk among the tunnel dwellers had it that he had been killed by a drug dealer he owed. Others believed he had been arrested. Sheila checked the hospitals and police stations and found out nothing. Sheila never gave up believing that Willie would come back, though other tunnel dwellers tried to convince her that he was gone for good.

Fran and Shorty

SHEILA AND WILLIE'S RELATIONSHIP WAS COMPLETELY DIFFERENT FROM their tunnel neighbors, Fran and Shorty. Fran is a plump white woman in her mid-twenties, blond and small-boned, looking more a teenager than a woman. She is a Nebraska farm girl with blue eyes sometimes wide with innocence. Shorty is about forty, short, and black. He is barely able to walk because of all the needles that have been stuck behind his knees and into his knee caps to inject drugs.

Both live for drugs. Shorty sends Fran into Broadway to turn tricks to support their addiction while he does crossword puzzles in the park. She is afraid to refuse, even to talk much. He often beats her, mostly if he sees her speaking to another person in the tunnel. Twice he has fractured her jaw.

"Why do you take this shit from this man?" Bernard demands almost every time we meet her, whether Shorty is present or not. He detests Shorty and is furious that Fran shows no will to resist him. Fran only sits passively and stares at the ground, and the light from the campfire at the tunnel's mouth exaggerates the multitude of needle scars up and down the insides of her soft white arms.

Cathy and Joe

CATHY AND JOE LIVE IN A BUNKER IN THE SOUTH END OF THE WEST Side Amtrak tunnel. She is an attractive woman, shy but with a bright and easy smile. He is nervous at times, but understandable for anyone living underground. In fact, they seem out of place in the tunnels, clean and well dressed. Neither use alcohol or drugs, at least not obviously. Her mother, a homeless woman living on a park bench, introduced me to the couple. Joe was occupying a nearby bench, and Cathy was living with her father outside Manhattan. They married, and now both are homeless, a condition about which she is embarrassed. He is looking for work, but refuses to allow her to do the same.

For some time, tunnel dwellers have thought Cathy is pregnant, partly because of her appearance but also because of the way she has been behaving. Bernard doubts it, however. "I think she is just acting that way to try to get Joe to move them out of the tunnels," he says.

LIFE TURNS OUT UNPREDICTABLY AT TIMES. FRAN AND SHORTY, against high odds, have returned to her Nebraska farm. They leave a mess of syringes and human waste, but the community cleans it up almost without complaint, pleased they have gone away. Everyone hopes they make it, but doubts they will.

Life also turns out totally predictably, too.

Sheila never doubted that Willie would come back, although everyone else suspected he had been killed or just died elsewhere. Few believed he had left for another woman. "I love him," she would say. "I still do. I know he's gonna come back, so I'm just waiting. He used to tell me this was no place for me, that I deserve to be a queen somewhere."

Willie did return, and took Sheila to live in a Single Rent Occupancy (SRO) hotel near Riverside Park. He was drug-free and had a job. He refused to let her bring any old belongings from the tunnel. They were to build a new life, with fresh things. He bought her new clothes, and told her she should never go into tunnels again.

"They were doing great," Bernard remembers. "They were like new people. Sheila was really pretty," he says, surprised by the effect of the new environment.

Soon after, Willie collapsed and a few weeks later died of AIDS. The day after he died, which was shortly after her thirty-first birthday, the hotel threw Sheila out for nonpayment of rent. The rent had been overdue for months, it turned out.

Willie's family refused to allow Sheila to attend the funeral. They believe she gave Willie AIDS. The strength she had before seems gone. She panhandles now, usually drunk. Bernard has sought her out several times, but she refuses to return to the tunnels.

"As bad as it is down here," says Bob, "it's a hell of a lot worse out there. She can't take care of herself. Down here at least she has somewhere to belong."

She refuses. "I promised Willie I'd never go back," she says while devouring a hamburger. She puts it back on the plate carefully and dabs her trembling mouth with a flimsy paper napkin. "He said I was better than the tunnel, that he was sorry he brought me down."

"But he took me higher than anyone ever did," she says after a pause.

Even in the tunnel? I ask.

"Even in the tunnel, or on the roof, or in the park. Everywhere," she says, picking at her glistening french fries. "He loved me, and that doesn't happen much in this world. I would never have known what it's like to be happy without Willie."

23

Jamall's Story

WHEN CHER DIED, THE SKY CRIED ALL DAY. IT CRIED DUSTY tears, sometimes full and heavy, other times as light as mist coming from the clouds. She said she was glad the sky wasn't bright and laughing at her, sparkling at her with its freshness. That always made her feel like she was missing out on some great wonder that was right before her but beyond her reach. But the day she died, the sky was sad for her. She told Jamall that she felt like just another tear from the sky, and that when the sun came up, it would pick her way up into the sky. That was her funeral, Jamall says. She delivered her own eulogy as he held her hand. He watched her smile when she took her last breath. That night her cat howled something fierce. It upset Jamall so much that he had to leave. He wandered through the night, trying to decide which authority to tell of her death and what to do with her body. He believed he was having a nightmare. He couldn't feel the rain or the cold, so he was sure it was only a nightmare. He hoped he would awaken in the decayed and decrepit but cozy house in the Bronx where he and Cher and about a dozen others had been squatters, diverting a bit of electricity from other lines until a spark lit a fire, which caved in part of the roof. City workers boarded up the house for good and they were back on the street.

When morning came, Jamall turned his back to the sun and returned to the tunnel. He half-expected Cher's body to have been picked up by the sun, but it was still there, like a shell with a strong shaft of sunlight falling a few feet away. He thought it was giggling. It had taken her to the sky.

Jamall left that tunnel and never went back.

"At first I wanted to jump that sunbeam and kill it for taking her. Then I begged it to take me too. Then, now you ain't gonna believe this, I know, but I'll tell you anyway because it's the only thing in this whole fucking world that makes sense. There was something in that sunbeam smiling at me and saying 'Man, it's gonna be alright now. Just ride life the rest of the way, you're halfway there, ride all the way through. Cher's OK now. You got no more responsibility.' and I thought, yeah, you got nothin' more to lose; it's gone already. Just ride life through. I got my ticket right here," he says, slapping the bottle sandwiched precariously between his shaking thighs.

Jamall is thirty-nine but looks about fifty. "I'm just watching now. I done my living. I'm just watching and it's a funny shit scene. All these people, shit. They do dumb-ass things. It's hilarious, it really is."

Jamall talks louder and more aggressively as he gets midway through the bottle. Toward the last few sips he looks straight and forward, strangely sober.

"Sure I'll tell you my story," he said. "But let me tell you one thing first: If that sunbeam come by, I'm jumping on that ride, girl. I've been waiting for it to take me for a long time now. So just so's you understand me, I make no commitments," not even for a couple of hours to tell his story.

"If that beam comes for me, I'm gone lickety-split," he repeats. He leans back for a moment and takes a long drag out of a tired cigarette crusting with gray ash. Within a few minutes his thoughts glaze into a mumbling sleep. Pulling an old blanket over him, he smiles a childlike smile, dreaming, I think, of the sunbeam and Cher. He's saving his story for another day.

BUT JAMALL IS NOT EASY TO TRACK DOWN ANOTHER DAY. HE WAN-
ders the tunnels searching for his sunbeam, but refuses to settle
into one of them again.

"He's a man who tried to make it up there," says Sam, the
former social worker turned underground mayor. "He went
through rehab several times, and he beat it all until Cher died.
Then he reached for the bottle and never let go.

"You'll think he's over the edge, and up there, most people
would say he is. He talks to himself, to the sunbeam like it's Cher.
But you gotta remember that sanity down here is different from
sanity up there. If someone doesn't cry and scream down here,
they're insane. If they do it up there, they're insane.

"But he knows the tunnels better than most, and he'll tell you
stories. I doubt you'll be able to verify many of them, but I vouch
for him because I know people down here, those who lie and those
who don't," Sam says.

I find Jamall sitting on a crate watching the scene in Times
Square with a couple of drinking "associates." He stands out in the
signature green knit cap he wears even on hot days. It's well before
noon and his friends are well on their way to being drunk.

"You ain't going to rob us are you?" one of them asks. "You
white girls are dangerous in this neighborhood," he laughs, a gold
tooth flashing.

We chat for a while until Jamall stands, ready for the promised cup of coffee. He's fully sober, not a hint of whiskey on his
breath. "I try not to start drinking until the afternoon," he explains.

His personal story, like so many other homeless men I know,
centers on his mother.

"I was maybe eight and my mama brought us up north to get
away from Alabama and the bigotry. My papa disappeared from the
farm in 1962," when the civil rights marches were breaking segre-
gation barriers. "They say the KKK got him, but they never found
his body."

Jamall's mother came to New York first. "My mama was a
beauty and she had the voice. She used to talk about having a shot

at the Apollo Theatre [in Harlem] and she left to become a star,"
he smiles sadly. After a year she returned, told her family she was
a secretary, and brought Jamall and his older sister to New York.
"We loved New York before we even see it," he remembers. "It
was a freeman's land. Everyone was supposed to be free and equal
under the law. Course it wasn't like that."

His mama was not a secretary either. "I remember coming
home from school one day and I was crying. Mama asked what was
wrong. Kids told me she was a hooker, I said, and she got mad and
slapped me. She weren't no hooker or no prostitute, she said, she
was a call girl. Then she slapped me and said I was too old to cry.
That's when she started drinking."

Yes, he says with lowered head, he still feels responsible for
his mother's drinking.

Soon his mother began bringing men home and his sister,
then fifteen years old and "almost as pretty as my mama," decided
to run away. "The last time I saw her, she was standing at the fire
escape window with a pillow case of clothes, begging me to come
with her. I told her I had to stay and take care of Mama," he says.

For all her problems, Jamall's mother insisted that he finish
high school. He worked at odd jobs, never getting into trouble.
He never took any money from her hands, he says. "I told her it
was dirty money," he tells me, "and that made her drink more."

Jamall enlisted in the army, where he learned to drink, he
says. When he was discharged, he got into drugs. "No, I don't do
drugs anymore—unless you got some," he smiles eagerly. "I don't
have the money for it anymore."

On the promise of a job if he broke the drug habit, an army
friend got him a job as a garbage collector, but, with the money,
he went back to drugs. He met a girl who sent him to rehab. "We
did great, best time in my life. I took good care of her and my
mother. Thing was," he laughs, "she looked better when I was
stoned than when I was sober." He got fired, reentered rehab a
fourth time, and landed a post office job. He got married and had
two children, whom he refuses to discuss.

"And I started drugging again. My woman wanted no part of

me. This time I landed on the street," living in cardboard boxes on the streets. "I was tired and I just wanted peace, but I didn't want to be on the streets where my kids' friends would see me and make fun of them. That's why I went into the tunnels."

There he met Cher, who was six years his elder. "The first thing she told me was she was dying," he remembers. "I didn't believe her because she didn't look that bad. I mean she looked like she'd been on the streets, a bit beaten up, but she didn't look like dying."

They spent two years together. "At first it was for company," he says. "She didn't bug me about my habits and I didn't bug her. But she was a lady," he adds quickly. "She didn't do drugs or nothing. Drank some, when the pain got bad. We didn't plan to stay together, just worked out that way. She was like a mother, a sister, a friend, and then a girlfriend. I stopped doing drugs and laid low on the drink because she needed me. She'd make me go get baths and she'd sew my clothes. She didn't ask about my past, but I told her anyway. She didn't say anything, but last year she bought a Christmas card for me to send to my kids. I wouldn't. They're better off thinking I'm dead, I told her. They should know you love them, she said. I told her I'd kill myself before I signed that card. That was the only fight we ever had," Jamall says.

Cher never told him about her illness. She coughed a lot toward the end, and he tried to get her into a hospital against her wishes.

"She said she didn't want to die ignored," he says. "The hospitals, see, when you're on the street, they make you feel like dirt. But a couple of times she was so weak I carried her, and she cried all the way. When they weren't looking, she'd sneak back. Even if they were nice to her, and some were, she wouldn't have stayed. So she died with me, the way she wanted. I think she even picked the day."

"You're gonna ask, but I ain't going to tell you Cher's story. That's her's to keep in her grave. All I'll say is she was a good person. She thought she was bad, but she was the best I ever known."

Drink keeps him immune from pain, he says. If the cost of drink is dying, he'll take the drink. He doesn't care whether he's believed or not about his life or anything else.

"When I walk them tunnels, I see things no one would believe," he says. "I even met the devil down there. He got these fiery eyes, baby, you wouldn't believe! He couldn't get me, though, cuz Cher looks out for me."

He's visited the Dark Angel's den, Jamall says, but more frightening is "Ghost's Cliff," which he found at the end of a natural tunnel, or a cave that opens midway up a sheer cliff. The cliff overlooks a river far below, he says, presumably the Harlem River on the Upper West Side.

Homeless people, according to him, make their homes in the cliffs. "They're like little birds," he says. "You can hardly see them. They don't talk to each other with words. They use noise that sound like birds or maybe the wind." He lets out a hollow screech to mimic the sounds he heard.

"It's a weird place," he adds, with tales of human sacrifice and cannibalism. "I didn't hang around long enough to find out."

Whether Jamall's birdlike people are real, natural caves are likely to run through the Manhattan bedrock of schist. Geologists describe schist as crystalline rocklike granite that has a folded structure and cleaves along parallel planes or slabs like the layers of mica. The shifting earth leaves gaps between slabs, which rain and spring water widen into huge caverns. The schist almost reaches the surface under the grass of Central Park before dropping a hundred feet or more below the surface elsewhere on Manhattan. Workers digging the subway tunnels early in this century are said to have found a ten-thousand-year-old standing forest buried deep under the Upper West Side, presumably inundated in a mud slide and driven into a cavern by an Ice Age glacier.

More plausible than Ghost Cliff is the huge underground room "with a piano and tiled floor and mirrors all around" that Jamall says he found. An elderly homeless woman later described to me a similar room in which about fifty homeless people live. She added a fountain to the decor. "Fantastic," she said. "It was just beautiful." The two compartments could be the same, although Jamall and the woman placed them in different regions of the city, one in lower Manhattan and the other in Mid-Town on the West Side. These rooms are probably remnants of compartments dug and drilled out more than a century ago as part of the subway and rail systems and long abandoned and forgotten.

Jamall has come across communities in the tunnels that he has felt uncomfortable with, but he adamantly believes that no one in the tunnels should be evicted.

"They make a life for themselves," says Jamall. "They take care of each other better than up here. They sleep in places everyone up here has forgotten, and that's not stealing; that's being resourceful and surviving. Why take them out of there? They're not hurting no one. Give them some space and some time to heal."

24

Blade's Piece

"Be the inferior of no man, nor of any man be the superior. Remember that every man is a variation of yourself. No man's guilt is not yours, nor is any man's innocence a thing apart. Despise evil and ungodliness, but not men of ungodliness or evil. These, understand. Have no shame in being kindly and gentle, but if the time comes in the time of your life to kill, kill and have no regret."
— *William Saroyan, Epigraph,* The Time of Your Life

THERE WAS AN EXTRAORDINARY DEPTH TO BLADE'S CHARACTER that I never really understood. In his kindness and warmth, as well as in his cold cruelty, he taught me most about the extremes that tunnel life can bring out in a person. He also exposed a dark part of myself I had not believed existed.

By treating me as a tunnel dweller, Blade brought me down to the psychological level of tunnel life, a more dangerous and unpredictable level. Exploring the tunnels as an observer, an outsider, had its physical risks. However, when I became accepted as an insider, privy to the anger and violence that are almost hourly events underground, the tunnels exposed me to another dimension, beyond fear and danger, inside myself.

Blade had warned me. Early in one of his guided tunnel tours for me, he said, "The people down here are just like people topside, only tunnels bring out a different part in them. A part of them that topside people in fancy suits don't think they got. But they got it all right. It's inside everyone. Everyone's got the power to kill."

Blade never analyzed a situation or weighed the consequences of an action before he acted, whether on instinct or whim or some other irrational emotion. He never doubted himself. If strange sounds came from a tunnel, we would enter it. If hostile men seemed to bar a tunnel's entrance, we would go in if Blade felt "comfortable." However, if a tunnel, no matter how peaceful it appeared to me, "felt bad" to Blade, we would quickly turn and walk out. That was our basic understanding. He showed me tunnels as he chose. I listened, and followed. Our friendship grew from there.

He once scaled a thirty-foot tunnel wall to rescue a crying kitten, shivering on a high beam. Two hours later, he kicked an old man lying on the street because he hadn't moved quickly enough out of Blade's path. One night he carried a bleeding stranger, a victim of a robbery, fourteen blocks to a hospital because cabs refused to take an obviously nonpaying fare. (One cab did stop, but sped off when the driver spotted blood.) The next day Blade pulled a knife on a thirteen-year-old boy who was talking with friends, because Blade didn't like the youth's "attitude."

I SHOULD NOT BE EXPLORING TUNNELS, OR ANYTHING ELSE, WITH such a dangerously unstable person, but I still do not believe him dangerous. He explains events in tunnels and relationships between homeless underground communities with clarity and incisiveness.

"Anger does strange things to me," Blade says after I witness his confrontation with the teenager. "Feels like the pot of gumbo Mama used to make," he says, "simmering and maybe gonna boil over, but not sure it will drop down the side to the flame and sizzle or explode." Most tunnel people feel the same way, he suggests. Everyone here is suicidal, not fearing death and almost welcoming it, but with a primeval instinct for survival. On the surface, a bad day may lead to angry words, even violent outbursts, he says, but underground, it could mean someone's life, perhaps your own.

Perhaps my own, as it turned out.

BLADE IS IN HIS EARLY THIRTIES. HE ISN'T SURE EXACTLY WHERE IN his early thirties, but thirty-three sounds like a good number, he says. He is very large, six foot four and about two hundred hard pounds. He lost the sight in his left eye in a fight; it is milky white rather than brown, like his right eye. He creates an imposing presence with a street smart aura, a frightening effect that he turns up or down as needed.

His past is sketchy. He remembers only the bright red lipstick of his biological mother. He lived with a grandmother, his father's mother, and considers her his mother. She died when he was nine. He grew up quickly after that, he says. Though he always minded his manners, he says, because his grandma told him to always be polite, he got into trouble, first with kids in the same housing project in the Bronx. He was passed from relative to relative, then foster home to foster home. He never uses his name, Wilson. "I was Wilson when I was seven, but I'm Blade now." Blade became his name when he was part of a Brooklyn gang. "They call me that cuz I'm sharp and quick with the blade," he says proudly.

He tried to join the Marine Corps several times, he says, but was rejected. He claims to have been a Guardian Angel briefly, although the Angels have no record of him as a member.* He tells

---

*The Guardian Angels patrol the streets and subways in red berets and tough attitudes. Most members are between twenty and twenty-three years old and volunteer ten to fifteen hours a week to help protect commuters in the more dangerous areas of New York. They were organized in 1979 by Curtis Silwa, one of a group of young men picking up trash in the Bronx and recycling it and, in the process, intervening to help people from being mugged. After some heroic responses to crime, Silwa organized the thirteen-member Guardian Angels. Though commuters seemed to appreciate their help, the city government was skeptical of their intentions. Some city politicians went so far as to dismiss them as thugs. Today, they are a nonprofit volunteer organization with five thousand members around the world with branches in forty-five U.S. and ten foreign cities, including London, Liverpool, Sydney, Berlin, and Milan. They are still strong and generally respected despite a few scandals in which Silwa himself came forth and admitted that the Angels staged some rescues.

me at first that he is a graffiti artist, and as we pass graffiti in the
tunnels, he points out his tag, or signature logo. Sometimes as we
go he pauses to spray his tag on someone else's work. He has many
stories: Now he is just a hustler who spent his money on crack and
lived in the tunnels. Now he has cleaned himself up and works at
several odd jobs, and lives aboveground with lovers and friends.

I MET BLADE AT ST. AGNES' SOUP KITCHEN NEAR GRAND CENTRAL
Station. Blade is friendly and laughs often and openly, with a
happy-go-lucky air. He is a gentle and familiar face at the basement
kitchen, which serves soup and maybe a little hope to the homeless.
He is remembered because he always thanks the servers.

The tables are emptier than usual this late afternoon, probably
because the weather has turned warm and clear with springtime,
as I pour green Kool-Aid into cups. I bend down to get another cup
for a pregnant woman.

"Don't look at her that way, man," says a voice in a low and
threatening tone. I recognize the voice as Blade's and stand up
smiling, but instead of the woman a man stands in front of me,
lips slightly pursed and jaw askew, in a leering pose that makes
me uncomfortable, then immediately angry. He looks me up and
down, then reaches out to touch my arm as I hand him Kool-Aid.

"Don't touch her, man," Blade orders loudly, but the man,
who is probably drugged out, hasn't heard or ignores the warning.

A tray of tinny utensils clatters suddenly to the floor and Blade
is standing before me, too, his powerful hand gripping the man's
shoulder in what looks like a very painful squeeze.

"I said, don't do that!" he hisses. The man just turns and
walks away in a daze. Blade picks up his tray and continues in the
line as if nothing has occurred. The kitchen staff, which had rushed
forward anticipating a fight, drifts back to the pots and pans.

Later, as I leave St. Agnes' that night, Blade is hanging out
at the corner with a group. The few pedestrians make wide detours
around them. I can barely identify his face behind a cigar as I thank
him.

"No problem," he says carelessly. "My mama raised me right," he adds. "Nothin' to do with you."

The following week when he comes to St. Agnes', Blade advises me coldly not to bend over with my back to the line, rear in the air, but rather always keep my face forward.

"And don't smile at people in line," he says. I thank him.

I next encounter Blade while walking home one night. I have an uneasy feeling about a man following me, and I hold my can of mace tightly. Abruptly, Blade is beside me, and we stop. The man hastily crosses the street.

This was to be the first of many times Blade became angry at me. "You shouldn't be walking the streets this late," he says. "That man was after you. Just cuz he's white don't mean he ain't gonna hurt you."

I'm angry and tell him so, first because he thinks I'm racist and second because he thinks I'm stupid.

"If I thought that way, I wouldn't be standing here with you at night. I've been in a lot more dangerous situations," I blurt out, "and I've been just fine."

"I know you done stupid things getting stuff for that book, but you been lucky. Someone must be watchin' over you, girl," he shakes his head. "You better believe, because you have no business in those tunnels. You don't know the rules down there.

"By rights you should be dead by now. Better believe it. You're lucky you made so many friends, but one day you won't be so lucky," he warns.

After that, he begins to instruct me about tunnel life, telling me of tunnel communities he knows. I ask him to take me to them, but he refuses. "A girl shouldn't go down there," he says. I intend to go down with or without him, I say, and he concedes. We are to meet at an entrance to Central Park.

Blade doesn't keep the date. I wait two hours that day, and the same on the next day. When next I see him at St. Agnes', I tell him he's unreliable. He laughs and says he showed up both days but just watched me to decide if he trusted me. I challenge him to tell me what clothes I wore, what color shoes, how I fixed my hair. He does, correctly.

Over the next several weeks he calls me "kid sis" and often pats my head. He takes me into the tunnels, where we visit many communities. He is usually cold and aloof to the people there, and I asked him why.

"They'll kill if they want, don't forget that," he says.

No one has ever come close to threatening me, I retort. Maybe you just don't want to see good in them.

"Maybe you're afraid to see the bad. You don't live with them. You don't have to. It don't matter how much time you spend with those people, you will never understand them because you're not one of them. You don't know. I do. I know how to kill people. You don't," he says intensely, as if willing me to understand.

"I know how easy it is to kill people, and I know that it don't usually bother you after you do it. You just go get something to eat and forget it. You can kill for a cigarette, for five dollars, for anything you want. You don't think that way up on the street, but down there, it don't make any difference if you kill or you don't. You don't think twice about it," he explains earnestly.

I offer to pay Blade for escorting me the first time. He is insulted.

"Never do that again," he says flatly.

Why are you spending so much time showing me the tunnels? I ask.

"Because I'm crazy," he replies. "And you remind me of a girl I sat next to in the first grade.

"I always thought if she was black, she'd be cute. But she was white, transparent like," he cringes. "White skin just looks bad to me. Anyway, she was a weak little kid. But one day this kid came over and ripped up a picture I was drawing for my mama, and she bit him. There was blood on her teeth and everything."

"Besides," he goes on after a pause, "you're funny and I like to keep an eye on you. You do stupid things."

Blade likes the responsibility of guiding me, I decide. He

sometimes walks me in a huge circle underground and claims we are in a new tunnel, just to make me confused and more dependent.

After finding communities with him, I go by myself to interview the underground homeless. With him nearby, people are less free to talk, glancing nervously at him. They are even more anxious when I'm with him than when I'm with a policeman.

One day I tell Blade that I've heard of a new tunnel to investigate and describe its location. He immediately says no one lives there, but later I learn that Blade sometimes sleeps there himself, so I avoid mentioning the tunnel again. He has said that he no longer lives in tunnels.

So on one fateful day, a Thursday, I go into that tunnel alone. I find no one, although there are mattresses and garbage bags that suggest it is used nightly. I resist the temptation to look for Blade's clothes. He had become more than just a guide and protector; he was a friend and it would be treacherous to search for his home in this unhappy place.

I go away from the city for the weekend, but on Monday, I visit a familiar tunnel community. Sneakers, a small man who earned his nickname by being fast and quiet, tells me that Blade is looking for me. "In a bad way," he adds pointedly.

I laugh, wondering if he is angry at me because I left town without telling him. But Sneakers is obviously worried, so I ask why Blade wanted me.

"Dunno," Sneakers says, looking away.

Another camp member, George, freezes when he sees me. It is in sharp contrast to the great warm smile I usually get. He stares at me for a minute before turning to Sneakers.

"You tell her?" he asks.

"No man, I jus' tell her he was lookin' for her," Sneakers replies, kicking the ground.

"You gotta get outta here," George says urgently. "He's not messin'. He's looking for you bad."

George drops the garbage bags in which he has been collecting soda cans, takes my arm, and walks me toward the exit.

"It's no joke," he says, looking into my face. "He's after you." He was visibly upset, so much that he could barely speak clearly.

Why? I ask, but George just shakes his head. He doesn't know, but it doesn't matter why, he says. Just go. I wonder if he just doesn't want to tell me.

That afternoon, still not believing the danger, I visit another community. Tyrone, one of its runners, frowns.

"It's on the street that someone's looking for you," he says severely. A large man named Blade is looking to kill me, he says, "and he ain't messin'." He says that I should stay out of the tunnels from now on.

I can't believe any of this. They are serious, I know, but it is a huge misunderstanding. When I last saw Blade, on a subway platform, he patted me on the head as usual and was laughing. The image was crystal clear. Now I am standing on the same platform, at 33rd Street on the Lexington Avenue Line, and a homeless woman comes up—I've never seen her before—and warns me to be careful. "Blade is looking for you," she says in a terrible repetition of the words I've heard all day.

By now I have become thoroughly frightened. I know it is not a joke. Blade is angry, but about what, I have no idea. I must find out and set him straight.

In the next few days I speak to other tunnel people, but they also warn me about Blade without offering any information about his anger. I should stay away from the tunnels for a very long time, they say.

Tyrone agrees to try to learn why Blade wants to kill me. A few graffiti artists do, too, particularly Chris Pape, who has painted many underground murals and is accepted by tunnel people.

Chris asks if I saw drugs in Blade's tunnel, on the theory that Blade may have been dealing or storing drugs there. Perhaps he saw me, or suspected I saw him with drugs, and now he is scaring me away from any thought of talking to the police about it. No one really knows.

Then Blade phones me at home. I have never given him my

phone number. On my answering machine he says he wants to see me. He sounds angry and distant. Even when he has been angry before, he has not sounded so cold.

"I need to talk to you," he says coldly. He calls again, his messages increasingly frustrated and furious.

"I need to see you. You need to talk cuz I know what you done." I have never given him my address either, but he says he knows it.

"I know where you live and I'm gonna come visit you. We need to get something straight finally."

The phone wakes me up, but no one speaks. I'm certain it is Blade.

Tyrone calls me at the office. He wants to meet in Queens. I am now badly frightened, and, although I know Tyrone, I don't know him as well as I know—or knew—Blade. So I ask Tyrone to meet in Central Park and he agrees.

The story he tells me is that Blade has killed a man in his tunnel, a "crackhead" who was harassing a woman passing through. It happened on the Saturday I was out of the city, but Blade thought he saw me witness the killing, and that I ran away. He chased me but I escaped, and then he saw me speaking to a policeman. When he was unable to reach me by phone on the weekend, he became convinced that I had gone to the police. Because I am not a tunnel person and don't live by tunnel rules—the chief one of which is never to inform to the police on another tunnel person—I am dangerous to Blade and will be dangerous to him for years.

This is what Blade believes, according to Tyrone. I believe Tyrone.

Tyrone shakes as he tells me. "You gotta understand how dangerous he is," says Tyrone. "You gotta leave the city, go home." My rapport with tunnel people has ended. Some will refuse to talk to me, and others will hide from me, he says.

"It's not you, baby," explains a homeless woman I particularly like. "It's that people could get killed just talking to you. We want you to be OK. We love you, but we want you to leave. I don't want to see you die, and if you keep coming into these tunnels like this, someone's gonna go fetch Blade to get on his good side. There's eyes all over this place, you know that. So go home, baby, please go home."

Blade's phone calls by now are even more terrifying. He tells me he will come to my apartment.

"I'm gonna come over with my blade. It's better than some piece gun. It got ya name on it and it thirsty. Ready to talk?" His words are blurred by street sounds from a booth, but his voice is steady and hard in a quick cold environment.

That night, going down to do laundry in the basement of my apartment building, his scribbled tag is painted on the green wall of my elevator. I am hardly able to think, seeing strange colors. His signature had once been so reassuring to me, comforting; if I feared trouble, I could drop his name and I'd be left alone. Now his tag means he is close to me. I am afraid even to go outside, even for groceries.

An officer tells me I should get a gun. No matter what happens, if I kill a man in my apartment, the case would never go to trial. I wonder if I could kill Blade. Within a few days of sleepless terror, I know I can if he comes into my apartment. I wish he would stand in my doorway so I could kill him—a man whose face I still remember only with a smile.

A week later, I leave New York.

It was exhilarating, walking a tightrope, exploring the underground while living aboveground. I had been part of two worlds, but I came to know the tunnel world too well, enough to be caught up in its irrational behavior and volatile emotions. I was no longer privy and at the same time immune to tunnel life with the guise of an outsider. I had already been slapped around when I tried to stop a man from battering his woman. Now I might be killed, and now I know that I could also kill.

As many tunnel people have told me, the line between them and people who live on the surface is very thin, much thinner than people on the "topside world" like to realize. I felt I could step over that line. I could also escape, and I did. I hope some of them will escape, too.

Epilogue

MONTHS HAVE PASSED SINCE I WAS LAST IN THE TUNNELS. Every time I hear about New York, I see a picture in my mind of the city in lights, sparkling with promise and excitement, and I think of the people I left behind in its shadow. Willie, Frederick, and Sane (David Smith) died before this book was published. Brenda is missing. Mac is still roaming the tunnels in search of track rabbits, and whistling. Seville's hobble healed into a steady limp. He is still smiling, using his humor to help him and others cope while looking for the welding job to free him from tunnel life. Bernard continues to meet at his campfire with Bob, Tony, and the other members of his vibrant community. They talk about trying to retrieve Sheila, who is lost to alcohol and the streets. Sheila keeps true to her promise to Willie, and says that no matter how bad things get on the streets, she won't live in the tunnels again. She misses the people down there, she says. She misses caring for them and being cared for. John moved out of the tunnel to live with a girlfriend on West 72nd Street. He met her with the help of John Tierney's article in *The New York Times* in which he spoke openly about his quest for love. He left Mama in the tunnel with Joe. Chris is spending months' worth of pay on paint for tunnel murals, he tells me, shaking his head. The one he's currently working on, his most ambitious yet, will cost about $1,000. He's planning to spread Sane's ashes at the foot of the mural on the tunnel ground. Smith sprinkled the other half of his brother's ashes along the No. 1 subway line, Sane's favorite. Roger is slowly recovering from his brother's death. Dolly is living with a man three times her age "for security until my rich man finds me," she says, her eyes blackened by drugs. She heard on the streets that Frank is in jail, but she doesn't know where the other members of the runaway community are now. Many more of those interviewed for this book may now be lost or dead.

When I began this book, I did my best not to interfere with the lives of the people in the tunnels. I never gave them money, but sometimes brought them food or warm clothes I bought from street vendors and thrift shops. I tried to avoid handing out cigarettes, but sometimes I did. I gave advice on which shelters to go to and what programs to join and sometimes helped them get there. I tried to limit such advice only to the times I was asked. I never reported children to authorities, mostly because I wanted to establish trust within the communities. I'll always wonder if I made the wrong decision.

Nightmares from the tunnels have followed me. One in particular still haunts me. It's of a girl in the tunnels living with her parents and two brothers. In my nightmare she wakes itching from the bugs and disease in the tunnels. She scratches, which only makes the itch rise into sores. She wakes her brother, who is just a year older, and they whisper so as not to wake their parents or younger brother.

"I'm sorry I woke you," she tells her brother. She shows him the sores, which have spread over her arms and soft face. He's surprised but also tired and tells her not to worry about it until the morning. The girl turns in her sleep until she can't stand the itch and pain any longer. She finds a crack razor on the tunnel floor and uses it to carve out each of her sores. It relieves the itch, but then she sees the blood running over her body and she touches her face, slippery with warm blood. She wakes her brother again. He looks shocked and frightened.

"Don't worry," he says soothingly. "Maybe you'll die by morning." And he turns over to go back to sleep. She lies on her back, thinking of the people walking above her, and accepts this as she accepts the rest of her life. She thinks that she will never be able to join their lives aboveground now that her scars from the tunnel are so obvious. She worries about her family. She closes her eyes, hoping that she'll die by morning. And then I wake up in a sweat.

As MY YEAR OF RESEARCH IN THE TUNNELS CONTINUED, I GATHERED more nightmares and concerns for the people I met there. I found it increasingly difficult to stay on the periphery of their lives. Several people became more than subjects; they became my friends. They'd give me advice on everything from office politics to how to handle my boyfriend. They taught me more than I thought I could learn. They opened avenues of thought I had no idea existed.

Their lives became very much a part of my own life. In exploring their world, I sometimes lost my own. They could understand and even help explain some of the changes going on inside of me better than my topside friends. Very early on, I recognized that they gave me more than I could give them. They showed me warmth in their cold, often mean world, which gave me hope, not only for them, but for all things. They even showed me happiness in what first seemed to me a void of darkness. They showed me a beauty to their world that saved me from a deep unhappiness. Most of all, they showed me that, even in the worst conditions, people can care for each other over themselves.

But some also showed me how they can extinguish whatever hope they have and chances they are given. I watched too many people destroy themselves with drugs or alcohol, or neglect to care for themselves in basic ways. They were people who lost the future and had not had the guidance to see how to live the life they wanted. For too many, happiness was anticipating their next hit. I saw drugs overtake love. I witnessed how responsibility is not easily understood by those who have never grown under its protection. Some people with self-destructive ways made me angry—not for the material things I gave them, but for things they took from within myself. They took from me unrelenting optimism. At times, they took my happiness. They brought an emptiness to my adventure, turning a great story into a human one that I might never put to rest.

As much as I trusted the people who talked with me, I always walked into the tunnels clutching the can of mace my father gave me, realizing it was more for luck than protection. I was often terrified walking the tracks alone, so frightened I could not turn back to look for the eyes I felt watching me. Once inside a community, I was safe from the random violence of tunnel life. Even without the aboveground law, there was a network of protection. Violence came more from people who felt threatened. If a stranger in the tunnel approached me and I dropped a name of someone in the tunnels, I was often welcomed.

In some communities, I became a fixture and I could watch people in the tunnels act in ways I was not privy to at the beginning. But by then I began to care too much, and I began to interfere with their behavior.

My last trip into the tunnels was one that I won't forget. I visited a couple, Tina and Melvin. I didn't write about this couple in the book because I felt I became too much a part of their story. When I first met them, Tina was panhandling and sometimes turning tricks near Times Square to support "her man," which actually meant his habit. Watching Melvin's declining health, Tina steered away from drugs. She said she realized that someone had to care for Melvin and she couldn't do it high.

Tina and I often spoke about what she wanted in the future. I encouraged her to join a cleaning agency and helped her get a false residential address to aid her in applying for the job. Her work gave her a glowing confidence. She walked tall and smiled frequently and told me that her work gave her back the self-respect she lost to the tunnels. She didn't want to leave Melvin, but many times I would find her rocking back and forth in her chair in the tunnel, crying.

"He's dying," she would tell me. I'm watching him die and I'm killing him." With the money she made with her new job, Melvin was able to buy heroin. He was only a skeleton of the man with the wide smile I had first known. Melvin refused treatment because he said he didn't want to leave Tina. I convinced Tina to pretend she also had a drug problem and sign the two of them up on a long waiting list for a six-month drug rehabilitation program. We had talked about doing this for several weeks, and one day she had the confidence to do it. On our way back, we picked up a bucket of fried chicken to celebrate. As she and her man ate and talked, I stood in the corner and watched what I thought would be the unfolding of a success story.

Instead, Melvin became furious. Believing that the city would now take away their welfare because they admitted to drug use, he began to hit Tina and throw her around. I stood up and walked into the brawl between Tina and her man, and I tried to explain that I had been the one to tell Tina to sign up for the program. In an attempt to get to Tina, Melvin threw me against the wall. I woke up a little dizzy, Tina crying over me. She was terrified that I was dead. She asked me to leave and never come back.

I REMEMBER A MAN IN THE TUNNELS WARNING ME WHEN I BEGAN the project that there is a point at which you feel so much you become numb. I was numb for several months and I broke through the numbness by fighting. Still, only now that I am out of the tunnels for good can I let myself be frightened.

When I sat down to write this epilogue, I felt drained and hollow, afraid that I have failed to accomplish what I set out to do. Thoughts of the people swirl around my head. There are many stories left untold. I offer this work as research into this tragedy of our times, notes for the present and future, to prevent more souls from being lost to the tunnels, and perhaps to stir more hope in bringing them back home.

CAMPFIRE AT NIGHT
TOO DARK TO DRAW
ANYTHING BUT FEET.

12/87

Acknowledgments

I AM GRATEFUL TO MY LITTLE BROTHER, JOHN, FOR URGING ME to go after this story when I was gently steered away from it three years ago. And my sister Jessica, for always believing I could do it and for masterminding the computer grant form Toth, Toth, Toth, Toth and Erturk.

I'd also like to thank my mother for making sure I ate well and exercised even in the darkest days, and for nursing me when I was sick. And my friends Angela and Greg Copenhaven, Annie Hung, Christine Sharp, Cathy Miley, Karen Cade, and Anne Rosenquist for calling to make sure I was still sleeping aboveground and for making me laugh. Most of my thanks go to Windley, for getting me through the tunnels and bringing me back to the wonders aboveground.

Los Angeles Times editor Roger Smith and reporters Karen Tumulty and Josh Getlin were wonderful in believing in the story and giving me the confidence to pursue it. Pat Welsh, Steve Clark, and Philip Ruiz were a great help with research and computers. Computer wizard Hank Kehlbeck also helped remarkably in converting the text on the twelfth hour.

Bill Adler, Mark Lewyn, and Dean Silvers were fantastic in believing in me and this book before I was ready to. Mark, in particular, pushed me into action. I was also extremely lucky to have Amy Teschner at Chicago Review Press edit the book, not

255

only because of her great talent, but because she sincerely cares about the people of the underground.

I can't thank Chris Pape, Roger Smith, Bernard Isaacs, and all the others in this book enough for sharing their underground with me, not just for this book but also for enriching my life.

I'm especially thankful to my father for reading, rereading, getting angry, and setting a brilliant example.

Bibliography

Abood, Edward F. *Underground Man.* San Francisco: Chandler and Sharp Publishers, Inc., 1973.

"ADAPT/MTA Outreach-Case Management Project Annual Report." 1991 (unpublished).

Association for Drug Abuse Prevention and Treatment, Inc. "Pennsylvania Station and Grand Central Terminal ADAPT Outreach Case Management Homeless Project Monthly Report." 1991 (unpublished).

Bahr, Howard M. *Skid Row: An Introduction to Disaffiliation.* New York: Oxford University Press, Inc., 1973.

Barak, Greg. *Gimme Shelter: A Social History of Homelessness in Contemporary America.* New York: Praeger Publishers, 1991.

Baum, Alice, and Donald Burnes. *A Nation in Denial: The Truth About Homelessness* (preview copy).

Beard, Richard. *On Being Homeless: Historical Perspectives.* Museum of the City of New York: 1987.

Beckford, William. *Vathek.* London: Oxford Press, 1970.

Brickner, Philip. W., Linda Keen Scharer, Barbara A. Conanan, Marianne Savarese, and Brian C. Scanlan, eds. *Under the Safety Net: The Health and Social Welfare of the Homeless in the United States.* New York: W. W. Norton & Company, 1990.

Burt, Martha R. *Over the Edge: The Growth of Homelessness in the 1980s.* New York: Russell Sage Foundation, 1992.

Castleman, Craig. *Getting Up: Subway Graffiti in New York.* Cambridge, Massachusetts: The MIT Press, 1984.

Caton, Carol L. M. *Homeless in America.* Oxford: Oxford University Press, 1990.

Cheibel, James, Suellen L. Stokes, and Mary Ellen Hombs. "Telling the Truth About Homelessness." *Washington Post,* Jan. 2, 1993, A17.

Cohen, Carl I., and Jay Sokolovsky. *Old Men of the Bowery: Strategies for Survival Among the Homeless.* New York: Guilford Press, 1989.

Cohen, Neal L. "Psychiatric Outreach to the Mentally Ill," *New Directions for Mental Health Services.* Winter 1991.

Cohen, Neal L. *Psychiatry Takes to the Streets.* New York: Guilford Press, 1990.

Dear, Michael, and Jennifer Wolch. *Landscapes of Despair: From Deinstitutionalization to Homelessness.* Princeton: Princeton University Press, 1987.

de Sant-Fond, Faugas, quoted in Pennick's *The Subterranean Kingdom.*

Dostoyevsky, Fyodor. *Notes from Underground/The Double.* Translated by Jessie Coulson. London: Penguin Books, 1972.

Dwyer, Jim. *Subway Lives: 24 Hours in the Life of the New York City Subway.* New York: Crown Publishers, Inc., 1991.

Ellison, Ralph. *Invisible Man.* New York: Vintage Books, 1972.

Fischler, Stan. *Uptown Downtown: A Trip Through Time on New York's Subways.* New York: Hawthorn/Dutton, 1976.

Fowler, Raymond D., ed. "Special Issue: Homelessness." *American Psychologist.* The American Psychological Association. Vol. 46, Number 11. Nov. 1991.

Garner, Robert. "Modern Troglodytes," *The Reliquary,* London: John Russell Smith, 1865.

Gissing, George Robert. *The Nether World.* Rutherford, N.J.: Fairleigh Dickinson University Press, 1974.

"Going About Town." *The New Yorker,* Nov. 23, 1992, p. 23.

Gonzalez, David. "For Some, Shelters Mean Chaos and Home." *The New York Times,* July 17, 1992, B1.

Gould, Jennifer. "Moscow Subways." *Moscow Times,* Nov. 11, 1992.

Granick, Harry. *Underneath New York.* Introduction by Robert E. Sullivan, Jr. New York: Fordham University Press, 1991.

Hager, Steven. *Hip Hop: The Illustrated History of Break Dancing, Rap Music, and Graffiti.* New York: St. Martin's Press, 1984.

Harrison, Michael. *London Beneath the Pavement.* London: Peter Davies, 1961.

Hoch, Charles, and Robert A. Slayton. *New Homeless and Old: Community and Skid Row Hotel.* Philadelphia: Temple University Press, 1989.

Hugo, Victor. *Les Miserables.* Revised and edited by L. Fahnestock and N. MacAfee. New American Library, 1987.

Kafka, Franz. "The Burrow." In *Complete Stories.* New York: Schocken Books, 1971.

Kaufman, Michael T. "A Middleman's Ventures in the Can Trade." *The New York Times,* Sept. 23, 1992, B1.

Kennedy, Shawn G. "Housing List in New York Hits Record: 240,000 Families Seek Space in City Projects." *The New York Times,* Dec. 27, 1992, p. 31.

Maclellan, Alec. *The Lost World of Agharti: The Mystery of Vril Power.* London: Trinity Press, 1982.

Miller, Henry. *On the Fringe: The Dispossessed in America.* Lexington: Lexington Books, 1991.

Momeni, Jamshid. *Homelessness in the United States.* New York: Praeger Publishers, 1990.

National Association of Social Workers. *Findings from a National Survey of Shelters for Runaway and Homeless Youth.* Oct. 1991.

National Research Council. *Inner-City Poverty in the United States.* Laurence E. Lynn, Jr., and Michael G. H. McGeary, eds. Washington, D.C.: National Academy Press. 1991.

Neibacher, Susan L. *Homeless People and Health Care: An Unrelenting Challenge.* United Hospital Fund. Dec. 1990.

Pennick, Nigel. *The Subterranean Kingdom: A Survey of Man-Made Structures Beneath the Earth.* Wellingborough, Northamptonshire: Turnstone Press, Ltd., 1981.

Rossi, Peter H. *Down and Out in America: The Origins of Homelessness.* Chicago: University of Chicago Press, 1989.

Salerno, Dan, Kim Hopper, and Ellen Baxter. *Hardship in the Heartland: Homelessness in Eight U.S. Cities.* 1984.

Schwartz, Rita. *The End of the Line: The Homeless and the Transportation Industry.* Metropolitan Transit Authority, 1992.

Susser, Mervyn, William Watson, and Kim Hopper. *Sociology in Medicine*. Oxford: Oxford University Press, 1985.

"Taki 183 Spawns Pen Pals." *The New York Times,* July 21, 1971, p. 37.

A Task Force Report of the American Psychiatric Association. "The Homeless Mentally Ill." Edited by H. Richard Lamb. Washington, D.C.: American Psychiatric Association, 1984.

Tierney, John. "Mole Returns to Hole; Lost: Job and Movie. Found: Love." *The New York Times,* Nov. 30, 1991, p. 21.

The United States Conference of Mayors. *A Status Report on Homelessness in America's Cities: 1992*. Dec. 1992.

The United States Conference of Mayors. *A Status Report on Hunger and Homelessness in America's Cities: 1991*. Dec. 1991.

Verne, Jules. *A Journey to the Center of the Earth*. New York: Heritage Press, 1966.

Wells, H. G. *Time Machine and Other Stories*. London: Ernest Benn, 1917.

Williams, Rosalind. *Notes on the Underground: An Essay on Technology, Society, and the Imagination*. Cambridge, Massachusetts: The MIT Press, 1984.

Zettler, Michael D. *The Bowery*. New York: Drake Publishers Inc., 1975.

Index

Abood, Edward F., 176
ADAPT. *See* Association for Drug
  Abuse Prevention and Treatment
  (ADAPT)
Agharthi legend, 170
Ali M. (mayor), 195–96, 198, 199–
  200, 202; on light, 195; reasons
  for seeing author, 191–92; on
  writing, 201
All Saints' Soup Kitchen, 90, 95, 96
April, 206, 207, 209, 211
Armenians, 36
Armory shelter, 57
Association for Drug Abuse Preven-
  tion and Treatment (ADAPT), 70,
  151, 155–63, 167; Deamues's
  work with, 67, 84, 158–59, 160,
  161, 162, 163; final report of,
  157, 162; on Project HELP, 152–
  53
Auden, W. H., 61

Bacon, Francis, 172
Bass, Gary, 56
Baum, Alice, 40
Beach, Alfred Ely, 45
Beard, Richard, 50

Beckford, William, 171
Beeper, 206, 209, 210, 211
Bellevue Hospital, 56, 57, 155
Bernard's tunnel, 75, 97–118. *See
  also* Isaacs, Bernard
Bethea, Michael, 67, 152, 153,
  156–58; optimistic views of,
  162–63
Big D, 12
Bill, 91–92, 93
Bingo, 186, 188, 189
Blade, 5, 237–47; on anger, 238–
  39; background, 239; depth of
  character, 237–38; and the Har-
  lem gang, 183, 184, 185, 187,
  188, 190; on killing, 242
BMT. *See* Brooklyn Manhattan Tran-
  sit (BMT)
Bob, 88, 105–9, 237, 249
Boggs, Joyce (Billy), 154
Borges, Jorge Luis, 171
Bowery, 49–58; history of, 49–50;
  Romero on, 51–54
Brenda, 116, 117, 213–19, 249
Bridges, Jeff, 216
Broadway-Lafayette Station, 54
Bronze Age, 36

Brooklyn Bridge Station, 131
Brooklyn Manhattan Transit (BMT), 45
Brown, Claude, 201, 202
Buckley, Rob, 90–91, 95–96; on underground communities, 91, 94
"Burma's Road," 47
Burnes, Donald, 40
"Burrow, The" (Kafka), 169
Butch (Brenda's boyfriend), 116, 117
Butch (tunnel birth observer), 78, 79, 80
Buxton, Derbyshire, 37

Candy, 18
Cannibalistic Human Underground Dwellers (CHUDS), 74, 205 Carlos, 137, 138, 140–41; on hope, 148–49
Castleman, Craig, 134
Cathy and Joe, 225–26
Central Park, 192, 213, 215, 216, 234, 245
Cher, 229–30, 233
children underground, 77–86; adaptability of, 84; in J.C.'s community, 82; Julie, 82–84; Teresa's family, 84–86
Chitthum, Samme, 99
Chud, 205, 206
CHUDS. See Cannibalistic Human Underground Dwellers (CHUDS)
Cimmerians, 35–36
Cindy, 24–25
"city of friends," 203–11; and Rex, 209–210; and Sam, 207–9, 210–11
Coalition for the Homeless, 88, 104. See also homeless advocates; tunnel outreach
Columbia University, 1, 2

"Condos, the," 20–21, 47; Henry's discovery of, 66–67
Covenant House, 136, 140, 145
Creation (Michelangelo), 125
Crimeans, 36
Crump, Daniel, 161

Dale, 56
Dameon, 137
Dante, 170
Dara, 84, 85, 86
Dark Angel, 165–68; Jamall on, 234
Dart, 187, 188
David, 136–37, 138
Deamues, Harold: on children underground, 84; on the Dark Angel, 167–68; on the mole people, 159, 161; work with ADAPT, 67, 84, 158–59, 160, 161, 162, 163
Demetrius ("Taki 183"), 132
Denise, 57
Dericka, 223, 224
de Sant-Fond, Faugas, 37
Dickens, Charles, 173
Dirty Slug, 129, 133
Doc (Fabulous Five member), 129, 133
Doc (Harlem gang member), 186, 188, 189
Dolly, 145–46, 148, 250
Don, 109–10
Dopey, 209
Dostoyevsky, Fyodor, 176, 177
Douglas Housing Project, 224
Dunsley Rock (Gibraltar), England, 36–37
Dwane, 84, 85
Dwayne, 89
Dwyer, Jim, 44

Edwards, Dee, 88
Eleanor Kennedy shelter, Fairfax, Virginia, 40

Eliot, George, 173
Ellison, Ralph, 177

Fabulous Five, 129–31
Farrell, Neil, 49, 57
Fay, 206, 210
Felicia, 138–39, 143–44, 146, 147
Fisher King, The, 215
Flacko, 11, 26
Flip, 111, 112
Fort Washington shelter, 56, 57, 116
Fran and Shorty, 225
Frank (runaway), 141–42, 143, 146, 148, 250
Frank (Virginia's boyfriend), 95–96
Franko, 23
Fred, 79
Frederick, 135–39, 249
"Freedom." *See* Pape, Chris ("Freedom")
Freud, Sigmund, 173–74

Garner, Robert, 36–37
Gayle, Kristen, 1–2, 82–83
George (Blade's associate), 243, 244
George ("city of friends" resident), 204–5, 206, 207, 211
Getting Up: Subway Graffiti in New York (Castleman), 134
Ghost, 51
"Ghost Cliff," 234
Gissing, George, 173
Goya, Francisco José de, 126
graffiti artists. *See* graffiti writings and writers; tunnel art and artists
graffiti writings and writers, 119, 121, 122, 127, 129–34; Fabulous Five, 129–31. *See also* tunnel art and artists
Grand Central Station, 3, 4, 57, 84, 122, 151, 161, 219; estimate of underground population, 39; evic-

tions from, 47; J.C.'s community under, 61, 82, 191–202; Williams's residence under, 12, 13, 19, 21, 23, 26–27
Granick, Harry, 43, 46
Guardian Angels, 230, 239n.
Guernica (Picasso), 126

Hammer, 48
Harlem gang, 183–90
Hector, 99–101
HELP. *See* Homeless Emergency Liaison Project (HELP)
Henry, Sergeant Bryan, 5, 12, 43, 59–63, 65–67, 82; and "the Condos," 21, 66–67; on the Dark Angel, 166–67; frustration experienced by, 59–61; initial meeting with author, 3–4; and J.C., 61–63, 66; and Michelle, 219–20; photograph of, 60; Williams on, 26
History of Graffiti (Pape), 125
homeless advocates, 4–5, 40, 104–5. *See also* Coalition for the Homeless; tunnel outreach
Homeless Credo, 109
Homeless Emergency Liaison Project (HELP), 151–55
HRA. *See* New York City Human Resources Administration
Hudson Street, 49–50
Hugo, Victor, 172, 173
"human morality," 209
"human religion," 209

Interborough Rapid Transit (IRT), 183, 184
International Encyclopedia of Social Sciences, 89
Invisible Man (Ellison), 177–79
Iris, 16–18

IRT. *See* Interborough Rapid Transit (IRT)

Isaacs, Bernard, 5, 88–89, 249; and Bob, 88, 105–9; on David, 137; and Don, 109–10; and Flip, 111; and Hector, 99–101; on homeless advocacy groups, 104–5; and John, 113–15; photograph of, 118; on the Rotunda community, 94; and Sheila, 226, 227; and Shorty, 225; source of income, 102–3, 107; and Tim, 110–11; and Tom, 116–17; and Tony, 111–13; and tunnel art and artists, 119–20, 124–25, 126, 127; tunnel community of, 75, 97–118; on underground people, 117

Israely, Beverly, 90

Jamaica, 189
Jamall, 166, 168, 229–35
Japan, 38
J.C., 4, 89; community of, 82, 191–202; and Henry, 61–63, 66
Jeff, 147, 148
Jeffers, Chris, 107–8
Jess, 221
Jesus, 103
Jimmy, 144–45, 146, 147, 148
Joe, 50–51
Joey, 112, 113
John, 113–15, 249
Journey to the Center of the Earth, A (Verne), 174
Juan, 78
Julie, 1, 2, 77, 82–84

Kafka, Franz, 169
Klambatsen, Sergeant Steve, 54, 55

Lady Pink, 132
Lafayette Street Station, 47
LaJoy, 69–70

law and underground homeless, the, 59–71; police brutality stories, 63–64; and social workers, 67–69
Lee, 129–30, 131, 132–34
Leon, 101
Lexington Avenue Line, 55, 244
Little Man, 182
Logan, Al, 53, 54
London, 38
Los Angeles Times, The, 4

Mac, 29–34, 249
Malcolm, 13
Manchild in the Promised Land (Brown), 201, 202
Martin, Marsha, 39
Marx, Karl, 173–74
Mary, 89
Meitus, Robert, 2
Melvin, 252, 253
Mental Hygiene Law, 154
Metropolitan Transit Authority. *See* New York City Transit Authority
Metropolitan Transit Police, 12, 43, 61
Michelle, 219–20
Middle Ages, 171, 175
Les Miserables (Hugo), 172
"Modern Troglodytes" (Garner), 36
Moe, 184, 185
Monica, 138–39, 145, 148
Mono, 129, 130, 131, 133
Morningside Park, 2
Moscow, 38
Mosley, Walter, 183
Murphy, Ken, 68
Museum of Modern Art, 125

National Association of Social Workers, 69
Need of Roots, The (Weil), 87
Nell, 81
Neolithic period, 36

Nether World, The (Gissing), 173
New Alliance Party, 183–84
New York City, 2, 6, 73; underground population in, 38–42; underground spaces in, 43–48
New York City Human Resources Administration, 26, 52, 68
New York City Transit Authority, 46, 48, 51, 67, 129; outreach programs sponsored by, 151–53, 156
New York Daily News, The, 99
New Yorker, The, 134
New York Health and Human Services Department, 39, 81
New York Mental Health Association, 40
New York Times, The, 26, 68, 108, 115, 132, 249
No Exit (Sartre), 171
Notes from Underground (Dostoyevsky), 176, 177
Notes on the Underground (Williams), 170–71, 172–73

On Being Homeless: Historical Perspectives (Beard), 50
On Walden Pond (Thoreau), 31
outreach programs. *See* tunnel outreach

Papa, 221
Pape, Chris ("Freedom"), 100–101, 119, 122, 244, 249–50; and Bernard, 111, 124–25; and Bob, 106; collaboration with Smith, 126–27; on David, 137; on graffiti writing, 132; self-portrait, 120, 123
Paris, 37–38
Paul, 83
Pennick, Nigel, 35, 36, 37
Penn Station, 13, 20, 47, 55, 135,

136, 144, 151, 192, 203, 210; estimate of underground population, 39
Peppin, 63–64
Picasso, Pablo, 126
Plato, 97
Polhemus, Guy, 107
Port Authority Station, 13, 47, 55, 57

Quinones, Jorge Lee. *See* Lee

Rambo, 204
Razor, 78
Reese, 51
Reliquary, The, 36
Renaissance, 171, 172
Republic, The (Plato), 97
Rex, 206, 209–10, 211
Rico, 167, 168
"Riker's Island," 47
Riley, Sergeant Steve, 49
Riverside Park, 107, 135, 181, 215, 224, 226; Bernard's tunnel community under, 88, 101, 103, 116; Pape's graffiti writing under, 124, 125 *Road Warrior*, 34
Rodney, 68–69
Rome, 38, 131
Romero, Lieutenant John, 51–53, 54
Ronda, 79, 80
Roosevelt, President Franklin D., 45
Rotunda community, 92–94, 221, 222
runaways underground, 135–49; Carlos, 140–41, 146; Dolly, 145–46; Frank, 141–42, 143, 146, 148; Frederick, 135–39; Jimmy, 144–45, 146, 147; Monica and Felicia, 139–40; Teddy, 142–44, 147, 148, 149

St. Agnes' Soup Kitchen, 3, 240, 241 Sally, 79
Sam (All Saints' Soup Kitchen customer), 94–95
Sam ("city of friends" mayor), 206, 209, 210; on "human morality," 208–9; on Jamall, 231; on listening, 211; management style, 207–8
"Sane." See Smith, David ("Sane")
Saroyan, William, 237
Sartre, Jean-Paul, 171
Scientific American, 45
Scott, Gwendolyn (Gwen), 221–23
Second Avenue Station, 47
Secret City of Ivan the Terrible, Moscow, 38
Seville. See Williams, Seville
Serrano, Yolanda, 70–71, 153
79th Street, 103, 221
Sheila, 100, 101, 223, 226–27, 249
Shorty (Fran's boyfriend), 225
Shorty (Seville's friend), 11, 23
Shorty (tunnel birth observer), 77–78, 79, 80
Silwa, Curtis, 239n.
Slam, 182
Slave, 129, 130, 133
Slim ("city of friends" resident), 206
Slim (Harlem gang member), 188, 189
Small Talk, 187, 188, 189
Smidge, 33, 34
"Smith." See Smith, Roger ("Smith")
Smith, David ("Sane"), 119, 125, 249; death of, 120–21, 250; lawsuit against, 121–22
Smith, Roger ("Smith"), 4, 51, 73–74, 119, 122, 125, 250; collaboration with Pape, 126–27; lawsuit against, 121–22

Sneakers, 243
social workers, 67–69
Sonya, 68–69
Squeeze, 39
Stash, 101
"Stealth," 181–82
"STIPSO" statute, 154
Stokes, Suellen L., 40
Stone, 221
Subterranean Kingdom: A Survey of Man-Made Structures Beneath the Earth, The (Pennick), 35–36, 37
Subway Lives (Dwyer), 44
Sullivan, Robert E., Jr., 43, 44, 46

"Taki 183." See Demetrius ("Taki 183")
Teather, 11
Teddy, 142–44, 147, 148, 149
Teresa, 84–86
Thackeray, William, 173
Third of May (Goya), 126
Thoreau, Henry David, 31
Tierney, John, 115, 249
Tim (member of Bernard's community), 110–11
Tim (Sally's boyfriend), 79, 80
Time Machine (Wells), 174–75, 176
Time of Your Life, The (Saroyan), 237
Tina, 252, 253
Tom (Butch and Brenda's friend), 116–17
Tom (Denise's friend), 57
Tony, 111–13, 249; on tunnel art, 128
Tracy, 134, 168
Transit Workers and Mechanics Union, 161
Trey, 69–70
Tripper, 95, 96
Tsemberis, Dr. Sam, 153–54, 155, 159–60, 163

Tumulty, Karen, 4
tunnel art and artists, 119–28; Bernard's involvement with, 119–20, 124–25, 126, 127; May Third mural, 126–28; Pape's work, 122–26; Tony on, 128. *See also* graffiti writings and writers
tunnel outreach, 151–63; ADAPT's efforts, 151, 152, 153, 155–63; Project HELP, 151–55. *See also* Coalition for the Homeless; homeless advocates
Tweed, Mayor Boss, 45
Tyrone, 244, 245

underground communities, 87–96; Bernard's tunnel, 75, 97–118; Buckley on, 91, 94; communication network in, 89–90; "families" in, 87; J.C.'s, 191–202; Rotunda, 92–94, 221, 222
underground in history, literature, and culture, 169–79; and the Agharthi legend, 170; in Ellison's *Invisible Man,* 177–79; in Hugo's *Les Miserables,* 172, 173; in the nineteenth century, 175–76; and the underground man concept, 176–79; in Wells' *Time Machine,* 174–75, 176
Underground Man (Abood), 176
underground population, 35–42; Cimmerians, 35–36; in England, 36–37; estimates of, 39; life expectancy of, 41; in New York City, 38–42; in Paris, 37–38
underground spaces, 43–48
Underneath New York (Granick), 43, 46

van Hollar, Roderick (Rick), 221, 222
Vathek (Beckford), 171
Verne, Jules, 174
Vicky, 96
Virginia, 95–96
Volunteer Services for the Grand Central Partnership Social Services Corporation, 90
Volunteers of the Bathroom, 13–14

wanderers, 181–82
Washington Post, The, 40
"We Can," 107
Weil, Simone, 87
White, Patrick, 32
Whitman, Walt, 211
Williams, Robin, 215, 216
Williams, Rosalind, 170–71, 172–73, 174
Williams, Seville, 11–27, 73, 249; childhood, 15–16; children, 17–18; on dealing drugs, 25–26; and humor, 12–13; and Iris, 16–18; medical treatment, 25; on Peppin, 63–64; on track workers, 75; on tunnels, 20, 27
Willie, 100, 224–25, 226–27, 249
Wilson. *See* Blade
women underground, 213–27; Brenda, 213–19; Cathy and Joe, 225–26; Dericka, 223; Fran and Shorty, 225; Gwen, 221–23; Michelle, 219–20; Sheila and Willie, 224–25, 226–27

Zack, 192

OUACHITA TECHNICAL COLLEGE